HOW TO FOSTER CREATIVITY IN ALL CHILDREN

DA Ma'Jah

Join us on the web at

EarlyChildEd.delmar.com

HOW TO FOSTER CREATIVITY IN ALL CHILDREN

MARY MAYESKY, PH.D.

THOMSON

DELMAR LEARNING

Australia Canada Mexico Singapore Spain United Kingdom United States

THOMSON

™

DELMAR LEARNING

How to Foster Creativity in All Children
Mary Mayesky

Strategic Business Unit Director:
Susan L. Simpfenderfer

Executive Production Manager:
Wendy A. Troeger

Executive Marketing Manager:
Donna J. Lewis

Acquisitions Editor:
Erin O'Connor Traylor

Production Editor:
J.P. Henkel

Channel Manager:
Nigar Hale

Editorial Assistant:
Ivy Ip

Technology Project Manager:
Joe Saba

Cover Design:
Andrew Wright

Library of Congress Cataloging-in-Publication Data
Mayesky, Mary.
  How to foster creativity in all children / Mary Mayesky.
    p.cm.
  Includes bibliographical refences and index.
    ISBN 1-40189-783-5
    1. Creative thinking in children--Problems, exercises, etc. 2. Creative ability in children--Problems, exercises, etc. I. Title.

BF723.C7 M29 2002
372.13--dc21   2002035044

NOTICE TO THE READER

CONTENTS

ABOUT THE AUTHOR

Mary Mayesky, Ph.D., author of this book is a certified preschool, elementary, and secondary teacher. She is a former professor in the Program in Education at Duke University, former director of the Early Childhood Certification Program, and supervisor of student teachers. She has served as assistant director for programs in the Office of Day Services, Department of Human Resources, State of North Carolina. She is also the former principal of the Mary E. Phillips Magnet School in Raleigh, North Carolina, the first licensed child care magnet in the Southeast. She has served several terms on the North Carolina Day Care Commission and on the Wake County School Board.

Dr. Mayesky has worked in Head Start, child care, kindergarten, and YWCA early childhood programs and has taught kindergarten through grade 8 in the public schools. She has written extensively for professional journals and for general circulation magazines in the area of child development and curriculum design. She is a member of Phi Beta Kappa, and was named Woman of the Year in Education by the North Carolina Academy of the YWCA. Her other honors include being named Outstanding Young Educator by the Duke University Research Council, receiving the American Association of School Administrators Research Award, and being nominated for the Duke University Alumni Distinguished Undergraduate Teaching Award.

A marathon runner, Dr. Mayesky has completed nineteen marathons and received many awards in road races and senior games. She is an active member of the Raleigh Host Lions Club, having served as its first woman president. She thanks her Yoga instructors for helping her get through the writing tasks undertaken thus far in her life.

PREFACE

You are the key to how children view their creative efforts in the arts as well as in all curricular areas. This book is written for you.

How to Foster Creativity in All Children is designed for the person who is dedicated to helping young children reach their full potential. It is written for people who want to know more about creativity, creative children, creative teaching, and creative activities in *all* areas of the curriculum.

In our world of rapidly changing technology, it is even more crucial to encourage and cherish creativity in each and every child. It is not enough to know facts and figures. Young children need to know how to ask questions, how to search for their own answers, how to look at things in many different ways, and how to create their own sense of beauty and meaning in life.

Creativity does *not* end in the art area. Creativity and a creative approach to learning is possible in *every* curriculum area. This book is written to help you present creative learning opportunities for children throughout the curriculum.

How to Foster Creativity in All Children is written for anyone who is interested in children. However, since it is written especially for busy people who work with children, the following points are emphasized:

■ Creativity is the focus in *all* curriculum areas, not just the arts.
■ The approach to creativity is a practical one. A wide variety of activities is included in each chapter. All activities have been classroom tested.
■ Ages/grades are not attached to activities, as your own knowledge of children's ability is the best way to guide your use of any activity.
■ All activities include *why* the activities should be carried out; goals for each activity are provided.
■ All activities give information on how to get ready for the activity, as noted in the Preparation section.
■ All activities include *how* to carry out the activity, including lists of Materials and Procedures for each activity.
■ Variations (more and different ways to present an activity) are listed where applicable.
■ Additional Information to enhance understanding of an activity is provided where needed.

Part 1 presents a brief discussion of child development and art theories as they relate to creativity, aesthetics, and social-emotional and physical-mental growth. Part 1 sets the stage for application of these theories in specific curriculum areas, while Part 2 covers the early curriculum in Sections 2, 3, and 4.

Some additional features of *How to Foster Creativity in All Children* are:

■ Inclusion of children through grade 5 to provide activities for after-school child-care programs. This also addresses the fact that in many states early childhood programs go through grade 5.
■ Activities for middle to upper elementary age children (grades 4–5), called "Activities for Older Children" in the book. However, you will need to use your knowledge of each child's ability as a guide to using any of these suggested activities.
■ "This One's for You" and "Food for Thought" sections, which are included in each chapter, provide interesting extra activities and information related to the chapter.
■ Sugar-free and reduced-sugar recipes in the "Creative Food Experiences" chapter are designated by the symbol of a large smiley face.

It is the author's sincere hope that you *use* and *enjoy* this book along with the children!

To Casper, with love
and gratitude

Mary

PART 1

CHILD DEVELOPMENT AND CREATIVITY

Part 1 presents an overview of theories of child development and creativity. It sets the stage for the application of developmental theories in the more specific subject areas presented in Part 2. Also included is a section on art and how it is related to the physical, mental, and social-emotional development of young children.

Also included are chapters for both two- and three-dimensional activities. The final section of Part 1 covers the concept of play and its relationship to a child's overall development, as well as development of creativity in play.

At the end of each chapter in Part 1 you will find a wide variety of field-tested activities for young children up to and including grade 5.

SECTION 1

Fostering Creativity and Aesthetics in Young Children

CHAPTER 1

CREATIVITY

Take a few minutes to watch a four-year-old child in action. At one moment he is building a tower out of blocks. Suddenly he spots one of his friends playing with a homemade finger puppet. He wants to make one, too. A bit later he is playing with a guinea pig, stroking its fur and tickling its chin. Next, he is placing long, wide strokes of color on a piece of paper and getting spots of paint on everything in sight.

What is this? Now he is at the sand table building a sand castle with a high sand tower that keeps falling over. He seems to have discovered something. It is easier to build a tower out of blocks than out of sand; so he is back building with wooden blocks. It looks as though he is back where he started, except that the new block tower does not look anything like the one he started earlier.

It is exciting to watch active young children studying the world around them. A couple of things become clear almost immediately. First of all, children are full of curiosity. They enjoy investigating and finding out things. Second, they seem quite capable of doing this successfully. They are very creative in finding answers to problems that arise from their curiosity. Young children have a natural ability to come up with creative answers, creative approaches, and creative uses of materials.

People who work with young children need to understand creativity and have the skills to help and encourage children express their creative natures. They should realize the importance of creativity for both children and teachers. They need to be able to identify creativity in children and be able to help them develop a willingness to express this creativity.

 ## WHAT IS CREATIVITY?

Perhaps the most important thing to realize about creativity is that everyone possesses a certain amount of it. Some people are a little more creative, some a little less. No one is totally uncreative.

Young children tend to be highly open and creative. Unfortunately, many adults want children to conform. As outside pressures from adults grow, the children's environment closes in on them. They find it less and less rewarding to express interest in things, to be curious, and to be creative in investigating their world. To avoid this, it is important to know ways of encouraging a child's creativity. To begin with, one should understand the meaning of the term **creativity.**

The following definition may help you understand the concept better. Creativity is a way of thinking and acting or making something that is original for the individual and valued by that person or others. A person does not have to be the first one in the world to produce something in order for it to be considered a creative act.

THE CREATIVE PROCESS

When someone is creating something, there are usually two parts to that person's activity. The first part has to do with originality—the discovery of an idea, plan, or answer. The second part has to do with working out, proving, and making certain that the idea or answer works or is possible. The first part, *discovering,* involves using the imagination, playing with ideas, and exploring. The second part, *process,* involves using learned skills, evaluating, and testing.

Young children are naturally industrious and involved in learning new skills.

Children enjoy activities in which they participate freely and openly.

THOUGHT PROCESSES AND CREATIVITY

There are two kinds of thinking that produce solutions to problems. One of these types is called **convergent thinking.** The other type is called **divergent thinking.** Convergent thinking usually results in a single answer or solution to a question or problem. Divergent thinking opens things up and results in many answers to a single problem.

For example, if a child is asked to count the number of fish in an aquarium, there is only one correct answer. This is a question that leads children to convergent thinking. However, if a child is asked to tell as many things as possible about the aquarium, there are obviously many correct statements that can be made. Questions such as this encourage divergent rather than convergent thinking.

In dealing with young children, the focus should be on the *process* (i.e., developing and generating original ideas). This focus on the process encourages the development of creativity across the curriculum, instead of being confined to art and music activities.

CREATIVITY AND OLDER CHILDREN

With older children, creativity involves more of an emphasis on the criteria of high-quality, original products or solutions. The development of creative products comes about later in the child's development. An example of this is seen in the fourth and fifth grade science fair projects. It becomes apparent that some projects are more creative than others. For example, a student who created and tested a new chair design seems to have an idea of a

different quality from another student who tested cleaning products to see which worked best on stains.

PROCESS OVER PRODUCT

When working with young children you need to focus on the *process* and *not the product*. Remember that young children do not always have the skills to make a creative product (an elaborate painting or a workable invention), and so the process that leads to originality is the focus of creative potential.

 ## CHARACTERISTICS OF CREATIVITY

The kind of behavior teachers identify as desirable in children does not always coincide with characteristics associated with the creative personality. For example, teachers who think they value uniqueness may find that, when a child has spilled her milk because she tried an original method of holding the cup with her teeth, they don't like creative exploration as much as they thought they did!

This lack of conformity can be inconvenient, but teachers should realize that some creative individuals possess character traits that aren't always easy to appreciate.

Ideally, understanding creativity will result in increased acceptance and valuing of creativity in young children. Acceptance is vitally important because it will encourage children to develop their creativity further. Let us now summarize the ways to encourage creativity in all young children.

THIS ONE'S FOR YOU

Free Yourself—To Be Creative

One of the pioneers of research into children's creativity, Paul Torrance (1965), felt that we had to free ourselves to be creative before we can ever really be creative teachers. Here are some of his suggestions to free yourself to be creative.

- Don't be afraid to fall in love with something and to pursue it with intensity.
- Know, understand, take pride in, practice, develop, exploit, and enjoy your greatest strengths.
- Learn to free yourself from the expectations of others and to walk away from the games they impose on you. Free yourself to play your own game.
- Find a great teacher or mentor who will help you.
- Don't waste energy trying to be well-rounded.
- Do what you love and can do well.
- Learn the skills of independence.

How many of these apply to you? Are you free to be a creative teacher? Pick one or two of the suggestions that you most want to work on and then go!

Identifying Creativity

Creativity isn't always recognized by teachers and peers. Actually, history is full of examples of people whose creativity wasn't recognized in their school or work experience.

Consider that . . .

- Albert Einstein was four years old before he could speak and seven before he could read.
- Beethoven's music teacher once said of him, "As a composer, he is hopeless."
- F. W. Woolworth got a job in a dry goods store at age 21, but his employers would not let him wait on customers because he "didn't have enough sense."
- Leo Tolstoy flunked out of college.

- A newspaper editor fired Walt Disney because he had "no good ideas."
- Abraham Lincoln entered the Black Hawk War as a captain and came out as a private.
- Louisa May Alcott was told by an editor that she would never write anything that had popular appeal.
- Winston Churchill failed the sixth grade.
- Isaac Newton did poorly in grade school.
- Thomas Edison's teachers told him that he was too stupid to learn anything.
- Admiral Richard Byrd had been retired from the Navy, declared "unfit for service," when he flew over both poles.

HELPING CHILDREN EXPRESS CREATIVITY

There are at least eight things that can be done for children to help them express natural creative tendencies:

Help children accept change. A child who becomes overly worried or upset in new situations is unlikely to express creative potential.

Help children realize that some problems have no easy answers. This may help prevent children from becoming anxious when they cannot find an immediate answer to a question or problem.

Help children recognize that many problems have a number of possible answers. Encourage them to search for more than one answer. Then they can evaluate all the different answers to see which ones fit the situation best.

FOOD FOR THOUGHT "Unpackaging" Your Life

No teacher I've ever known became a teacher to stifle creativity in young children. Somewhere along the way, teachers become affected by the "package" syndrome: using "packaged" curricula, using "packages" of ideas, and—worst of all—expecting young children to come to the classroom in neat, tidy, predictable "packages."

To help restore your own joy of teaching, try this:

- List the reasons why you became a teacher.
- List what you like about young children.
- List what you like about yourself.
- List what you think is creative about you (in teaching and in your life in general).
- Go over these lists whenever you are making choices that will directly affect young children—choices such as materials, texts, and curricula. See how your choices fit your lists.
- Use your lists as a guide to "unpackaging" your life.

Help children learn to judge and accept their own feelings. Children should not feel guilty for having feelings about things. Create an environment where judgment is deferred and all ideas are respected, where discussion and debates are a means of trying out ideas in a nonthreatening atmosphere.

Reward children for being creative. Let children know that their creative ideas are valued. In fact, the more creative the idea or product, the greater they should be rewarded. It is also useful to help children realize that good work is sometimes its own reward.

Help children feel joy in their creative productions, and in working through a problem. Children should find that doing things and finding answers for themselves is fun. The adult should establish the conditions that allow this to take place.

Help children appreciate themselves for being different. There is a tendency to reward children for conforming. This discourages creativity. Children should learn to like themselves because they are unique.

Help children develop perseverance—"stick-to-itiveness." Help children by encouraging them to follow through. Provide chances for them to stick with an activity even if everyone else has moved on to something different.

In all creative activities for young children, the process is more important than the product.

THIS ONE'S FOR YOU

Are You a Creative Doer or a Spectator?

Painter Stanley A. Czurles feels that the modern person has contracted the dreaded sickness called "spectatoritis," which leads to increased feelings of boredom, lack of satisfaction, and apathy. In his view, only the creative person can experience true fulfillment in life. Czurles presents the following comparison of the two contrasting approaches to life. See if you can find yourself in either (or maybe both) of the following two lists.

SPECTATOR

- Kills time
- Is an observer
- Has few self-sufficiency interests
- Seeks to have something happen to or for him or her
- Is involved in a merry-go-round of prestructured activities
- Has only temporary enjoyment, with little or no lasting product
- Is swept into activities
- Has fractionated experiences
- Is prone to boredom
- Experiences no deep challenge
- Accomplishes nothing very distinguished
- Curtails self by a focus on pessimistic personal concerns
- Has increased hardening of opinions and attitudes
- Achieves superficial trappings of culture
- Is subject to early spiritual-mental aging
- Experiences primarily what is

CREATIVE DOER

- Uses time to develop self
- Is involved, experiences personal achievement
- Is rich in self-enriching activities
- Is self-stimulating; is at home and in control of many conditions
- Enjoys selected relevant activities
- Experiences continuous satisfaction, achieves tangible results, and becomes a more efficiently functioning person
- Selects planned participation
- Has completeness and continuity of involvement
- Is stimulated by challenging interests
- Aspires more as he or she achieves new goals
- Grows in potential through unique achievements
- Is enlivened by a recognized freedom to pursue creative interests
- Continued being flexible through continuous new insights
- Experiences the essence of a culture
- Enjoys an extended youthful spirit
- Experiences what might be

(Adapted from *More Creative Growth Games* by Eugene Raudsepp. Copyright © 1980 by Eugene Raudsepp. Used by permission.)

ACTIVITIES FOR CHILDREN

Creative Thinking— Changing the Known

GOALS: To encourage divergent thinking
To develop children's creative thinking

MATERIALS: Assortment of common objects such as a cotton ball, paper clip, key, belt, cup, book, and so on.

PREPARATION: Choose one of the above listed objects to show the children.

PROCEDURE:

1. Show the children the object.
2. Have the children tell you as many uses as they can for the object.
3. Accept all suggestions, even those that seem silly to you.
4. For older children, you may want to list all of the suggested uses on a chart or blackboard for later use in language arts or science lessons.
5. Choose another item and repeat the activity.

VARIATION:

■ Have the children choose objects for this exercise. Repeat the activity using these objects.

■ Have children draw or paint a picture about creative uses for the object(s) from this activity. Older children may write a short story on the same topic.

ACTIVITIES FOR CHILDREN

Just Suppose . . . Creative Imagining

GOAL: To encourage creative thinking

MATERIALS: Paper, pencils, crayons

PREPARATION: Set aside a large block of time for this activity. Time limits can discourage the creative process.

PROCEDURE:

1. From the chart of "Just Suppose" possibilities on page 9, choose one to use with the children.
2. Read the item to the children.
3. Discuss the item and answer any questions the children may have on it.
4. Have the children draw pictures or write down all their ideas to the "Just Suppose" item.
5. Have the children share their work.

VARIATION:

■ Have the children make up their own "Just Suppose" items for this activity.

■ Have the older children write a story based on their ideas from this activity.

Just Suppose . . . Creative Imagining

Here are some suggestions to use with this activity:

■ "Just suppose" that there is nothing made of wood in the room. What would change? What would things look like? What dangers might exist? What would you be unable to do?

■ "Just suppose" you cannot use words, either written or spoken. How can you communicate? What is frustrating about it? What is pleasing about it? What would it mean if it continued forever?

■ "Just suppose" you receive a million dollars and must spend all of it. Make a list or drawing of ways to spend the money.

■ "Just suppose" you were the first person to meet a man from Mars and could ask him only three questions. What would they be?

■ "Just suppose" you could be any person in the world for one hour. Who would it be? What would you do?

■ What would happen if all people woke up tomorrow morning to find themselves twice as large?

ACTIVITIES FOR CHILDREN

Objects of Art

GOALS: To encourage creative thinking
To develop divergent thinking

MATERIALS: Collection of objects that children may use as inspiration for an art or writing project (examples include rocks, feathers, twigs, fabrics, pieces of wood, bottle caps, corks, and so forth), paper, pencils, paste, scissors, markers, and playdough

PREPARATION: Display the collection of objects for all children to see.

Allow children to touch as well as see the objects.

Provide children with the art supplies listed above.

PROCEDURE:

1. Ask the children to describe the objects they see.
2. Have the children state which they like best.

3. Have each child choose at least three of the displayed objects to use in a picture, a collage, or in any other art form he or she chooses to make.
4. Encourage children's artistic work. Make comments such as "That feather looks so good where you glued it on your paper."

VARIATION:

■ Have the children bring in "art objects" of their own choice for this activity.

■ Go on a walk with the children and collect "art objects" for this exercise.

ADDITIONAL INFORMATION: Be sure to have a wide variety of objects and many of the same items. This will avoid too much disappointment or disagreements when several children want the same type of item.

ACTIVITIES FOR CHILDREN

Using All Your Senses

GOALS: To encourage creative thinking

To be more open to an everyday experience

To use all five senses in eating an apple

MATERIALS: Apples, one for each child

PREPARATION: Discuss the five senses. Have the children give examples of each.

PROCEDURE:

1. Give each child an apple.
2. Have the children use all five senses in eating the apple.
3. Have the children describe what they see, feel, hear, and smell.
4. Have the children use the last sense—the sense of taste—by actually eating the apple.

VARIATION:

■ Go outside and do the same activity with a tree (except the eating part!)
■ Use a different fruit or vegetable and repeat the process.

REFERENCES

Raudsepp, E. (1980). *More creative growth games.* New York: Pedigree Books, G. P. Putnam's Sons.

Torrance, E. P. (1965). *Rewarding creative behavior: Experiments in classroom creativity.* Englewood Cliffs, NJ: Prentice-Hall.

CHAPTER 2

PROMOTING CREATIVITY

C reative thinking is not a station one arrives at, but a means of traveling. Creativity is fun. Being creative, feeling creative, and experiencing creativity is fun. Learning is more fun for children in settings where teachers and children recognize and understand the process of creative thinking. Incorporating creative thinking into all areas of the curriculum contributes to a young child's positive attitude toward learning. As one teacher commented, "I used to think that if children were having too much fun they couldn't be learning. Now I understand how they are learning in a more effective way." This chapter covers the relationship of creativity and the classroom environment, providing guidelines for encouraging creative thinking in the early childhood program throughout the day. In subsequent chapters, the same emphasis on creativity is applied to specific curriculum areas.

A child who meets with unquestionable acceptance of her unique approach to the world feels safe expressing her creativity.

 ## PROMOTING CREATIVITY THROUGH POSITIVE ACCEPTANCE

Adults who work with young children are in an especially crucial position to foster each child's creativity. In the day-to-day experiences in early childhood settings, as young children actively explore their world, adults' attitudes clearly transmit their feelings to the child. A child who meets with unquestionable acceptance of her unique approach to the world will feel safe in expressing her creativity, whatever the activity or situation.

The following are guidelines on how to help transmit this positive acceptance to children, which in turn fosters creativity in any situation.

■ Openly demonstrate to young children that there is value in their curiosity, exploration, and original behavior.

■ Allow the children to go at their own pace when they are doing an activity which excites and interests them.

■ Let children stay with what they are making until they feel it's done.

11

FOOD FOR THOUGHT   Right-brained Children

I have always found children who "marched to a different drummer" a joy and a challenge to work with. They make me re-examine my teaching methods and open up my mind to alternate views. These children approach life and learning in a truly unique manner. One specific group of these special children has been named right-brained (or "alpha") children.

When we talk about a right-brained or a left-brained person we are referring to learning preferences based on functional differences between the hemispheres (sides) of the brain.

Right-brained or "alpha" children are those whose right hemisphere of the brain is dominant in their learning process. This is in contrast to the majority of children, whose left hemisphere is dominant in their learning style. As we will see later in this section, each hemisphere of the brain has distinctly different strengths and behavioral characteristics.

All of us use both hemispheres of the brain, but we may use one side more than the other. For instance, you might have a dominant right hemisphere, which simply means that it is your preferred or stronger hemisphere. It is the one in which you tend to process first most of the information you receive. That does not mean you don't use your left hemisphere. You may use your right hemisphere 60 percent of the time and your left hemisphere 40 percent. Similarly, when we talk about right-brained or left-brained children, we do not mean they use only one hemisphere but simply that they use one hemisphere to a greater extent than the other.

The right and left brain hemispheres have specialized thinking characteristics. They do not approach life in the same way. The left hemisphere approach to life is part-to-whole. It sequences, puts things in order, and is logical. The right hemisphere learns whole-to-part. It does not sequence; it does not put things in order; it looks at things in an overall way or holistically. Let's consider specific skills and in which hemisphere that skill is best developed.

LEFT HEMISPHERE

The skills best developed in this side of the brain are handwriting, understanding symbols, language, reading, and phonics. Other general skills best developed here are locating details and facts, talking and reciting, following directions, listening, and auditory association. These are all skills children must exercise on a day-to-day basis in school. We give children symbols; we stress reading, language, and phonics. We ask for details; we insist upon directions being followed, and mostly, we talk at children. In short, most of our school curriculum is left-brained. We teach to the child who has a dominant left brain.

RIGHT HEMISPHERE

The right hemisphere contains a whole other set of skills. The right hemisphere has the ability to recognize and process nonverbal sounds. It also displays a greater ability to communicate using body language.

Although the motor cortex is in both hemispheres, the ability to make judgments based on the relationship of our bodies to space (needed in sports, creative movement, and dance, for instance) is basically centered in the right hemisphere.

The ability to recognize, draw, and deal with shapes and patterns, as well as geometric figures, lies in the right hemisphere. This involves the ability to distinguish between different colors and hues, as well as the ability to visualize in color.

Singing and music are right-hemisphere activities. Creative art is also in debt to the right hemisphere. While many left-brained children are quite good in art, the "art" they make is structured; it must come out a certain way. They are most comfortable with models and a predictable outcome. Their pictures, or the things they create, are drawings made for Mother's Day or turkeys drawn for Thanksgiving. Left-hemisphered children are good at other-directed art.

(Continued)

Right-hemisphered children create "mystery" pictures. They show the pictures to you but they aren't quite sure what you are looking at until they start talking about it. For example, they may show raindrops falling and the sun shining at the same time.

After listening to a story, when you ask right-brained children what they heard, they can retell the story in their own words without any difficulty. However, they are so creative that they usually add their own details and ending. You think they are exaggerating and they may be, in adult terms. But in their terms, they are simply being what they are. They change stories, add details, and alter endings to meet their emotional needs. Feelings and emotions appear to be most dominant in the right hemisphere.

A further way to understand the right-brained child is by the behavioral characteristics associated with this group of children. While not all right-brained children will display all of these characteristics, you will find many of them easily recognizable in certain right-brained children. The following is just a sampling of right-brained behavioral characteristics.

Right-brained children:

- appear to daydream.
- talk in phrases or leave words out when talking.
- have difficulty following directions.
- make faces or use other forms of nonverbal communication.
- display greater-than-average fine motor problems (cutting, pasting, and so on) when asked to conform or do structured tasks. Fine motor problems rarely appear when children are doing something they have selected.
- are able to recall places and events but have difficulty recalling symbolic representations such as names, letters, and numbers.
- are on the move most of the time.
- like to work partway out of their chairs or standing up.
- like to take things apart and put them back together again.
- are much messier than other children.
- like to touch, trip, and poke other children.
- display impulsive behavior.
- get lost coming and going, even from familiar places such as the classroom.
- may forget what they started out to do.
- will give the right answer to a question, but can't tell you where it came from.
- often give responses unrelated to what is being discussed.
- may be leaders in the group.
- may chew their tongues while working.

Now, armed with all of this information on right- and left-brained children, you need to reflect on your own work with children and ask yourself if your curriculum is directed toward only one type of learner. Are you in tune with the right-brained learners? You may find it helpful to go to the library and take out books with specific curricular ideas for right-brained children. At the very least, you need to be aware of yet another way in which each young child is uniquely different (Vitale, 1982).

Given appropriate, open-ended materials, children know how to create their own fun.

- Let children figure out their own ways of doing things if they prefer to do so.
- Keep the atmosphere relaxed.
- Encourage guessing, especially when the answers make good sense.

WORKING WITH OLDER CHILDREN

In the upper elementary grades, teachers have an even greater challenge to promote creativity since the curriculum often dominates the program. There are often state level guidelines for what to teach, at what level, with specific books and materials. Even in this situation, you can encourage creativity in your classroom. Here are some suggestions to help you get started.

To encourage creativity with older children:

- Use tangible rewards (stickers, prizes) as seldom as possible; instead, encourage children's own pride in the work they have done.
- Avoid setting up competitive situations for children.
- Downplay your evaluation of children's work; instead, lead them to become more proficient at recognizing their own strengths and weaknesses.
- Encourage children to monitor their own work, rather than to rely on your surveillance of them.
- Whenever possible, give children choices about what activities they do and about how to do those activities.
- Make intrinsic (internal) motivation a conscious factor of your discussions with children. Encourage them to become aware of their own special interests and to take their focus *off* the extrinsic (external rewards).
- In order to build children's intrinsic (internal) motivation, help them build their self-esteem and help them focus on and appreciate their own unique talents and strengths.

THIS ONE'S FOR YOU   Cherishing Each Child

Creativity thrives in an environment that cherishes the individual. Each person in such an environment feels special. I've used this idea at the beginning of the program year to encourage this "special" feeling in each child.

On my classroom door, I first put up a big sign that said "Special Person." I waited for the children's questions as to what it said. I read them the two words, pointing to each as I said it. Some children imitated me and "read" the sign as well. I kept up the large sign for a week, arousing the children's natural curiosity. They all eventually asked me who was the special person? I told them they would all know the answer on the next Monday morning.

When the children arrived on that Monday morning, they each saw themselves reflected in a mirror I had attached to the door under the title "Special Person." Each child was indeed a "special person" that day and every day of the year in my room.

Young children actively explore their world in day-to-day experiences in early childhood settings.

- As much as possible, encourage children to become active, independent learners rather than to rely on you for constant direction. Encourage them to take confident control of their own learning process.
- Give children ample opportunities for free play with various materials, and allow them to engage in fantasy whenever possible.
- In any way you can, show children that you value creativity—that not only do you allow it, but you also engage in it yourself.
- Whenever you can, show your students that *you* are an intrinsically motivated adult who enjoys thinking creatively.

Just the way a question is phrased or asked sets the stage for creative replies. For example the question, "Describe (or tell me about) the sky. . ." would certainly get different answers than "What color is the sky?" In the first, more open-ended (divergent) question, children are encouraged to share their personal feelings and experiences about the sky. This might be color or cloud shapes, or even how jets, birds, and helicopters can fill it at times. The second question is phrased in such a way that a one-word (convergent) reply would do. Or even worse, it may seem to children that there is one and only one *correct* answer! In asking questions, then, a teacher can foster children's creativity.

 MOTIVATING SKILLS FOR TEACHERS

Some children need help in getting started. The fact that the activity is labeled "creative" does not necessarily make the child "ready to go." All teachers, even those with good ideas, face this problem. There are several ways to help children become motivated for the creative process.

Physical needs. Make sure children are rested and physically fit. Sleepy, hungry, or sick children cannot care about creativity. Their physical needs must be met before such learning can be appealing.

Interests. Try to find out, and then use, what naturally interests the child. Children not only want to do things they like to do, they want to be successful at them. Whenever children feel that they will succeed in a task, they are generally much more willing to get involved. Parents may be good resources for determining the child's interests.

Friends. Permit children to work with their friends. Some teachers avoid putting children who are friends together in working situations. They worry that these children will only "fool around" or disturb others. When this does happen, one should question the task at hand, since it is obviously not keeping the children's interest.

Activities for fun. Allow the activity to be fun for the child. Notice the use of the word "allow." Children know how to have their own fun. They do not need anyone to make it for them. Encourage child-initiated activities and self-selection of creative materials. Emphasize voluntary participation of the children in activities. Teachers are giving children opportunities for fun if they honestly can answer "yes" to these questions:

Is the activity exciting?

Is the activity in a free setting?

Can the children imagine in it?

Can the children play at it?

Is there a gamelike quality to it?

Are judgments avoided?

Is competition deemphasized?

Will there be something to laugh about?

Goals. Permit children to set and reach goals. Most of the excitement in achieving a goal is in reaching for it. Children should be given opportunities to plan projects. They should be allowed to get involved in activities that have something at the end for which they can strive. If the completion of an activity is not rewarding to a child, then the value of that activity is questionable.

Variety. Vary the content and style of what the children can do. It is wise to consider not only what will be next, but how it will be done, too. For example, the teacher has the children sit and watch a movie, then they sit and draw, and then they sit and listen to a story. These are three different activities, but in each of them, the children are sitting. The content of the activity has changed, but not the style. This can, and does, become boring. Boring is definitely *not* creative.

Challenge. Challenge the children. This means letting them know that what they are about to do is something that they might not be able to do, but that it will be exciting to try. An example of this is letting the children know that their next activity may be tricky, adventurous, or mysterious. It is the "bet you can't do this" approach with the odds in favor of the children.

Reinforcement. Reinforce the children. The basic need here is for something to come at the end of the activity that lets the children feel they would like to do

it again. It could be the teacher's smile, a compliment, reaching the goal, hanging up the creation, sharing with a friend, or just finishing the activity. The main thing is that the children feel rewarded and satisfied for their efforts.

The children's feelings. Try to make certain the children feel good about what they are doing. Some teachers feel if a child is working intensely or learning, that is enough. This may not be so. The most important thing is not what the children are doing but how they feel about what they are doing. If children feel bad about themselves or an activity while doing it, this is a warning. If a child is made to continue the activity, it may be damaging, as it tends to lower self-concept and security. This means the teacher must be continually in touch with how the children are feeling. It is done by listening, watching, and being with the children in a manner that is open and caring.

ACTIVITIES FOR CHILDREN

Make Things Better with Your Imagination

GOALS: To encourage children to think more creatively
To develop divergent thinking skills

MATERIALS: Paper, pencils, crayons, and markers

PREPARATION: Gather children in a group.
Discuss what imagination is.
Have children give examples of imagination.

PROCEDURE:

1. Ask children to "make things better with their imagination."

2. Ask children to change things to make them the way they would like them to be.

3. Use the chart below for examples of questions to use for this activity.

4. Have the children share their ideas on how to "make things better with imagination."

VARIATION:

■ Have the children make a drawing, painting, collage, or any other art form to express their ideas on how to "make things better."

■ Have the children act out their ideas.

■ Let the children come up with things they can make better with their imaginations.

Making Things Better with Your Imagination—Suggested Questions

■ What would taste better if it were sweeter?

■ What would be nicer if it were smaller?

■ What would be more fun if it were faster?

■ What would be better if it were quieter?

■ What would be more exciting if it went backwards?

■ What would be happier if it were bigger?

ACTIVITIES FOR CHILDREN

Using Other Senses

GOAL: To develop creative thinking

MATERIALS: Piece of foam rubber, small rock, a grape, a piece of sandpaper, and any other interesting objects

PREPARATION: Keep items in a box or bag out of the children's sight. Have the children sit in a circle.

PROCEDURE:

1. Explain that children have to guess what's been placed in their hands.
2. Have one child close his eyes.
3. Take one item out of the bag and place it in this child's hand.
4. Have the child guess what's in his hand.

VARIATION:

- Have the children close their eyes and guess what they hear.
- Use sounds like shuffling cards, jingling keys or coins, rubbing sandpaper, crumbling newspaper, or ripping paper.

ADDITIONAL INFORMATION: When doing this exercise, children should be asked for reasons for their guesses. It results in a more fun and better learning experience for them.

ACTIVITIES FOR CHILDREN

Water Play Activities for Creative Thinking

GOALS: To develop creative thinking
To encourage divergent thinking

MATERIALS: Tub of water (water table), plastic squeeze bottles, objects to float in water, plastic play objects (measuring cups, bowls, spoons, funnels, and so on)

PREPARATION: Choose a small group of three to four children for this activity. Gather around the water table or tub of water.

PROCEDURE:

1. Ask children thought-provoking, divergent-thinking questions. (See chart on page 18 for some suggestions.)
2. Pose one problem to solve with water and play objects.
3. Have the children work with materials and water to answer the questions.

VARIATION:

- This is a great outdoor activity.
- Let the children come up with more water play challenges of their own.

Suggested Questions for Creative Water Play Activities

- Can you make the water in your squeeze bottle shoot out like the water from the hose?
- Can you make a water shower for the plants?
- Can you catch one drop of water on something? How many drops of water can you put on a jar lid?
- Can we think of some words to describe what we do with water (sprinkle, pour, drip, trickle, drizzle, shower, deluge, torrent, splash, spank, stir, ripple, and so on)?

- Can we collect some rainwater? How?
- How far can you make the water spray?
- Can you make something look different by putting it in water?
- Can you find some things that float (or sink) in the water?
- Can you make a noise in the water?

ACTIVITIES FOR CHILDREN   Space Explorers

GOALS: To develop creative thinking

To encourage creative movement

MATERIALS: None required

PREPARATION: Gather children in an indoor or outdoor space large enough so they can move freely without bumping into each other.

PROCEDURE:

1. Ask the children to pretend they are on a planet in space where they are much *heavier* than on earth.
2. Have the children lift their arms as though their bodies are twice as heavy as they actually are.
3. Have the children walk as though they are twice as heavy as they actually are.
4. Next, try dancing at that heavy weight.

VARIATION:

- Have the children pretend they are on the moon, where their bodies are much *lighter* than on earth.
- Have the children move their body parts as though they are very light.
- Have the children select a familiar activity (such as walking, dancing, moving to rhythms) and pretend they are doing it on a strange planet, using slow motion.

ACTIVITIES FOR CHILDREN

Becoming an Object

GOALS: To develop creative thinking
To encourage creative movement

MATERIALS: None required

PREPARATION: Gather children in an indoor or outdoor space large enough so they can move freely without bumping into one another.

PROCEDURE:

1. Name inanimate objects, such as a chair, ball, lamp, shoe, pencil, and so on.

2. Have the children make the shapes of the various objects named with their bodies.

3. Have the children show, with their bodies, how objects would move by an external force. See the chart below for examples of these motions.

Suggestions for Becoming an Object

Challenge the children to move like:

- an orange being peeled.
- a standing lamp being carried across the room.
- a wall with a vine growing over it.
- a paper clip being inserted on paper.
- an ice cube melting.
- a balloon with air coming out of it.
- a cloud drifting through the sky, slowly changing shapes.
- smoke coming out of a chimney.
- a twisted pin being thrust into paper.
- a rubber ball bouncing along the ground.
- a boat being tossed by the waves.
- an arrow being shot through the air.
- a steel bar being hammered into different shapes.

ACTIVITIES FOR OLDER CHILDREN Telling Tableaus
(Grades 4–5)

GOAL: To develop creative thinking

MATERIALS: None required

PREPARATION:

1. Explain that tableaus are "frozen pictures" in which a group of students freeze or pose to act out a scene, a saying, a book title, a movie title, a CD title, and so on.
2. Discuss the skills necessary to be a good "freezer," such as staring eyes, no movement, a frozen expression, and so on.

PROCEDURE:

1. Have children work in small groups.
2. Name a captain for each group.
3. Better yet, have the children choose their own captain.

4. Give the children 5–10 minutes (more if needed) to develop their scene and practice their frozen poses.
5. Don't allow any props.
6. For the performances, have the first group come to the front of the room.
7. Turn off the lights and have the children close their eyes as the first group sets up their scene.
8. When the scene is set, turn on the lights and have the children open their eyes.
9. Read the caption or have the rest of the children guess the title.
10. Continue through the tableau scenes until all groups have had a chance to perform.

ACTIVITIES FOR OLDER CHILDREN Television Drama
(Grades 4–5)

GOALS: To develop creative thinking
To encourage use of imagination

MATERIALS: VCR, TV, and tape

PREPARATION: Pre-record a part of a television show that will interest your children. Children will be able to tell you which are their favorite shows if you're not sure.

PROCEDURE:

1. Show children a couple of minutes of the tape and then turn it off.

2. Discuss the creativity the characters are using.
3. Show more of the program.
4. Stop it at a critical point in the story.
5. Have the children work in pairs to brainstorm decisions the characters could make.
6. Turn the show back on to see what decisions the characters actually made and what happened as a result of those decisions.
7. Have the children identify if the characters came up with creative decisions and why or why not.

ACTIVITIES FOR OLDER CHILDREN
(Grades 4–5)
Fairy Tales for Creativity

GOALS: To develop creative thinking
To encourage divergent thinking

MATERIALS: Paper, pencils, crayons, and markers

PREPARATION: Read several fairy tales to the group. Ask the children to recall other fairy tales.

PROCEDURE:

1. Each child chooses one fairy tale to use for the creative activities suggested in the chart below.

Suggested Activities Using Fairy Tales

Creative fairy tale puppet shows. Create a puppet show to retell your favorite fairy tale to the class. Change one thing about the story and see if the class can guess the change.

Fairy tale rating. Read four fairy tales of your choice. Rate them in order of your most-to-least favorite and explain why you rated them as you did. Using your favorite fairy tale, write a short review explaining why everyone should read it.

Fairy tale journal. Pretend you have been put into one of the fairy tales, and in journal form discuss the events and characters you meet. Discuss what you like and dislike about the characters. Include at least eight entries.

Fairy tale logic. Choose a song that you think tells a story similar to one of the fairy tales you've read, and then write a short essay explaining why you chose this song and why it relates to your fairy tale.

Fairy tale music. Compose a song that tells the story of one of the fairy tales. Perform it for a group of students, and have them guess which fairy tale your song represents.

Fairy tale picture book. Create a picture book for your favorite fairy tale. Read it to another class.

Fairy tale day. Plan a fairy tale day for the class, including activities for the entire day. This may include dressing up as your favorite character, eating fairy tale foods, playing games, and reading fairy tales.

Fairy tale rewrite. Rewrite a fairy tale from the perspective of one of the minor characters in the story. Read your story to the class.

Fairy tale game. Create a board game with a fairy tale theme. Include all of the main parts of the story in the game. Let students play the game and give you feedback. Make any changes that would make it more fun to play.

ACTIVITIES FOR OLDER CHILDREN What Would Happen If?
(Grades 4–5)

GOALS: To develop creative thinking
To encourage the use of imagination

MATERIALS: Paper, pencil, and markers

PREPARATION: Talk about how imagining can make things more fun.

PROCEDURE:

1. Ask one of the following questions:
   - What would happen if all the trees in the world were blue?
   - What would happen if everyone looked alike?
   - What would happen if all the cars were gone?
   - What would happen if everybody wore the same clothes?
   - What would happen if every vegetable tasted like chocolate?
   - What would happen if there were no more clocks or watches?
   - What would happen if you could fly?
2. Have children share their ideas.
3. Continue asking questions as children's interest continues.

VARIATION:

■ Have children draw a picture, paint a painting, or use any other art form to express their answers to the questions.

■ Have children act out their responses to the question(s) posed.

■ Have the children come up with imagination questions of their own.

REFERENCES

Goleman, D. (1995). *Emotional intelligence.* New York: Bantam Books.

Vitale, B. (1982). *Unicorns are real.* New York: Ablex.

CHAPTER 3

AESTHETICS

The term **aesthetics** refers to an appreciation for beauty and a feeling of wonder. It is a sensibility that uses the imagination as well as the five senses. It is seeing beauty in a sunset, hearing rhythm in a rainfall, and loving the expression on a person's face. Each person has an individual personal sense of what is or is not pleasing.

Aesthetic experiences emphasize doing things for the pure joy of it. Although there can be, there does not *have* to be any practical purpose or reason. Thus, you may take a ride in a car to feel its power and enjoy the scenery rather than to visit someone or run an errand. In the same way, a child plays with blocks to feel their shapes and see them tumble rather than to build something.

Young children benefit from aesthetic experiences. Children are fascinated by beauty. They love nature and enjoy creating, looking at, and talking about art. They express their feelings and ideas through language, song, expressive movement, music, and dance far more openly than adults. They are not yet hampered by the conventional labels used by adults to separate each art expression into pigeonholes. Young children experience the arts as a whole. They are creative, inquisitive, and delighted by art.

The purpose of aesthetic experiences is to help develop a full and rich life for the child. It does not matter whether an activity is useful for anything else. There does not have to be a product. Doing just for the sake of doing is enough. Teachers must be careful to allow for and encourage such motivation.

Children gain an aesthetic sense by doing. This means sensing, feeling, and responding to things. It can be rolling a ball, smelling a flower, petting an animal, or hearing a story. Aesthetic development takes place in secure settings free of competition and adult judgment.

AESTHETICS AND THE QUALITY OF LEARNING

Aesthetic learning means joining what one thinks with what one feels. Through art, ideas and feelings are expressed. People draw and sculpt to show their feelings about life. Art is important because it can deepen and enlarge understanding. All children cannot be great artists, but children can develop an aesthetic sense, an appreciation for art.

Teachers can encourage the aesthetic sense in children in a variety of ways. For example, science activities lend themselves very well to beauty and artistic expression. Since children use their senses in learning, science exhibits with things like rocks, wood, and leaves can be placed in attractive displays for children to touch, smell, and explore with all of their senses. They can experience with their senses artistic elements such as line, shape, pattern, color, and texture in these natural objects.

The arts are developed best as a whole. After hearing a story, some children may want to act it out. Some may prefer to paint a picture about it. Others may wish

When children are allowed freedom to choose and evaluate, they are developing their aesthetic sense.

A happy balance must be established between structured and nonstructured activities.

to create a dance about it, and some may want to make the music for the dance. These activities can lead to others. There should be a constant exchange, not only among all the art activities, but among all subject areas. This prevents children from creating a false separation between work and play, art and learning, and thought and feeling. The environment can be set up to encourage this type of aesthetic discussion by implementing the suggestions presented in "This One's For You" box on page 25, and in the chart on page 27.

SUGGESTIONS FOR AESTHETIC EXPERIENCES WITH OLDER CHILDREN

Children experience a developmental shift around ages 7–8 which allows them to deal with more abstract ideas (more information on this is in Chapter 5). At this point, older children are able to not only experience the arts aesthetically, but are able to begin discussing their own opinions, aesthetic tastes, and experiences. Thus, the teacher can engage children in grades 4–5 in discussions

FOOD FOR THOUGHT

Ways to Encourage Aesthetics in the Classroom

- In addition to the typical art center, include books about artists in the reading area.
- Include "real" art books in the reading and quiet areas of the room. These do not necessarily have to be children's books, since young children will enjoy looking at artwork in any book.
- Display fine-art prints on bulletin boards and walls so that children can easily see them. Be sure to change them regularly. If they are up too long, they will quickly fade into the background.
- Include art objects on the science table, where appropriate. Geodes, shards of pottery, and crystals are all good starting points.
- Invite guest art educators into the classroom to show the children art objects to look at, touch, and talk about.
- Give children an opportunity to choose their favorites from a selection of fine-art prints.
- Display fine-art prints near the writing and art centers.

about what is art and why they consider something to be art or not.

The best type of environment for older children is one in which questioning is valued. In such an environment students will feel comfortable raising questions about art and their reactions to it. Teachers of older children need to encourage rather than suppress discussion of aesthetic questions as they emerge. This is done by providing them the time and environment for art-related experiences and discussions.

AESTHETIC EXPERIENCES

Aesthetic experiences for young children can take many forms. They can involve an appreciation of the beauty of nature, the rhythm and imagery of music or poetry, or the qualities of works of art. Far from being a specialized talent, the recognition of aesthetic qualities comes quite naturally to children.

In the early childhood classroom, children are introduced to new experiences. Teachers have a responsibility to provide the very best that our culture has to offer by introducing a range of good art, not merely what is easiest or most familiar. Most children have plenty of exposure to cartoon characters, advertising art, and stereotyped, simplistic posters. These do not foster aesthetic development and are sometimes demeaning to children. Teachers often say, "children like them," but the fact that children like something—for example, candy and staying up late at night—does not necessarily mean it is good for them.

THIS ONE'S FOR YOU
Suggestions for Improving Aesthetics in the Environment

For young children, giving special attention to the environment can help develop their aesthetic sense. Here are some suggestions on how to enhance the environment to develop children's aesthetic sense:

Color—Bright colors will dominate a room and may detract from art and natural beauty. If there is a choice, select soft, light, neutral colors for walls and ceilings. Color-coordinate learning centers so that children begin to see them as wholes rather than as parts. Avoid having many different kinds of patterns in any one place—they can be distracting and overstimulating.

Furnishings—Group similar furniture together. Keep colors natural and neutral to focus children's attention on the learning materials on the shelves. When choosing furnishings, select natural wood rather than metal or plastic. If furniture must be painted, use one neutral color for everything so that there is greater flexibility in moving it from space to space. Periodically give children brushes and warm soapy water and let them scrub the furniture.

Storage—Rotate materials on shelves rather than crowding them together. Crowded shelves look unattractive and are hard for children to maintain. Baskets make excellent, attractive storage containers. If storage tubs are used, put all of the same kind together on one shelf. If cardboard boxes are used for storage, cover them with plain-colored paper or paint them.

Decoration—Mount and display children's artwork. Provide artwork by fine artists and avoid garish, stereotyped posters. Make sure that much artwork (by both children and adult artists) is displayed at children's eye level. Use shelf tops to display sculpture, plants, and items of natural beauty like shells, stones, and fish tanks. Avoid storing teachers' materials on the tops of shelves. If there is no other choice, create a teacher "cubby" using a covered box or storage tub.

Outdoors—Design or arrange play structures as extensions of nature rather than intrusions upon it. If possible, use natural materials like wood and hemp instead of painted metal, plastic, or fiberglass. Provide adequate storage to help maintain materials. Involve children, parents, and staff in keeping outdoor areas free of litter. Add small details like a garden or a rock arrangement to show that the outdoors also deserves attention and care.

(Adapted with permission from the National Association of Young Children, S. Feeney and E. Moravcik, "A Thing of Beauty: Aesthetic Development in Young Children," in *Young Children,* Sept., 1987, 11.)

Aesthetic development begins early in a child's life as he expresses his personal preferences.

Children can also gradually learn about the concepts of design (see Figure 3–1 on how to talk with children about this and other art elements). During group discussions, children should be encouraged to talk about the design qualities of a specific color, the movement of lines, the contrast of sizes and shapes, and the variety of textures. They should be helped to think and feel, as individuals, about a certain art object or piece of music. Their understanding of aesthetics, and their willingness and ability to discuss its concepts, will increase with experience.

FOOD FOR THOUGHT

Develop Your Own Aesthetic Sense

Teachers need to cultivate *their own* aesthetic sensitivity if they are going to help children develop theirs. And that's not always easy! I always searched for something of beauty to inspire me, especially in the dreary days of seemingly endless midwestern winters.

The following ideas helped boost my aesthetic sense, which in turn benefited the young children in my care.

■ The weekly purchase of a single, fresh flower (usually costing under $2), which I displayed on my desk in a small vase. It perked up my and the children's spirits.

■ The purchase of a new set of brightly colored markers for *my* use. I made up my lesson plans in several gorgeous colors. I even used some metallic colors and glitter markers for a real spark!

■ An inexpensive prism, hung in a sunny window. The light designs cheered all our hearts.

■ A borrowed instant camera to take pictures of us in our everyday routine. I posted them all over the room. Our smiling faces couldn't help but inspire us.

■ A wallpaper sample book gave me almost a year's supply of placemats. Each week, each child had a new and different placemat for snack time.

■ The radio, tapes, or CD played during rest time for *my* pleasure. I chose the music that pleased me that particular day: pop, western, rock, rap, and hip-hop, or classical.

Colors can be called by name or hue—red, scarlet, turquoise, magenta—that add richness to children's experience. They can be pure—primary colors (red, blue, yellow), white, and black—or mixed. Different hues have temperature—coolness at the blue end of the spectrum and warmth at the red end. They have different degrees of intensity or saturation (brightness or dullness) and value (lightness or darkness). Colors change as they mix, are related to one another (orange is related to red), and appear to change when placed next to each other.

Examples of things to say:
Hue—I saw a lavender sunset last night.
Intensity—The ball is bright red; the bricks are a duller red color.
Temperature—The blue in your painting makes me feel icy.
Value—The pale green reminds me of jade: it's a soft, misty color.
Relationship—My car looks orange next to the school bus, but yellow by the truck.

Line is a part of every work of art. Every line in a piece of art has length, beginning, end, and direction (up/down, diagonal, side-to-side). Lines have relationships with one another and with other parts of the work. They can be separate, twined, parallel, or crossed.

Examples of things to say:
Kind—Michael's socks have zig-zags; Thad's have stripes.
Direction—I see wide, heavy lines in the wallpaper.
Length—Mary Ann filled her paper with short lines.
Relationship—The paint strokes cross each other.

Form or **Shape** in art is more than geometric shapes. Artists combine regular with irregular shapes. Some have names. All can be filled or empty, separate, connected, or overlapping. One shape may enclose another. When the boundaries are completed, the shape is closed; if uncompleted (like a U or a C) it is open. Three-dimensional shapes may be solid (like a ball) or incorporate empty space (like a tire). Empty and filled spaces have shape. Shapes can be large or small and be compared (bigger, smaller, rounder, more angular, and so on).

Examples of things to say:
Size—You used a necklace of tiny circles to make a pattern.
Name—The ridge of the dragon's back has triangles on it.
Solidity—We can walk through the bead curtain.
Relationship—Zach's picture has a person on each side of the house.
Open/Closed—Can you take one block away and open your structure?

Space refers to the distance within or between aspects in artwork. It can be crowded, sparse, full, or empty, creating feelings of freedom or enclosure. Space can have balance with other forms. Boundaries, inclusion, and exclusion are spatial qualities. Space can be solid or permeable.

Examples of things to say:
Location—The birds are in the top corner of the picture.
Boundaries—Some animals are inside the house and some are outside.
Feeling—I feel free when I can see such a long way.

Design is the organization of artwork. Children initially work without a plan; as they gain experience they design. Design includes use of an element (like a circle) repeated or varied. The ways color, line, shape, and form are placed give the work a visual effect. Symmetry, balance, repetition, and alternation are design characteristics.

Examples of things to say:
Symmetry/Asymmetry—The wings of the butterfly mirror each other.
Repetition—Every one is filled with circles.
Alternation—There is a stripe after every heart.
Variation—In all of your pictures you used different shades of red—each one a little different.

FIGURE 3–1 | Talking with children about art elements. From "A Thing of Beauty: Aesthetic Development in Young Children," by S. Feeney and E. Moravcik, Sept., 1987, *Young Children*, 11. Adapted with permission.

THIS ONE'S FOR YOU   Virtual Museum Trips

You don't have to plan and execute a field trip to visit a museum. You can provide children opportunities to visit museums via museum Web sites. These "virtual" visits will spark their imagination and inspire them to learn more about art and artists. A list of some Web sites or contact points of some of the national children's museums, along with their Web sites or contact points, follows. Enjoy the trip!

SMITHSONIAN INSTITUTION

Smithsonian Institution Building
Room 153
Washington, D.C. 20560-0010
www.si.edu

THE VIRGINIA DISCOVERY MUSEUM

524 Main Street
Charlottesville, VA 22902
www.vadm.org

HANDS ON CHILDREN'S MUSEUM

Corner of 11th Avenue and Capital Way
Olympia, WA 98501
www.hocm.org

HUDSON VALLEY CHILDREN'S MUSEUM

21 Burd Street
Nyack, NY 10960
www.hvcm.org

CHILDREN'S PROGRAMS AND INTERACTIVE GALLERY FROM THE CALIFORNIA MUSEUM OF PHOTOGRAPHY

3824 Main Street
Riverside, CA 92510
www.cmp.ucr.edu/Sundays

CANADIAN CHILDREN'S MUSEUM

Canadian Museum of Civilization
P.O. Box 3100
Station B
Hull, Quebec J8X 4H2
www.civilization.ca

CHILDREN'S DISCOVERY MUSEUM OF SAN JOSE

180 Woz Way
San Jose, CA 95110
www.cdm.org

INTERNATIONAL CHILDREN'S ART MUSEUM

World Wide Trade Center, Suite 103
San Francisco, CA 94111
www.sanfrancisco.sidewalk.com

KOHL CHILDREN'S MUSEUM

165 Green Bay Road
Wilmette, IL 60091
www.kohlchildrensmuseum.org

CHILDREN'S MUSEUM OF MANHATTAN

The Tisch Building
212 West 83rd Street
New York, NY 10024
www.cmom.org

(Continued)

THE CHILDREN'S MUSEUM OF INDIANAPOLIS

3000 North Meridian Street
Indianapolis, IN 46208-4716
www.communic@childrensmuseum.org

BROOKLYN CHILDREN'S MUSEUM

145 Brooklyn Avenue
Brooklyn, NY 11213
www.Newyork.sidewalk.com

THE NEW CHICAGO CHILDREN'S MUSEUM

417 South Dearborn Street, Suite 500
Chicago, IL 60605
www.chichildrensmuseum.org/kid_kids.html

ACTIVITIES FOR CHILDREN   Art Talk

GOALS: To encourage children's aesthetic senses
To expose children to fine art

MATERIALS: Art print of Van Gogh's painting "Starry Night"

PREPARATION: Display the print at children's eye level.
Gather children around the print.

PROCEDURE: Ask the children the following questions about the painting:

■ What do you see in the painting?
■ What do you notice about the colors and lines?
■ Show me what you think is the most important thing in the painting. Why?
■ How does this picture make you feel?

■ What do you think the artist was feeling when he was painting this picture?

VARIATION: Ask the children to imagine they are in the painting. Then ask them these questions:

■ If you were in the painting, where would you want to be?
■ How would that feel?
■ What kind of things do you think you would smell?
■ What kind of animals might live there?

Additional Information: The previous two sets of questions could be used for any other painting of your choice.

ACTIVITIES FOR CHILDREN

Exploring Nature

GOALS: To develop children's aesthetic senses
To encourage the development of sense of design

MATERIALS: Index card for each child
Carton or paper bag for each child

PREPARATION: Draw a geometric shape or lines on each index card.
Check out in advance a good outdoor area for a short walk with the children.

PROCEDURE:

1. Give each child a card with a specific line or shape drawn on it.

2. Have each child look for his or her shape during a walk to an outdoor area.

3. Have the children trade cards during the walk.

VARIATION: After the walk, have the children draw a picture, make a painting, or create a collage using the lines or shapes they found during their walk.

CAUTION: Be sure to be alert so that children do not pick up glass or any other potentially harmful objects.

ACTIVITIES FOR CHILDREN

Aesthetics in the Environment

GOALS: To develop children's aesthetic senses
To encourage the appreciation of beauty in the environment

MATERIALS: None required

PREPARATION: Discuss colors with the children. Include words such as "brightness," "darkness," "cool" colors (blue, green, purple), or "warm" colors (red, orange, yellow)

PROCEDURE:

1. Help the children notice specific colors in the room.

2. Help them see the varieties of reds, blues, grays, and other colors.

3. For a display of color families, have the children who are wearing warm colors stand as a group.

4. Ask them to look at and describe the variety of warm colors they see.

5. Repeat this kind of exercise with the cool and the neutral color families.

ACTIVITIES FOR CHILDREN

Seeing Lines and Designs

GOALS: To develop children's aesthetic senses
To encourage closer observation of line and design

MATERIALS: Magnifying glasses; collection of natural objects such as shells, twigs, seed pods, acorns; paper, pencils, crayons, and markers

PREPARATION: Place objects collected into a box. Place a magnifying glass next to the box.

PROCEDURE:

1. Choose one object.
2. Show children how to examine this object with the magnifying glass.
3. Point out the lines, shapes, and designs seen with the magnifying glass.
4. Have the children use the magnifying glass to see the lines and shapes in objects of their choice.
5. Have the children draw what they see.

VARIATION: Have the children bring in objects from home or from a class walk for this activity.

ACTIVITIES FOR CHILDREN

Natural Artwork

GOALS: To develop children's aesthetic senses
To express creativity

MATERIALS: Balls of clay or playdough; pieces of Styrofoam; collection of natural objects such as dried weeds or plants, leaves, seed pods, pebbles, twigs, feathers, and so on.

PREPARATION:

Provide each child with a ball of clay or playdough or a piece of Styrofoam.

Discuss several of the natural objects they see with regard to lines, colors, shapes, and so on.

PROCEDURE:

1. Have the children choose objects and secure them into a design in the clay/playdough or Styrofoam base.
2. As children work, chat with them using terms that relate to the color, form, texture, pattern, and arrangement of space in their natural creations.

VARIATION: Glue objects to the tops of plastic margarine tubs or plastic yogurt containers for special child-made gifts.

ACTIVITIES FOR OLDER CHILDREN
(Grades 4–5)

Art Problem #1— The Pile of Bricks

GOALS: To develop children's aesthetic senses
To encourage the development and expression of artistic opinion

MATERIALS: None required

PREPARATION: Read the following problem to the class:

A famous artist, known to be a "minimalist" sculptor, buys 120 bricks and, on the floor of a well-known art museum, arranges them in a rectangular pile, two bricks high, six across, and ten lengthwise. He labels it *Pile of Bricks.* Across town, a bricklayer's assistant at a building site takes 120 bricks of the very same kind and arranges them in the very same way, unaware of what has happened in the museum—he is just a neat bricklayer's assistant.

PROCEDURE: Ask the students the following questions:
■ Can the first pile of bricks be a work of art while the second pile is not?
■ Does it matter that the two piles are seemingly identical?
■ Why or why not?
■ What *is* art in their opinion?
■ Is art representation?
■ Is art the expression and communication of emotions?

VARIATION:
■ Ask children if a painting of a soup can is art.
■ Ask the same questions posed above.

ACTIVITIES FOR OLDER CHILDREN
(Grades 4–5)

Art Problem #2— The Fire in the Louvre

GOALS: To develop children's aesthetic senses
To encourage the development and expression of artistic opinion

MATERIALS: None required

PREPARATION: Relate the following scene to the children:

The Louvre is on fire. (The Louvre is a very, very famous art museum in Paris.) You can save either the "Mona Lisa" or the injured guard who had been standing next to it . . . but not both.

PROCEDURE: Ask the students the following questions about the previous scene:
■ What should you do?
■ Who or what is more important?
■ Why?

VARIATION:
■ Make a poster representing your opinion on who or what should be saved.
■ Write and act out a TV ad representing your opinions.

ACTIVITIES FOR OLDER CHILDREN
(Grades 4–5)

Art Problem #3—Is Shakespeare a Real Writer?

GOALS: To develop children's aesthetic senses

To encourage the development and expression of artistic opinion

MATERIALS: None required

PREPARATION: Read the following to the children:

Lord Byron criticized Shakespeare as follows: Shakespeare's name, you may depend on it, stands absurdly too high and will go down. . . . He took all his plots from old novels, and threw their stories into dramatic shape, at as little expense of thought, as you or I could do.

PROCEDURE: Ask the children the following questions:

■ Is Shakespeare's use of familiar stories an aesthetic defect? Why or why not?

■ Is Byron a good critic of Shakespeare? Why or why not?

VARIATION:

■ Write and act out a TV ad presenting your opinions on this question.

■ Draw a poster that presents your opinions.

REFERENCE

Feeney, S. and Moravcik, E., "A Thing of Beauty: Aesthetic Development in Young Children." Sept. 1987, *Young Children*, 11.

CHAPTER 4

PROMOTING AESTHETIC EXPERIENCES

 ## FINDING AND ORGANIZING AESTHETIC MATERIALS

Every teacher has many ideas about what materials are best for children.

Here are some guidelines for choosing materials with good aesthetic potential.

- Choose materials that children can explore with their senses (touch, sight, smell).
- Choose materials that children can manipulate (twist, bend, cut, color, mark).
- Choose materials that can be used in different ways (thrown, bounced, built with, fastened, shaped).

Encourage children to find aesthetic materials. Children enjoy finding materials because it involves exploration and discovery. Finding materials usually involves more than looking. Children need to play with the found materials to try them out for weight, texture, structure, and so on. After the materials have been tested and shared, they may go into the classroom collection.

Sometimes the children's search can be focused on something, as in finding things for painting or building. As they find that their discovered materials make their day-to-day work more interesting, they become alert to new possibilities. For the teacher and the children, this can mean a constant supply of materials and new aesthetic experiences.

Children explore things in many ways to learn how things work.

Provide children with materials that are open-ended, and can be used in many ways.

Older children will enjoy this same experience of collecting materials, but can go further into associating materials with the elements of art. For example, the materials can be selected and collected according to their design possibilities. Objects can be classified into art categories such as those to be used for line, shape, texture, size, and color elements. The number and types of classifications will vary by the age level and interest of the children.

AESTHETIC USE OF MATERIALS

The uses of materials collected by the teacher and children are only limited by the collectors' interests and imagination. Of course, storage space and time to search can sometimes set boundaries on the exploration for

FOOD FOR THOUGHT

Promoting Aesthetic Experiences: Talking with Young Children about their Artwork

John Pete, age four, runs up to you with his dripping-wet painting. Beaming with pride, he thrusts his painting of several dark blotches at you and says expectantly, "Look what I painted!"

What do you say to him? Should you praise John Pete, encourage more painting, critique his work, or withhold any judgment at all? What is the best way to talk with young children about their art in a way to encourage their individual aesthetic experience? The following suggestions should assist you in answering this question.

1. The next time children show you what they have created, smile, pause, and *say nothing at first*. This serves two purposes. It gives you time to study the children's art and to *reflect* on what you want to say before you speak. It gives you time to think of a better response than an impulsive, stereotypical response like, "That's nice." Second, and more importantly, it will give children an opportunity to talk *first* if they so choose. This provides a lead-in and direction for your subsequent comments.

2. The elements of art provide a good framework for responding to children (for a description of the art elements, see Figure 3–1 in Chapter 3). You can comment on such things as design, pattern, color, line, shape or form, texture, and space. Figure 3–1 provides sample "things to say" to help you here.

3. Do *not* focus on representation in art ("What *is* it?"), but focus instead on the abstract or design qualities ("Look what a beautiful pattern these blue lines make!").

4. Use reflective dialogue in talking with children about their art. "You are so proud of your work, aren't you?" "You spent a lot of time making so many different shapes." "You worked very hard at drawing today."

5. Not all comments need to refer to the artistic elements. Your comments might also refer to other aspects of the project or to the child's specific interests as well. For example, a young artist hands you a drawing and says, "That's my house, and the painter is painting it." You may want to comment on other qualities of the work such as the amount of time and effort spent, how the materials were handled, or the meaning of the drawing to the child. For example, you might respond, "Your drawing really shows a lot of action!" or "How hard you worked to include the paint cans and brushes!" "I can tell by your drawing that you really enjoyed using so many different colors of crayons."

6. Do *not* attempt to correct a child's artwork or try to improve a child's art by having it more closely approximate reality. Children's art is not intended as a copy of the real world. Child artists may freely choose to add or omit details. Adults' criticism or corrections only discourage children and do not foster aesthetic experiences. Concentrate and comment on what *is* in the child's work and not on what *isn't!*

7. You may even want to simply ask the child "Do you want to tell me about your work?" Of course, with this question, "no" is as acceptable an answer as "yes."

aesthetic materials. However, what is most important is that the materials and what is done with them become personal statements of the children and teacher. This is not done by what is made, but by how it is made—whether it is an art project, a building project, or another activity. The *process* of making and the child's personal involvement in it are the keys here—*not* the finished product.

Children must have the opportunity not only to find materials but also to try them out. This means much experimenting with the materials to determine what the children feel they need. A question such as, "What would you like to say with these things?" might help both the children and the teacher get started. Checking with the children's moods may be helpful, too. Do they seem to feel happy, dreamy, sad, gentle, or aggressive? Such questioning can help the children reach their own purpose based on their experience and interests.

Another important consideration in the creative process is the number of materials. It is important to remember not to give children too many materials too often. Too much to choose from can overwhelm a child. The qualities of one material can be lost in the midst of so many others. An example of this would be to work with a certain color or a single material, such as clay or paper. In this way, the children can learn more about making their own aesthetic choices, as well as mastering specific skills.

While the *process* of exploring materials is the primary focus of aesthetic experiences, with older children (grades 4–5), the process usually involves the creation of more complex works of art. Children at this level pay greater attention to expressing specific ideas in their work. They are more intentional in their approach to using materials. Because they are not distracted by the quantity of materials as younger children are, a variety of interesting materials needs to be available for their aesthetic experiences.

DISPLAYING CHILDREN'S WORK

An important part of the teacher's role in developing children's aesthetic sensitivity is showing their work to parents and others. A good rule of thumb is that if the children feel good about their work, let them show it. The work does not have to be complete. It should be displayed at children's eye level so that they, as well as adults, may enjoy it. Not every child in the group has to have his or her work displayed.

Set up displays to show the different ways the children have used a medium, such as painting, collage, clay, and so on. Let the room reflect the children's di-

Has the child done something today that has helped him feel good about himself?

versity, their likes, their interests—much the way a well-decorated home reflects the interests and skills of the people who live in it. Children aren't clones, so we certainly don't expect to see 25 identical works of art with different names on them displayed in the room. How does this reflect the children's diversity?

Take time at the end of the day to show artwork to the children, letting them talk about each other's work. Model for the children how to make a positive comment, using the guidelines presented in this unit.

Be sure to send all artwork home in a way that shows your respect for the artist and the art. For example, paintings folded rather than rolled, or rolled when wet and therefore stuck together, tell children their work doesn't matter. (More specific suggestions on displaying children's work are covered in Appendix D.)

DEVELOPING YOUR SENSE OF AESTHETICS

Early childhood teachers need to protect the spirit, imagination, curiosity, and love of life and learning in young children as fiercely as we protect our environment. In a like manner, early childhood teachers need to develop and protect their own aesthetic sense.

As you read through this book you will most likely find some activities that catch your attention, that appeal to your spirit, and reflect your personality and philosophy. Indeed, it must be *your* personality and philosophy that determine how you use any activity. All of the ideas and activities in this book are to be shaped

FOOD FOR THOUGHT

Create a Classroom Museum

Provide children (of all ages) a year-round aesthetic experience by incorporating a classroom museum in your program. It's "show and tell" in a more meaningful, aesthetic sense. Here are the basics to get you started.

WHAT IS A CLASSROOM MUSEUM?

A **classroom museum** is a collection of items and artifacts on a specific theme. Items and artifacts are brought in by the children for display. Using this approach for show and tell, the theme or topic is motivating and the exhibit grows gradually and joyfully. Decision-making, problem-solving, and communicating are skills practiced as the children share/add their special selections. Treasures from home, a family-crafted item, or an occasional purchase—each contribution is worthy. The sharing is educational and enjoyable. Museum topics change each month, with teacher/child interest sparking the choice.

ESSENTIALS FOR SUCCESS

- Make a quality choice for the first museum of the year.
- Determine a clear purpose and definite goals for the museum as a curriculum tool appropriate for children's development.
- Invite family participation via an informative, friendly August newsletter, a September Parent's Night, and a special museum notice.
- Plan a simple but attractive museum area in the classroom. A suitable physical set-up includes a backdrop for hanging pictures and a display table.
- Highlight the children's artifacts and show and tell experience.
- Select a child as a curator to encourage responsibility.
- Guide children's selection for show and tell artifacts to help foster respect for all contributions and ensure their survival in the classroom (especially fragile or sentimental items).

A good place to start in the beginning of the program year is with a "Me Museum." This is a good topic to start with because it encourages a feeling of community as teacher and children learn more about each other.

STEPS TO SETTING UP THE "ME MUSEUM"

1. Awareness (with children)—Explore the concept of *museum*. Discuss possible items for a Me Museum. Plan ways that families can help. Frame a family museum notice. Establish routines for sharing.
2. Contributions (from children)—Me Museum artifacts are always surprises. Descriptions delight. Personal history in bits and pieces come alive. Students have shared: stuffed animals, baby journals, family photos, toys, travel souvenirs, books or stories, ballet slippers. . . .
3. Integration (with children)—Growth in vocabulary occurs. Expressive language expands. Thinking and problem-solving skills are nurtured.
4. Outcomes (for children)—Child by child, with each contribution, child-centered showing and sharing creates a caring community in which each child is important and friendships emerge.

TO CONTINUE THE MUSEUM

To create the next month's museum, brainstorm with the children some possible topics and themes. What do they want to learn about? What provokes their curiosity? What special interest do they want to share/explore with classmates? Inspired and motivated, many ideas are listed and voting follows (integrating math skills such as counting, graphing, predicting, and comparing).

First choice becomes the next museum, with second place a strong possibility for a future museum. The teacher also selects topics to coincide with curriculum or timely topics. Topics may vary from year to year. The steps listed above of awareness, contributions, integration, and outcome all facilitate museum planning.

and modified to suit your own needs with a particular group of children. Any idea will only be successful if you like it and are excited to use it with young children. You must mix a lot of *you* into all of your work with young children. Do not hesitate to mix in your philoso-phy and personality along with those of the children, add a good portion of energy (yours and the children's), stir in a large measure of imagination, and you are on your way to a truly creative environment for young children.

ACTIVITIES FOR CHILDREN

Sensory Experiences— Seeing

GOAL: To develop children's aesthetic sense of color

MATERIALS: None required

PREPARATION: Discuss colors with children. Topics may include how they are everywhere, and how they make our world beautiful, favorite colors.

PROCEDURE:

1. Have children look for colors in the room, using a question like, "How many red things can you see?"
2. Play a guessing game, such as "I am thinking of something green in this room. What is it?"
3. Ask how the color red can tell us important things (some possible answers are: red lights tell us to stop, red flags mean danger, red lights in a building mean an exit).

VARIATION:

■ Follow-up this activity by allowing children to experiment with mixing colors.

■ Blow soap bubbles and look for the rainbow of colors in them.

■ Hold a prism up to the light. Talk about the rainbow of colors seen.

ACTIVITIES FOR CHILDREN

What If?

GOALS: To encourage creative thinking
To develop children's aesthetic senses

MATERIALS: Crayons, pencils, markers, and paper

PREPARATION: Discuss giants: how big they are, how they would look, and so on.

PROCEDURE:

1. Ask the children, "How do you think the world would look to a giant?"
2. Encourage a wide variety of answers.
3. Have the children draw a picture of the world as a giant would see it.

VARIATION:

■ Have the children make a three-dimensional model of how the world would look to a giant.

■ Older children can write and illustrate a story about a giant's life.

ACTIVITIES FOR CHILDREN — New Ways to Go

GOALS: To develop children's aesthetic senses

To encourage creative thinking

MATERIALS: Pencils, crayons, markers, and paper; construction materials such as blocks, boxes, paste, and so on

PREPARATION: Discuss several types of transportation such as an automobile, truck, bus, or train.

PROCEDURE:

1. Ask the children, "If you could invent a new means of transportation, what would it be?"

2. Draw or construct how it would look.

3. Have each child explain his or her form of creative transportation.

VARIATION:

■ Have the children dramatize their new form of transportation, alone or with another child.

■ Write and act out a TV ad for your new form of transportation.

ACTIVITIES FOR CHILDREN — Feelings

GOALS: To develop children's aesthetic senses

MATERIALS: Art supplies for drawing or painting

PREPARATION: Discuss what the word "lonely" means.

Discuss how it feels to be lonely.

PROCEDURE:

1. Ask the children to draw or paint a picture showing how they feel when they're lonely.

2. Have the children share their work.

VARIATION: Use other emotions in this activity, such as things that scare you, things that make you happy, and so on.

ACTIVITIES FOR CHILDREN — Listening to Learn

GOALS: To develop children's aesthetic senses
To encourage awareness of sound

MATERIALS: Tape recorder, tape

PREPARATION: Record some of these sounds: children's voices, voices of others, classroom sounds, animal sounds, passing cars, steps in the hallway, or children skipping and running.

PROCEDURE:
1. Play the tape.
2. Have the children identify the sounds.

3. Ask questions to help the children tell the difference between sounds:
   - Do any of the animals sound alike?
   - Which of the sounds was the loudest? the softest?
   - How would you describe those sounds?
   - Which sound did you like the best? Why?

VARIATION:
- Have the children draw their favorite sound.
- Have them act out the sound.

ACTIVITIES FOR CHILDREN — Street Sounds

GOALS: To develop children's aesthetic senses
To encourage awareness of sound

MATERIALS: Tape recorder, tape

PREPARATION: Tape outside sounds in the street. Some examples are a car turning the corner, wind blowing past a sign, dog barking, rain dripping, wheels on wet pavement, animal footsteps, high heels on pavement, or sneakers on pavement.

PROCEDURE:
1. Play the tape.
2. Have the children identify as many sounds as they can.

3. Ask questions to help the children think about the differences between sounds:
   - Do any of the sounds hurt your ears?
   - Which sound was the hardest to figure out?
   - Which was the easiest sound to figure out?
   - Which sound did you like the best?

VARIATION:
- Have the children draw a picture of their favorite sound.
- Have the children act out their favorite sound.

ACTIVITIES FOR CHILDREN

Fun with a Stethoscope

GOALS: To develop children's aesthetic senses
To encourage awareness of sounds

MATERIALS: Stethoscope

PREPARATION: Discuss what a stethoscope is used for. Show children how it is used.

PROCEDURE:

1. Have the children listen to each other's heartbeats.
2. Listen to the teacher's and any other adult's heartbeat.
3. Have the children listen to each other's stomach after a snack.

VARIATION:

■ Scratch different objects on a table top (floor, rug, and pipe) and listen to the sound through the stethoscope.

■ Listen to a child as he hums or sings, listening with the stethoscope on the child's back.

ACTIVITIES FOR CHILDREN

Taste and Smell

GOALS: To develop children's aesthetic senses
To encourage awareness of smells

MATERIALS: Ingredients for a recipe to make with the children. (See chapter 15 for recipe suggestions.)

PREPARATION: Gather the required ingredients and utensils for the recipe.

PROCEDURE:

1. Make the recipe with the children.
2. Taste the ingredients.
3. Identify what's cooking by the smells.

VARIATION:

■ Have the children guess what they will have for lunch from smells coming from the kitchen.

■ Make lemonade with and without sugar. Talk about the differences.

■ Squeeze tomatoes, apples, and oranges for juice. Ask the children what smells best, as well as what smells they don't like.

■ Draw a picture about smells from these activities.

ACTIVITIES FOR CHILDREN

Touching

GOALS: To encourage development of children's aesthetic senses

To develop the sense of touch

MATERIALS: Objects of varying textures such as silk cloth, burlap, feathers, rope, seashells, mirrors, balls, driftwood, beads, furry slippers, and so on.

PREPARATION: Have the children sit in small groups.

PROCEDURE:

1. Give each group an object.

2. Have each child in the group hold and feel the object.

3. Have each child in the group show how the object makes her feel. For example, a feather may stand in a straight line with arms and legs extended and then move "softly," with arms waving gently from side to side.

VARIATION:

■ Have the children draw a picture about the object.

■ Make up a song about it.

ACTIVITIES FOR CHILDREN

A Bulletin Board for Touching

GOALS: To encourage development of children's aesthetic senses

To develop sense of touch

MATERIALS: Bulletin board, objects with different textures—supplied by the teacher or children (examples: sandpaper, flannel, velvet, burlap, plastic, bottle caps, pebbles, paper clips, and so on).

PREPARATION: Gather objects onto a table near the bulletin board.

Provide each child with a small amount of paste or a small container of glue.

PROCEDURE:

1. Have each child choose one object to glue onto the bulletin board.

2. Before gluing it on, have the child describe the texture of the object.

3. Continue until all objects are glued on.

VARIATION:

■ Once the collage is complete, children can make "rubbings" using crayons on newsprint paper.

■ Have the child feel the texture of one of the objects on the bulletin board and act out the way it feels.

ADDITIONAL INFORMATION: This board should encourage the use of vocabulary-expanding words like "coarse," "smooth," "bumpy," "prickly," and so on.

ACTIVITIES FOR CHILDREN

Hidden Objects

GOALS: To develop children's aesthetic senses
To develop the sense of touch

MATERIALS: Boxes, collection of sets of objects for children to touch (examples include two rocks, two twigs, two marbles, two feathers, two pieces of tree bark, and sets of cloth pieces of different textures).

PREPARATION: Hide the sets of objects inside the boxes.

PROCEDURE:

1. Have the child reach into the box with his eyes closed.

2. Have the child feel and describe the object without seeing it.

3. Have the child match a given object by hunting for its mate in the box with his eyes closed.

4. Have the child pull the items out of the box to see what the match looks like.

VARIATION:

■ Put several objects in the boxes to make this activity more challenging.

■ Put more similar objects in the boxes to make the activity more challenging.

ACTIVITIES FOR OLDER CHILDREN

(Grades 4–5)

Color Optics—Afterimage

GOALS: To develop children's aesthetic sense
To explore the phenomena of color

MATERIALS: One large piece of solid colored construction paper, pieces of white paper for each child

PREPARATION: Have the children draw a dot in the center of the white paper.

Display the piece of colored construction paper so all children can easily see it.

PROCEDURE:

1. Have the children stare at the page of solid color for about 30 seconds.

2. Next, have the children look at the dot on the white page.

3. Their eyes will see *color* on the white page. This is called *afterimage.*

4. Usually they will see the complement or near complement of the color first looked at.

For example, they will see red if they first stared at blue-green. They will see blue or violet if they first stared at yellow.

VARIATION: Use different colors of construction paper.

ADDITIONAL INFORMATION: Afterimage is probably the best-known illustration of how our eyes react to color.

ACTIVITIES FOR OLDER CHILDREN
(Grades 4–5)

Lines, Lines, Everywhere—Verticals

GOALS: To develop children's aesthetic senses
To observe vertical lines in the environment

MATERIALS: Paper, pencils, crayons, and markers

PREPARATION: Discuss lines with the group. See the chart on page 45 for discussion ideas.

PROCEDURE:

1. Ask the children what they see in our environment that is made up of vertical lines (skyscrapers, trees, telephone poles, rain, soldiers standing at attention, and so on).

2. Ask the children what moods or feelings a series of vertical lines make (heavenward, of the sky, strong, straight, dignified, and so on).

3. Ask the children if they have ever leaned against a vertical? (The answer should be yes: a wall, a tree, a door, and so on.)

4. Ask when a body is vertical.

5. Have the children draw a picture using lots of verticals.

Some Points to Discuss about Lines

- Lines are basic to art.
- Lines can convey different moods.
- We see lines in our daily lives: telephone lines, clotheslines, lines of people, lines of music, the line of scrimmage.

- Where do we see more straight lines—in nature or in man-made objects?
- What do we associate with lines on a face?
- Which conveys more movement—a straight line or a curvy one?

ACTIVITIES FOR OLDER CHILDREN
(Grades 4–5)
Just Another Line— Horizontals

GOALS: To develop children's aesthetic senses
To observe horizontal lines in the environment

MATERIALS: Paper, pencils, crayons, and markers

PREPARATION: Discuss lines with the group. See the above chart for discussion ideas.

PROCEDURE:

1. Ask the children what in the environment is mostly horizontal (the horizon, the floor, a bed, a table, a still lake or pond, and so on).

2. Ask the children what feelings they get from horizontal lines (grounded, of the earth, relaxed, at rest, calm, and so on).

3. Ask the children when their body is horizontal (resting on a bed, lying on the grass, and so on).

4. Ask the children if they can stand or sit on a horizontal (yes, a sofa, the floor, the ground).

5. Have the children draw a picture using lots of horizontal lines.

VARIATION: Use diagonal lines for this activity. Ask the children:

- Where do you see diagonals (a slide, a plane taking off, a ramp, and so on)?
- What feeling do you get from diagonals (action, movement, and so on)?
- When is your body at a diagonal (when you are running, speed walking, leaning into the wind, and so on)?
- Have them draw a picture using lots of diagonals.

ACTIVITIES FOR OLDER CHILDREN **Zigzagging**
(Grades 4–5)

GOALS: To develop children's aesthetic senses

To observe zigzag lines in the environment

MATERIALS: Paper, pencils, crayons, and markers

PREPARATION: Discuss lines in the environment. Use the chart on page 45 for discussion points.

PROCEDURE:

1. Ask the children where they see zigzag lines in the world (lightning, a jagged tear, the earth after an earthquake, crimped hair).

2. Ask the children how zigzags make them feel (tense, anxious, frenzied).

3. Ask the children when their body forms a zigzag (while jumping on a pogo stick, doing calisthenics).

4. Have the children make a design using zigzag lines.

VARIATION: Use spiral lines for this activity with the following questions:

■ What do you see that is shaped in a spiral (a spring, water going down a drain, a staircase, a tornado, a snake, and so on)?

■ What feelings do you get from spirals (spinning, swirling, energetic)?

■ When is your body in a spiral (while twirling in a dance, doing a spin in a game, and so on)?

■ Have the children make a design using spiral lines.

SECTION 2

Art and the Development of the Young Child

CHAPTER 5

ART AND THE GROWING CHILD

 ## ART AND SOCIAL-EMOTIONAL GROWTH

The term **social-emotional growth** refers to two kinds of growth. Emotional growth is the growth of a child's feelings, and social growth is the child's growth as a member of a group.

Learning to be a member of a group involves many social skills. Young children, for example, must learn to relate to other children and adults outside the family. Often, a child's first experience of sharing an adult's attention with other children occurs in the early childhood setting. Of the social skills involved in learning to work in a group, children have to learn how to share materials, take turns, listen to others, and how and when to work on their own—to mention just a few!

Social-emotional growth occurs as a child grows in self-concept and self-awareness.

 ## SELF-CONCEPT AND SELF-ACCEPTANCE

Self-concept can be defined as the child's growing awareness of his or her own characteristics (physical appearance as well as skills and abilities) and how these are similar to or different from those of others.

All children like to feel good about themselves. This good feeling about oneself is called *self-acceptance* or self-esteem. Children who feel good about themselves and believe they can do things well have a good sense of self-acceptance.

Children who have positive self-concepts accept their own strengths and limitations. The early childhood program provides an environment which nurtures the development of a positive sense of self and a good self-concept in each child.

In the early childhood art program, children must continue to learn to accept and feel good about themselves. The art program can be of special help in this area. When children feel they can do things well in art, they grow in both self-confidence and self-acceptance.

The importance of a good self-concept is equally as important to middle and upper elementary students. They, too, need the same encouragement and emotionally safe environment in which to express themselves creatively. Just because they are physically bigger and appear more sure of themselves doesn't mean that a teacher can overlook the development of their self-concept in all creative activities.

A teacher needs to plan the art program in such a way that it gives each child a chance to grow in self-acceptance. To do so, the program should be *child-centered,* which means that it is planned for the age and ability levels of the children in it.

Naturally, if it is child-centered, it is, in turn, developmentally appropriate—meeting the specific individual needs of each child. The art program is planned around the developmental needs of the child. In this way, the teacher has clear guidelines for selections of appropriate materials and activities for the level of each child in the program. (Developmental levels in art and related activities for these levels are covered in Chapter 6.)

Learning to be a member of a group is an important milestone for young children.

When children are allowed to express themselves freely in art, they learn to accept their own ideas and feelings.

BUILDING RELATIONSHIPS

It is only after a child has developed self-acceptance that it is possible for her to accept other children. In the early childhood art program, there are many chances for a child to be with other children of the same age. Children who have had positive creative experiences are the ones who can honestly accept their own abilities and those of other children.

The art program is a good place for child-to-child relationships, where children can work, talk, and be together. If the art activities are developmentally appropriate for the children, they provide a relaxed time for exploring, trying new tools, and using familiar ones again. They also allow children many chances to interact with each other.

The freedom of art itself encourages children to talk about their own work or the work of other children. Working with colors, paint, paper, paste, and other materials provides children an endless supply of things to talk about.

A child learns new ways to be with an adult in the early childhood program. The teacher is an adult, but not the child's parent; therefore, a new type of relationship opens up. Of course, it is different in several ways from the adult–child relationship at home.

The school setting is unlike the home situation. Children learn how to be and act in a place other than the home. They learn how it is to be in a larger group than the family and how to share an adult's attention with other children.

The children learn about art as well as about themselves from the teacher. The teacher helps them feel that it is safe to be themselves and to express ideas in their own way. The sensitive teacher lets the child know that the fun of participating in and expressing oneself in art or other creative activities is more important than the finished product. With older children, the teacher encourages them to explore the many ways to express their ideas in the growing complexity of their work, which is characteristic of this age group.

ART AND PHYSICAL (MOTOR) DEVELOPMENT

The term **motor development** means physical growth. Both terms refer to growth in the ability of children to use their bodies.

In an early childhood program, activities like dance, drawing, painting, pasting, and other activities that exercise muscles aid a child's motor development. Exercising muscles in creative activities aids both small- and large-muscle development. Before we consider each of these types of motor development, let us look at the overall pattern of growth and development.

PATTERN OF DEVELOPMENT

The process of human development follows a general pattern that includes growth in three basic directions

FOOD FOR THOUGHT

Altruism—Teaching the Value of Helping, Caring, and Sharing

Why are some children more altruistic than others? The answer is complicated, since altruism is affected by many factors. During the past few decades, researchers have observed hundreds of adults and children in laboratories and in real-life situations to gain insight into three main altruistic behaviors—helping, caring, and sharing.

The beginnings of altruism are present at birth, research shows. In one study, babies only 18 hours old were more distressed by tapes of other infants' crying than by recordings of their own crying and would cry longer and more often when they heard human cries than when they were exposed to other loud noises.

Researchers also report that some people are innately more empathic than others. There are individual differences in temperament, so some children respond more intensely to other people's distress than others. But all children have the ability to be affected deeply by other people's emotional states.

Adults have a great deal of influence on children's altruism, experts say. Here's what you can do to teach children the value of helping, caring, and sharing.

■ Make your environment as nurturing as possible. By meeting children's physical and emotional needs, you free them psychologically to meet other people's needs.

■ Foster self-esteem by encouraging children to do things for themselves. Acknowledge children's accomplishments, and let them know they don't have to perform to be loved. Children with high self-esteem can behave altruistically because they are not preoccupied with their own perceived inadequacies.

■ Talk about the feelings of others. For example, if you see a bus driver snap at a passenger, say, "He seems upset about something. Maybe he's having a bad day today."

■ Assist children in defining their own feelings toward others. Ask them if they feel sad because they have to miss a birthday party or if they are excited about going to their grandparents' house. Research shows that children can't empathize the emotions of others until they understand their own.

■ Let children know how much you value helping, caring, and sharing, and model altruistic behavior yourself. In several studies, children exposed to generous models were more inclined to donate money and trinkets to others than children exposed to selfish models.

■ Establish clear behavioral standards for children and emphasize how misconduct hurts other people.

■ Explain why disciplinary measures are necessary and use emotion so youngsters know you really mean business, but discourage aggressive behavior and avoid spanking and belittling.

■ Welcome children's help, and stress how much you appreciate even the smallest effort. This will foster altruism by teaching youngsters to view themselves as caring individuals. But do not give children material rewards for helping, caring, and sharing. They should help because they want to, not because they expect rewards.

■ Minimize television viewing. Behavior experts say most children's television shows encourage aggression, rather than helping, caring, and sharing. Two exceptions are *Mister Rogers' Neighborhood* and *Sesame Street,* which have increased altruistic behavior among preschoolers.

■ Talk children through conflicts, step by step. For example, if a child is fighting about a toy with another child, empathize with her distress and ask how she thinks her friend is feeling. Praise her when she takes her playmate's point of view, and encourage her to solve the problem in ways that will benefit both children.

(Figure 5–1). The first of these is called large to small muscle or **gross** to **fine motor development.** Large (gross) to small (fine) motor development means that large muscles develop in the neck, trunk, arms, and legs before the small muscles in the fingers, hands, wrists, and eyes develop. This is why young children can walk long before they are able to write or even scribble.

The second direction of growth is from head to toe (or top to bottom). This growth pattern explains why a

THIS ONE'S FOR YOU

Collaborating with Children: Another Way to Build Self-Concept

Involving young children in decorating their room is a fun, productive way of building their self-concept and improving the room's appearance at the same time! Designing a bulletin board (or wall decoration) can involve many skills and can be a learning experience unlike any other. Here are some tried-and-true bulletin board ideas to involve children while building their self-concept, too.

- **Hands On**—Cover one wall with brown kraft (wrapping) paper. With bright paint (one color for each letter), write the title, "Hands On!" at the top of the paper. Children then place handprints randomly on the board by first pressing hands on a paint-coated sponge and then pressing directly on the paper. Label each print with the child's name and date.

- **Pattern Prints**—Prepare the bulletin board by measuring off horizontal lines on backing paper to create one horizontal stripe/space for each child. At the left end of the stripes, list the children's names. Then, offer the children a variety of materials for printing (cut fruits and vegetables, rubber stamps, printing letters, and so on) and an inked pad (or sponge soaked in tempera paint). Allow the children to create any pattern or design they would like to make.

- **Names**—Cover a large bulletin board with a bright, solid background. Divide paper evenly into a grid design, thus providing each child with a 12-inch square space on the board. With a marker, print each child's name in large letters at the top of the space, leaving at least 11 inches of paper exposed under each name. First, use the board as a basis for a matching game—children must match namecards to their name printed on the board. Children are then invited to decorate their name with markers, crayons, or paints. As the year progresses, children can copy their names in a variety of (for older preschoolers): yarn, sparkles, and so on.

- **Artwork**—Children are always being told not to write on the walls, but now they can have the freedom and the fun to write on at least one board in the room. Once again, cover a large bulletin board with kraft (or wrapping) paper. (You may want to tack several layers at first so that you can tear off the top layer to expose a fresh piece when needed.) Then, invite the children to draw to their hearts' content. If you share a special story, event, or trip, expose a fresh piece of kraft paper to create an instant mural!

Decorating the room with your children develops a sense of pride in them toward themselves and their environment. They will be proud to show off their room and the bulletin boards they all shared in creating!

---

baby is able to hold up his head long before he is able to walk, since the muscles develop from the head down.

The third pattern of development is from inside to outside (or from center to outside). This explains the ability of a baby to roll over before he is able to push himself up with his arms. Because the inner muscles of the trunk develop first, rolling over comes before pulling or sitting up. Understanding these basic principles of development, especially large to small motor development, is important in planning appropriate art activities for young children. Let us now consider large and small motor development.

LARGE-MUSCLE DEVELOPMENT

Since large muscles in the arms, legs, neck, and trunk develop first, by the time children reach the preschool age, they are able to use large muscles quite well. They can walk, run, sit, and stand at will. They can use their arms and hands quite easily in large movements like clapping and climbing. Most three-year-olds and many four-year-olds are actively using their large muscles in running, wiggling, and jumping. They are not yet as developed in small motor skills (like cutting, tying, or lacing) as five-year-olds.

The early childhood art program gives the child a chance to exercise large motor skills in many ways other than just in active games. Painting with a brush on a large piece of paper is as good a practice for large-muscle development as dancing. Whether it be wide arm movements made in brush strokes or arms moving to a musical beat, it is only by first developing these large muscles that a child can begin to develop small motor skills.

Creative activities in the early childhood program provide many opportunities for exercising large-muscle skills. Activities that exercise large muscles include

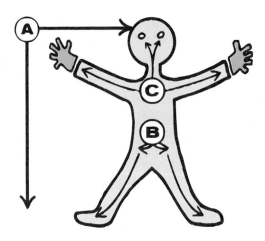

TOP (Head)	*Cephalocaudal Development*	BOTTOM (Toes)
INSIDE (Trunk)	*Proximodental Development*	OUTSIDE (Extremities)
LARGE (Trunk, Neck, Arms, Legs)	*Gross to Fine Motor Development*	SMALL (Fingers, Hands, Toes, Wrists, Eyes)

FIGURE 5–1 | The pattern of development.

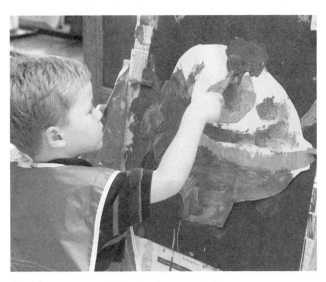

Small motor skills develop in art activities.

group murals, tracing body shapes, easel painting, clay-pounding, and crayon rubbings. (See end of chapter for more specific activities.)

SMALL-MUSCLE DEVELOPMENT

Small muscles in fingers, hands, and wrists are used in art activities such as painting, cutting, pasting, and clay modeling. These small motor art activities and any other activity that involves the use of small muscles help exercise and develop a child's fine motor control.

Small muscle skills are different for a child at different ages. For example, many three-year-olds do not have good small muscle development, so the muscles in their fingers and hands are not quite developed enough to enable them to use scissors easily.

Practice in crushing and tearing paper, and later practice in using blunt scissors, all help small muscles develop. The better the small muscle development, the easier it will be to cut with scissors. Small muscles can grow stronger only by practice and exercise. A teacher encourages a child to exercise these small muscles in small motor artwork, such as tearing, pasting, working with clay, making and playing with puppets, and finger painting.

Small muscles are often better developed in four- and five-year-olds. However, small motor activities are still

necessary for continued small muscle development. Drawing with pencils, crushing paper into shapes, modeling figures with clay, and making mobiles are examples of more advanced small motor activities.

LARGE AND SMALL MOTOR ACTIVITIES

The early childhood art program should have a good mixture of both small and large motor tools and activities. A child needs to develop both large and small muscles, and artwork provides this chance.

The teacher needs to respect each child's need to develop both large and small muscles at any age. This means a teacher needs the right equipment, but more important, the right attitude for the level of each child. The right attitude is one that lets the child know it is all right to try many large and small motor activities at any age. In this type of art program, not all four-year-olds are expected to cut well, to button a shirt successfully, or to be able to do either at all. Five-year-olds, as well as younger children, may enjoy pounding clay for no other purpose than the fun of pounding. Older children should also be allowed this same freedom of expression with both large and small muscle activities. Just because they may appear more grown, middle and upper elementary children still enjoy "messing around" with clay and even fingerpaints. In an art program with this type of freedom, a child naturally uses creative materials in a way that helps large and small muscles grow.

Appendix H contains suggested activities in art and other curriculum areas to develop children's large and small muscles.

This child is using the small muscles in her hands, fingers, and wrists.

Young children learn about their world in active ways.

 ## ART AND MENTAL DEVELOPMENT

As children grow physically, they also grow mentally. This is because young children learn by doing. Jean Piaget, in his work with young children, describes a child's learning by doing as "sensorimotor" development.

The word **sensorimotor** derives from the two words *sensory* and *motor*. Sensory refers to using the five body senses and motor refers to the physical act of doing. Sensorimotor learning involves the body and its senses (sensori) as they are used in doing (motor).

SENSORIMOTOR LEARNING IN ART

An example of sensorimotor learning in art is modeling with clay. In using clay (the motor activity), children use their senses (sensory), such as feel and smell, to learn about clay and how to use it. A teacher can tell the children how clay feels and how to use it; but children truly learn about clay by physically using it themselves. A child needs this sensorimotor exploration with clay and many other art materials.

In the art program, children learn many things in this sensorimotor way—learning by doing. Many ideas and concepts are learned from different art activities. Just as children exercise different muscles in art activi-

ties, they also learn new concepts in many kinds of art activities.

VOCABULARY AND ART

An expanding vocabulary about creative materials and processes is a natural partner to the activity itself. Children working with art materials will use descriptive terms for the media and the resulting creations. The teacher's use of particular words to compare size, weight, color, texture, and shape influences children's descriptions of their artwork.

As children grow and develop through art, they begin to use words such as *thick, thin, hard, soft, straight, curved, dark, light, smooth,* and *sticky.*

The teacher introduces words like *soft* and *smooth* to describe the feel of velvet material. Scraps of burlap are called rough, bumpy, or scratchy. Even the word *texture* is one that can be used with young children. As they feel the different kinds of cloth, the different "feels" can easily be called "textures." Children then put together in their minds the feel of the velvet with the words *soft, smooth,* and *texture.* This is sensorimotor learning—learning through sensing as well as by association.

Learning to notice the different way things feel teaches a child about concepts that are opposite, which are important in subjects like math and science. The difference between hard and soft is similar to the difference between adding and subtracting in math; both ideas are opposites. A child learns in art that soft is not the same as hard. In math, a child learns that adding is different from or the opposite of subtracting. Mastering opposite concepts used in doing artwork thus helps the child learn the mental concepts needed later in other school subjects.

Art helps a child grow through creative thinking and feeling, not only about art but about all other things. The confidence and good feelings about themselves and their work that children develop in art apply to other things in and out of school. Seen in this way, art cannot be thought of as a separate part of the program. It is and always must be an approach to learning inseparable from all the rest.

THIS ONE'S FOR YOU   Motor Development and Movement

As you are reading this chapter, have you sat still for an uninterrupted time? Or did you get up to move around some? Did you take a break for a while during your reading? Did you get up to call and talk with a friend on the phone?

Consider how adults learn. Sometimes when they are working, adults need to spread out materials on a floor or table. At other times, adults retreat to a "snug spot" to read and reflect. At other times, adults need to talk with friends to chat about work and ideas.

None of these facts are surprising to you. Yet they are surprising when we start to apply these same facts to children.

With children, do we allow the same flexibility in space and preferences that we, as adults, take for granted in our learning environment?

Children need the same access—access to a range of working spaces, and access to materials, access to other children and adults. We need to provide environments for children that have different working spaces to meet the demands of a child's particular task and way of making meaning.

Especially for older children, rather than having their own assigned seat or desk, children can be members of a wider creative workshop community, sitting where and with whom they need to for the task at hand.

In early childhood classrooms, children need the flexibility to change where they are working depending on the varied needs and nature of their tasks. Socially it allows them to work alone when they need undisturbed time or to seek out spaces that accommodate two or three others when they need to share ideas or to help each other. This in turn leads to far greater independence within the class. Children know they can turn to others besides the teacher for help and feedback, and they are likely to work toward solving their problems as part of a community rather than passively sitting at their desks, waiting for a teacher's help.

A classroom with this kind of flow and movement can be disconcerting to parents—and some teachers—the first time they experience it. But having watched this type of environment over the years, it is clear that these conditions add to children's abilities to work for longer periods of time than many adults imagine.

Just like adults, children need spaces to work, not one designated space. Assigning children to one work spot day after day doesn't give them the chance to learn how they work best. Children, in their workplaces and creative environments, need the same tools adults do. This doesn't mean that there is one magic formula for the physical layout of the classroom. Teachers create different environments with their children that set the stage for stimulating learning.

For example, one teacher used this arrangement: She set up her room with a variety of areas rather than centers. Over one small round table hung a sign, "Quiet! Genius at work." This was a place designated for children to work where they wouldn't be disturbed. Other tables were pushed together, in fours or twos, and there were several longer tables that would seat up to six children for larger group work. At one point in the year, this teacher's classroom included a listening area with many books created by the children and "published" in class as well as recordings of children reading their stories; a bird feeder outside the window with pads of paper and pencils for observations; and a long publishing table with enough room to spread out covers, glue, binding materials, and labels. Organizing the classroom with areas like these shows the thought this teacher put into planning for the resources that children might need. What a difference from an assigned seat and a set schedule!

ACTIVITIES FOR CHILDREN

"I Can" Scrapbook

GOALS: To develop child's self-concept
To develop child's self-awareness

MATERIALS: Construction paper, paste, samples of children's work

PREPARATION: Teacher and child choose samples of child's work to put in the scrapbook.

PROCEDURE:

1. Using samples of child's work, make an "I can" scrapbook.

2. Show "I can paint," "I can color," and "I can paste" with samples of work.

3. Illustrate "I know colors," for example, with samples of the colors the child can recognize, and "I can count" with drawings of the number of objects that the child can count.

ACTIVITIES FOR CHILDREN

Group Self-Esteem Activity

GOALS: To develop children's self-esteem
To develop children's self-awareness
To encourage children's creativity

MATERIALS: Table, crayons, markers, paper, and tape.

PREPARATION: Cover the top of the table with paper, attaching it with tape. In the middle of the paper write the title of the picture, for example, "Our Art Group."

PROCEDURE:

1. Allow the children to draw pictures on the paper during group or free-choice time.

2. When the picture is finished (to everyone's liking), take it off the table.

3. Tape it to the wall or put it on a bulletin board.

4. Give children time to talk about their individual drawings.

VARIATION:

■ Use different shapes or colors of paper.

■ Use paper cut in a tree or animal shape.

■ Use a round table or a rectangular table.

■ Try to have a special theme for the group artwork: nature, families, animals, and so on.

ACTIVITIES FOR CHILDREN

Mirror Activities—Toddlers

GOALS: To develop child's self-concept
To develop child's self-awareness

MATERIALS: Large, full-length mirror, or small hand-held mirror

PREPARATION: If using hand-held mirrors, have several available for this activity.

PROCEDURE:

1. Bring each child to the mirror.
2. Encourage them to look at the mirror.

3. Have them point to the parts of the body you name. Examples may include "Show me your nose," "Where is your tummy?" and "Point to your mouth."

VARIATION:

■ Have child point to *your* mouth, tummy, nose, and so on.

■ Play a game that involves body part identification, such as "Put your finger in the air" or "If You're Happy and You Know It."

ACTIVITIES FOR CHILDREN

Mirror Activities— Kindergarten—Third Graders

GOALS: To develop child's self-awareness
To develop child's self-concept

MATERIALS: Large, full-length mirror, or small hand-held mirror

PREPARATION: Have each child spend at least a minute looking at himself in the mirror.

PROCEDURE:

1. Ask the children, as they look at themselves, such questions as:
   - "Why do people look in mirrors?"
   - "Why do people look at themselves?"
   - "What do you like about you that you see in the mirror?"
2. Have two children look in the mirror together.
3. Have one child tell the other what is special about her, and what he likes about her.

VARIATION: Have children draw what they have seen or how they feel about what they have seen in the mirror.

ACTIVITIES FOR CHILDREN

Mirror Activities—Fourth and Fifth Graders

GOALS: To develop child's self-concept

To develop child's self-awareness

MATERIALS: Large, full-length mirror, or small hand-held mirror

PREPARATION: Have children spend at least one minute looking at themselves in the mirror.

PROCEDURE:

1. Ask the children questions such as:
   - What features do they see that are like their parents, siblings, a famous person, or other relatives?
   - What is special about what they see?
   - What lines and shapes do they see in their image?
2. Have two children look into the mirror.
3. Have them compare the lines and shapes they see in each other's face.
4. Ask them to tell each other what is special about their images.
5. Does either one look like a famous person?

VARIATION: Have the children draw a picture of themselves or of the child they looked into the mirror with.

ACTIVITIES FOR CHILDREN

A Self-Awareness Photo Album

GOAL: To develop child's self-awareness

MATERIALS: Large pieces of colored paper, paper punch, yarn, and paste

PREPARATION: Have each child bring in a photo of himself or herself.

PROCEDURE:

1. Use large pieces of colored paper.
2. Punch holes in the side of each sheet of paper.
3. Tie yarn through the holes to hold the pages together.
4. Have the child paste his photo on a page.
5. Print the child's name under the photo, if the child can't write his own name.
6. Leave the photo album out so the children can look at and enjoy the pictures.

VARIATION:

■ A personal picture sequence chart can be made for each child using photos taken at different times of the year (birthday, outings, holidays, and so on). Children will gain a sense of time, change, and growth in these photo charts.

■ During the year, children may want to dictate stories or short descriptive statements to accompany these photos. Older children can write their own stories. These "story pages" can be added to the book throughout the year.

ACTIVITIES FOR CHILDREN   Me-Mobiles

GOALS: To develop child's self-concept
To develop child's self-awareness

MATERIALS: Selection of magazines (school and department store catalogs; nature, sports, or any popular family magazines), scissors, paste, construction paper, wire hangers, yarn (or string), and name tags large enough to fit in the center triangle of the hanger.

PREPARATION:
Tie the child's name tag to the central portion of the hanger. Allow at least three strings to dangle from the bar of the hanger.

PROCEDURE:
1. Have the children look through the magazines and cut (or tear) out three or more pictures that reflect a favorite thing or activity in their lives.

2. Have the children paste the pictures on the construction paper.

3. Have the children tie or staple the mounted pictures to the strings attached to the hanger.

VARIATION:
■ Encourage the children to talk about their selections.

■ Hang the hangers on a "clothesline" in the classroom or in any other appropriate place.

ACTIVITIES FOR CHILDREN   Patty-Cake

GOALS: To develop child's self-concept
To develop child's self-awareness

MATERIALS: None required

PREPARATION: Review the song, "Patty-cake, Patty-cake, Baker's Man" with the children.

PROCEDURE:
1. Begin by singing and clapping: "Patty-cake. Patty-cake. Baker's Man. Bake me a cake as fast as you can. Roll it and pat it. Mark it with (use a child's initial). Put it in the oven for (use a child's name) and me."

2. Use all the children's names in the song.

3. Repeat the song often so that children learn each other's names.

VARIATION:
Have each child take a turn to sing the song and name another child in the group.

ACTIVITIES FOR CHILDREN   I Like

GOALS: To develop child's self-concept

To develop child's self-awareness

MATERIALS: Tape recorder, tape

PREPARATION: Ask children to think about things they really like or are interested in.

PROCEDURE:

1. Individually ask children to name something they like or are interested in.
2. Record these statements and create a pause on the tape.
3. After the short pause, ask each child to say his or her name and record it.
4. During group time, play the tape for the children.
5. Ask them to identify each child after each statement of interest.
6. Have the children check their guesses when they hear the name of the child recorded on the tape.

VARIATION:

■ As a follow-up to this activity, play the tape in the art center. Some children may want to express what they heard on the tape with paint, markers, clay, and so on.

■ Another possible use of the tape is in the book corner. Have earphones on the tape player so children can listen quietly to their own and their friends' voices and comments.

■ Some children might want to dictate a story about something they heard on the tape.

ACTIVITIES FOR CHILDREN   Tearing, Punching, and Stapling

GOAL: To develop small muscles in hands and fingers

MATERIALS: Supply of old magazines and newspapers, paper punch, variety of papers (such as smooth, bumpy, heavy and tissue-thin, all in different colors), and stapler

PREPARATION: Place all of the required materials within easy reach of the children.

PROCEDURE:

1. Give the children a variety of paper, along with the stapler and paper punch.
2. Challenge the child to tear a tiny shape, an enormous shape, a wide shape, and so on.
3. Have the child paste or staple all of the interesting ragged shapes on a long piece of paper for a big, colorful mural.
4. Tape the mural on an empty wall for all to see.

VARIATION:

If a paper punch is used, save the circles that the child punches from white waxed paper and put them in a jar full of water. After you fasten the lid on tightly, the child can shake the jar and make a "snowstorm" inside.

...TIES FOR CHILDREN   Shaving Cream Art

GOALS: To develop small muscles in hands and fingers

MATERIALS: Can of white shaving cream, and finger paint paper

PREPARATION: Cover the table with newspapers. Have the children put on smocks or paint shirts.

PROCEDURE:

1. Put a few squirts of shaving cream onto a piece of finger paint paper.
2. Take food coloring and dye the shaving cream the color the children choose.
3. Watch the shaving cream turn colors.
4. Have the children finger paint with the shaving cream.
5. Save the design by putting a clean sheet of white paper over the design and rubbing the paper. Then lift the paper off and hang it to dry.

VARIATION:

Shaving cream is also great to use when there are a few minutes until cleanup time and the children are bored with what they are doing. Squeeze a little dab of shaving cream on a table in front of each child. Show how it grows, changes, and how designs, mountains, and squeezy-feely shapes can be made from the cream. When art time is over, have each child clean up with a sponge.

ACTIVITIES FOR OLDER CHILDREN Body Outlines
(Grades 4–5)

GOALS: To develop child's self-awareness
To develop awareness of others

MATERIALS: Large sheets of paper, dark colored markers, other colors of markers, and tape

PREPARATION: Project a light onto a blank wall which has a large sheet of paper taped on it.

PROCEDURE:

1. Have the students trace each other's "standing shadow" with a large dark marker.
2. Have the students decorate the outline or fill it in with words or phrases describing that person.
3. Allow children to do another person's outline to learn more about that person.

VARIATION:

While children are tracing the body outline, they may want to ask questions about the child's favorite foods, clothes, TV or movie stars, cars, and so on. They can then fill in the outline with drawings of these favorite things.

ACTIVITIES FOR OLDER CHILDREN Talk Time
(Grades 4–5)

GOALS: To develop child's self-awareness

To develop child's awareness of others

MATERIALS: None required

PREPARATION: Let the children know they will have a "talk time." This is a time set aside to visit with their friends.

PROCEDURE:

1. Choose what time of the day you want to set aside for "talk time."
2. Set the length of time it will last.
3. Ask the children to spend some time in "talk time" getting to know more about each other.
4. Suggest they talk about what they did last night, their new item of clothing, what they are going to play at recess, or a book they have been reading—anything they feel is important to share with their classmates.

VARIATION:

■ Have the children keep journals of their talk times. It is fun to look back over the year and see what was important at different times of the year.

■ Teachers can join in the conversations, using this "break" as an information-gathering time.

ADDITIONAL INFORMATION: The development of strong friendships and a peer group are characteristic of this age group. This type of experience also provides an opportunity for developing social interaction and for finding out that their friends have special interests and mutual concerns.

Teachers who use "talk time" find that when children know they are going to have a time to visit freely, they refrain from visiting at inappropriate times.

ACTIVITIES FOR OLDER CHILDREN Rope Games
(Grades 4–5)

GOALS: To develop child's large muscles

To encourage motor development

MATERIALS: Long rope

PREPARATION: Put the long rope on the floor in a zigzag pattern.

PROCEDURE:

1. Have the children walk on the rope.
2. Note how many of the children can do this and how well they can do it.
3. Put the rope in a straight line and pretend it is a tightrope.
4. Have the children "walk the tightrope" with a real or pretend umbrella in their hands for balance.

5. Note the balancing ability of each child.

VARIATION:

■ Have two children take turns holding the rope very high at first and then gradually lower and lower. Have the rest of the children go under the rope without touching it.

■ Place the rope straight out on the floor. Have the children walk across it, hop on one foot across it, hop on two feet across it, crawl across it, jump across it, and cross it any other way they can think of. Note each child's physical control.

ACTIVITIES FOR OLDER CHILDREN Blanket Statues
(Grades 4–5)

GOALS: To develop large muscles
To develop motor control
To encourage child's creativity

MATERIALS: Blanket

PREPARATION: Large, open space

PROCEDURE:

1. Have the children make shapes using their bodies.
2. Have them experiment with as many shapes and forms as they choose.
3. Have the children make "blanket statues."
4. Have a child stay frozen in one position and place a blanket over her to create a statue.
5. Two children can create partner statues: one child rests on hands and knees and a second child rests on his back.
6. Let the children's creativity direct their movement.

VARIATION:

■ Use this activity as an opportunity to take photographs that can later be displayed.
■ Allow older children to write captions for their photographs, creating their own documentary of the activity.

ADDITIONAL INFORMATION: This activity is most suitable for kindergarten and up. Younger children may not want to be covered with a blanket. Never force a child to participate in this or any activity.

ACTIVITIES FOR OLDER CHILDREN Can You Guess What I Am?
(Grades 4–5)

GOALS: To develop motor control
To encourage child's creativity

MATERIALS: 15–20 different animal pictures

PREPARATION: Place the animal pictures in a box. Have a small group of four to five children seated on the floor.

PROCEDURE:

1. Choose one child to pick out a picture from the box.
2. Have the child act out the animal in the picture for the others to guess.
3. Allow whoever guesses the animal to be the next to pick out a picture to act out.

VARIATION:

■ Use transportation pictures such as a train, truck, jet, car, boat, bus, and so on.
■ Draw a picture of the experience.
■ Tape children describing their experience.

ACTIVITIES FOR OLDER CHILDREN   Painted Toast
(Grades 4–5)

GOALS: To develop fine muscles in the hands and fingers

To encourage child's creativity

MATERIALS: ¼ cup milk, a few drops of food coloring, slices of white bread, and clean paintbrushes

PREPARATION: Mix a few drops of food coloring into the milk. Distribute small containers of this mixture to the children.

PROCEDURE:

1. Give each child a clean paintbrush.
2. Give each child a piece of white bread.
3. Have the children paint designs or faces on the white bread.
4. Toast the bread in a toaster.
5. After the activity, the bread can be buttered and eaten or used as part of a sandwich.

ACTIVITIES FOR OLDER CHILDREN   Art, Dance, and
(Grades 4–5)   Physical Movement

GOAL: To challenge children to use motor skills in creative ways

MATERIALS: Art prints that show a good deal of movement. Some suggestions: Van Gogh's "Starry Night," Jackson Pollock's "Water Birds," Jacob Lawrence's "Strike," or Edgar Degas' "Ballet Scene," paper, pencils, and markers.

PREPARATION:
Review the elements of line and movement in art while viewing one of the prints. Discuss the ways the artist used lines to show movement.

PROCEDURE:

1. Tell the students that they will take turns modeling and drawing different movements.
2. Have volunteers pantomime individually or in small groups various kinds of movements such as those in dance, in a sport, or in a type of exercise.
3. Have the students observe the movement, then draw lines that represent or reflect the movements they are seeing.
4. Continue the activity until students have filled their sheet of drawing paper with colorful lines.
5. Have the students exchange roles.

ACTIVITIES FOR OLDER CHILDREN Shadowplay
(Grades 4–5)

GOALS: To develop understanding of the source of light

To develop creative thinking

MATERIALS: Ball, and flashlight smaller than the ball

PREPARATION: Place the ball on a surface in front of a fairly plain and darkened area so that shadows can be seen clearly.

PROCEDURE:

1. Place the flashlight in position (behind the ball) before turning it on.

2. Ask the students if they can guess where the shadow will fall.

3. Shine the flashlight on the ball from behind.

4. See how many children guessed correctly.

5. Use a variety of angles such as to the left of the ball, above the ball, and below the ball.

VARIATION:

■ Use this activity to help students determine the source of light in paintings.

■ Substitute a toy stuffed animal for the ball (this makes a good activity to do near Groundhog's Day).

ACTIVITIES FOR OLDER CHILDREN Paper Telescopes
(Grades 4–5)

GOALS: To practice looking carefully for details

To continue development of small muscles in the eye

MATERIALS: 4 × 6 index cards for each student, and art prints

PREPARATION: Explain that looking very closely is an important skill. It can be used when reading a book, examining a map, and looking at a painting.

PROCEDURE:

1. Have each child make a "telescope" by rolling up the index card into a tube.

2. Ask them to find certain things in the art print.

3. Determine by the angle of the telescopes if the child is looking in the correct place.

CHAPTER 6

DEVELOPMENTAL LEVELS AND ART

This chapter provides some important, basic information for teachers on the different stages children go through in art.

 DEVELOPMENTAL LEVELS/STAGES OF ART

Just as young children experience various stages of physical development, they also develop art abilities in a gradual process, going through specific stages. These stages are called **developmental levels.** A developmental level is a guide to what a child can do in art at different ages, but it is not a strict guideline. Some children may be ahead or behind the developmental level for their age. Developmental levels tell the teacher what came before and what is to come in the artwork of the young child.

There is no exact pattern for each age level. Not all three-year-olds behave alike, nor are they completely different from four-year-olds. But there is a gradual growth process, called *development,* that almost every child goes through. An understanding of developmental levels helps an adult accept each child at the child's present level, whatever it is.

 CHILDREN'S DRAWING

There are three developmental levels in drawing that are of concern to the early childhood teacher: the **scribble stage,** the **basic forms stage,** and the **pictorial** (or first drawings) **stage.**

 THE SCRIBBLE STAGE

Most children begin scribbling at about one and one-half to two years of age. They will scribble with anything at hand and on anything nearby. Their first marks are usually a random group of lines. Yet these first scribbles are related to later drawing and painting. They are related to art just as a baby's first babbling sounds are related to speech.

The crayon may be held upside down, sideways, with the fist, or between clenched fingers. Children may be pleased with this scribbling and get real enjoyment from it. However, they do not try to make any definite pictures with these marks. They simply enjoy the physical motions involved in scribbling. It is the act of doing—not the final product—that is important to the child.

EARLY SCRIBBLE STAGE: DISORDERED OR RANDOM SCRIBBLING

During the early scribble stage, the young child does not have control over hand movements or the marks on a page. Thus, this stage is called **disordered** or **random scribbling.** The marks are random and go in many directions. The direction of the marks depends on whether the child is drawing on the floor or on a low table. The way the crayon is held also affects how the scribbles look. But the child is not able to make the crayon go in any one way on purpose. There is neither the desire nor the ability to control the marks. (See Figure 6–1 for some examples of random scribbles.)

The child doesn't even realize that she is producing these scribbles. The connection between herself and the scribbles isn't made by the early scribbler. In fact, these children receive as much satisfaction from just handling the materials—dumping the crayons out of the box, putting them back in again, rolling them across the table or in their hands—as they do from scribbling!

Art is such a sensory experience at this age that children may use crayons in both hands as they draw, singing along in rhythm to the movements they are making. They may not even notice the crayon they're working with isn't leaving marks on the paper.

LATER SCRIBBLE STAGE: CONTROLLED SCRIBBLING

At some point, children find a connection between their motions and the marks on the page. This may be about six months after the child has started to scribble, but the time will vary with each child. This very important step is called **controlled scribbling.** The child has now found it possible to control the marks. Many times, an

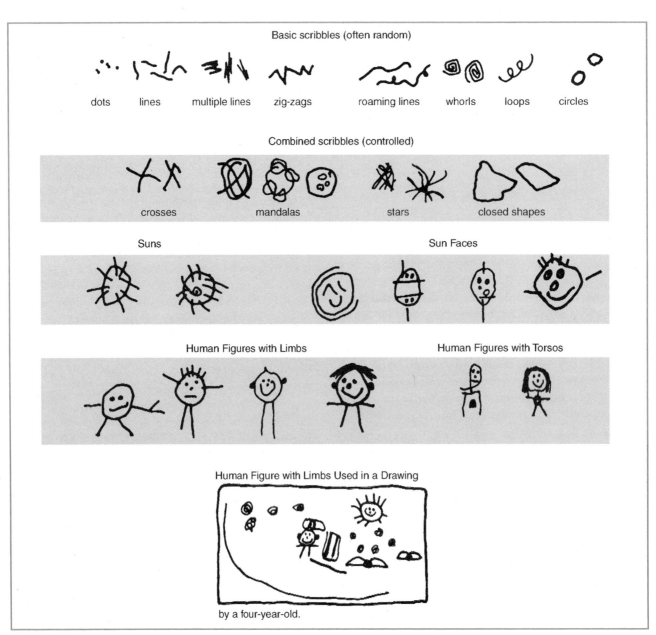

FIGURE 6–1 Examples of development in children's drawing (from Feeney et al., 1995).

adult cannot see any real difference in these drawings. They still look like scribbles—but they are different in a very important way.

The child's gradual gaining of control over scribbling motion is a vital experience for the child. She now is able to make the marks go in the direction desired. Most children scribble at this later stage with a great deal of enthusiasm, since coordination between seeing and doing is an important achievement.

Because children enjoy this newfound power, they are encouraged to try new motions. They now may scribble in lines, zigzags, or circles. When they repeat motions, it means they are gaining control over certain movements. They can become very involved in this type of scribbling.

TOOLS FOR THE SCRIBBLE STAGE

Children just beginning to scribble need tools that are safe and easy to hold and use. For a child between the ages of one and one-half and three years, large, non-toxic crayons are good tools for artwork. Pencils are dangerous for the young child and are also too difficult to hold and use. A good-quality, kindergarten-type crayon is the best tool. The crayon should be large and unwrapped so it can be used on both the sides and ends. Good-quality crayons are strong enough to hold up to rough first scribbles. They also make bright, clear colors, which are pleasant for the child to use.

Since motion is the chief enjoyment in this stage, the child needs large blank paper (at least 18″ × 24″). This size allows enough room for wide arm movements and large scribbles in many directions. The paper should always be large enough to give the child a big open space for scribbling. Paper can be in a variety of shapes, such as triangular, circular, oval, and so on.

If possible, a child in the scribble stage should use large white paper. Crayon scribbles show up better on white paper, so the child can see more easily the results of the scribbling. The classified section of the newspaper is also appropriate paper for beginning artists. The small print of the advertisements makes a neutral, non-intrusive background for scribbling, and this section of the paper provides a generous supply of material for young scribblers, which encourages the frequency of their scribbling.

The child needs only a few crayons at a time. Because motor control is the main focus in the early period of the scribbling stage, too many different crayons may distract the child in the scribbling process.

Painting is another good art activity for children in the scribble stage. Paintbrushes for two- and three-year-olds need to have 12-inch handles and 3/4-inch to 1-inch bristles. Paint for two- and three-year-old children should be mixed with a dry soap so it is thick enough to control. The paper for painting may need to be heavier than newsprint because children will repeatedly paint the paper until it disintegrates. Toddlers and two- and three-year-olds all enjoy experimenting with paint at the easel and table. Pasting, tearing paper, and soap and finger painting are also art activities enjoyed by most children of this age. A good deal of monitoring is required with toddlers because they are tempted to taste the materials and carry them about the room. For toddlers the major value lies in simple experimentation with the colors and textures.

 ## THE BASIC FORMS STAGE

Basic forms like rectangles, squares, and circles develop from scribbles as the child finds and recognizes simple shapes in the scribbles. More importantly, they develop as the child finds the muscle control and hand–eye coordination (use of hand(s) and eyes at the same time) to repeat the shape.

At this stage, the drawings look more organized. This is because the child is able to make basic forms by controlling the lines. A child in the age range of three to four years is usually in the basic forms stage.

During this stage children hold their tools more like adults and have a growing control over the materials. Children can now control their scribbles, making loops, circular shapes, and lines that are distinguishable and can be repeated at will. Children at this age value their scribbles. By age three or four, children will not draw if their marker is dry. Children now ask to have their names put on their work so it can be taken home or displayed in the room.

A child in the three- to four-year-old range is generally in the basic forms stage.

EARLY BASIC FORMS: CIRCLE AND OVAL

Generally, the first basic form drawn is the oval or circle. This marks the **early basic forms stage.** It develops as children recognize the simple circle in their scribbles and are able to repeat it. Both the oval and the circle develop from circular scribbles.

Another early basic form in this stage is the curved line or arc. This is made with the same swinging movement of an arm used in the early scribble stage. Now, however, it is in one direction only. This kind of line gradually becomes less curved, and from it come the horizontal and vertical lines. Making an intentional arc-shaped line reflects more developed motor control.

LATER BASIC FORMS: RECTANGLE AND SQUARE

As the muscle control of three- to four-year-olds continues to improve, more basic forms are made in their drawings. The rectangle and square forms are made when the child can purposefully draw separate lines of any length desired. The child joins the separate lines to form the rectangle or square. This indicates the **later basic forms stage.**

The circle, oval, square, and rectangle are all basic forms made by the child's control of lines.

TOOLS FOR THE BASIC FORMS STAGE

Children in the basic forms stage have enough motor control and hand–eye coordination to use different tools. In addition to crayons, the child may now begin to work with tempera paint. Tempera paint is the best kind for children because it flows easily from the brush onto the page. Large lead pencils are good for children in the later period of this stage; there is less danger of injury with these older children. A variety of papers can be supplied, from newsprint to construction paper.

Felt-tip pens or colored markers are an excellent tool for this stage. They provide clear, quick, easily made, and nice-looking marks. In the basic forms stage, when the child really enjoys seeing the marks come out as desired, these pens are best. They require little pressure to make bold marks. Felt-tip pens should be nontoxic and water-soluble so that most spots can be washed out of the child's clothes. (See "Food for Thought . . . Marker Maintenance" for suggestions on prolonging the life of colored markers.)

The largest paper size is not as necessary in this stage as in the scribble stage. Because the child now has better motor control, it is easier to keep marks on a smaller

When young children work with new forms or practice new skills, allow enough space and time for their total involvement.

space. Make available different colors and textures of paper and a variety of colored pencils and markers. Children in this stage like to make basic forms in many colors and ways as an exercise of their skill. Make available paper of many sizes and shapes.

 THE PICTORIAL STAGE

With the two earlier stages complete, the children now have the ability to draw the variety of marks that make up their first pictures; this occurs at the next developmental level in art—the pictorial stage. Many four-year-olds and most five-year-olds are at this level.

Pictures or first drawings are different from scribbling in that they are not made for pure motor enjoyment. Instead, they are made by the child for a purpose. The basic forms perfected in the preceding stage suggest images to the child that stand for ideas in the child's own mind. A new way of drawing begins. From the basic forms the child is able to draw, only particular ones are chosen. Miscellaneous scribbling is left out. In this way, children draw their first symbols. A **symbol** is a visual representation of something important to the child; it may be a human figure, animal, tree, or similar figure. Art in which symbols are used in such a way is called **representational art.** This means there has been a change from the sheer physical activity to attempts at making symbols. The child realizes that there is a relationship between the objects drawn and the outside world and that drawing and painting can be used to record ideas or express feelings.

FOOD FOR THOUGHT

Marker Maintenance

Markers are wonderful for young artists. But busy artists frequently lose caps from these markers, often resulting in dried-out markers. Replacing dried-out markers can be expensive, so here are a few hints on "marker maintenance" to help preserve markers as long as possible.

■ Solve the lost cap/dry-out problem by setting the caps with *open ends up* in a margarine or whipped topping container filled with plaster of Paris. Make sure the plaster does not cover the holes in the caps. When the plaster dries, the markers can be put into the caps and will stand upright until ready for use again.

■ Give new life to old dry felt markers by storing them *tips down with the caps on.* When the markers become dried out, remove the caps and put in a few drops of water. This usually helps "revive" them.

■ Recycle dried-out markers by having children dip them in paint and use them for drawing.

■ Make your own pastel markers by adding dry tempera paint (or food color) to bottles of white shoe polish that come with sponge applicator tops.

■ Use empty plastic shoe polish bottles or roll-on deodorant bottles to make your own markers. Wash the tops and bottles thoroughly and fill them with watery tempera paint (Warren, 1987).

The ability to draw symbols comes directly from the basic forms stage. The basic forms gradually lose more and more of their connection to body motion only. They are now put together to make symbols, which stand for real objects in the child's mind. Now the child is expressing in the scribble something of importance to her. It may seem to be a scribble, but it is now a "man" or a "dog"—a definite symbol representing something in the child's life.

The human form is often the child's first symbol. A man is usually drawn with a circle for a head and two lines for legs or body. Other common symbols include trees, houses, flowers, and animals. The child can tell you what each symbol stands for in the drawing.

TOOLS FOR THE PICTORIAL STAGE

Children need tools that can be easily controlled to help them more easily produce the desired symbols. Thinner crayons and paintbrushes and less fluid paints can now be made available so children can express their ideas and feelings with greater realism. Children over age five will want to be able to select colors that fit their symbols, so a variety of colors of paint, crayons, and markers are necessary.

Naming and owning the art produced are also important to children in this stage. These children may ask you to record the names of their paintings or drawings as well as write stories to go with their drawings. These children recognize other children's work at this point.

Notice how the child puts basic forms together in a drawing.

They will want to take their work home, as well as contribute some to display in the classroom.

IMPORTANCE OF FIRST DRAWINGS

Sometime in the pictorial stage, children begin to name their drawings. Naming a drawing is really an important

THIS ONE'S FOR YOU

Stages of Art Development— Grades 1–5

With elementary students, one of the major goals of art experiences is to cultivate students' abilities to create original and expressive art. At this level, children are usually able to produce pictorial drawings at will. Art experiences for children in grades 1–5 need to focus on prior creative experiences and build on these.

In order to set appropriate expectations and guide artistic growth, you should be familiar with the typical stages of development in creating artwork for this level of students.

The stages of artistic growth outlined below focus on skills portraying space, proportions and movement or action. Each stage is typical of many children at a particular grade level; however, it is not unusual to find a range of developmental levels within a class or within the work of single students during a year.

Similar variations can be expected in students' ability to respond thoughtfully to artwork. At each stage of development, some students will have greater interest and skill in responding to art than in creating art (or the reverse).

Stage 1 (usually Grades K–2). Children begin to create visual symbols to represent figures such as people, houses, and trees. The figures often seem to "float" in space. Proportions are related to the importance of a feature in the child's experience. Movement is often suggested by scribble-like lines. Three-dimensional artwork reflects the level of prior instruction and practice in using media and the physical coordination students have developed.

Stage 2 (usually Grades 1–3). In picture-making, lines or borders are often used to represent the ground below and sky above. Figures may be placed along a line or at the lower edge of the paper. Proportions are shown through relative size—a house is larger than a person. Action is implied by the general position of lines and shapes, rather than subtle shifts in direction. Students who receive instruction will show general improvement in using three-dimensional media and applying design concepts as they work.

Stage 3 (usually Grades 3–6). Students try out new ways to portray space in the pictures they draw and paint. These explorations often reflect remembered functional or logical relationships more than visual recall or observation. General proportions improve, as well as the use of diagonals to suggest action. Many students develop a strong affinity for three-dimensional work and are willing to try out new media and techniques that require several steps.

Stage 4 (usually Grades 4–6). In picture-making, students search for ways to portray recalled or observed space. Some students begin to use perspective to imply near and distant objects. Movement is suggested through more subtle angles and curves. Individual styles and preferences for two- or three-dimensional work become more evident, along with increased skill in applying design concepts to create expressive work.

step for children. It is a sign that their thinking has changed; they are connecting their drawings with the world around them. This is the beginning of a new form of communication—communication with the environment through art.

Soon a five-year-old may think: "My daddy is a big man; he has a head and two big legs." She then draws a head and two big legs and names her drawing, "Daddy." Through drawing, the child is making a clear relationship between father and the drawing. The symbol of a man now becomes "Daddy." Of course, a child will not verbally name all objects every time a picture is made.

In their use of schemas, children express their own personalities. They express not only what is important to them during the process of creating, but also how aware they have become in thinking, feeling, and seeing. From early drawings to the most complex, they give expression to their life experiences.

Older children enjoy further developing fine motor skills in drawings.

ACTIVITIES FOR CHILDREN

Variations on Easel Painting

GOALS: To encourage children's development in art
To encourage creativity
To stimulate children's interest in easel painting

MATERIALS: Tempera paint, brushes

PREPARATION: Prepare easels and paint using the procedures listed below.

PROCEDURE:
Try one or several of the following ideas:

1. Have the children use a number of shades of one color paint.

2. Have the children use colored paper—colored newsprint comes in pastel shades, or the backs of faded construction paper can be used.

3. Have the children use the same color of paint with the same color paper.

4. Have the children use various sizes of brushes, or both flat and floppy ones, with the same colors of paint.

VARIATION:

■ Have the children paint objects the children have made in carpentry, or paint dried clay objects.

■ Have the children paint large refrigerator-type boxes.

ACTIVITIES FOR CHILDREN — More Painting Ideas

GOALS: To encourage children's development in art

To stimulate children's interest in painting

To encourage creative thinking

MATERIALS: Long pieces of paper, paint, brushes, and crayons

PREPARATION: See the Procedures below for preparation steps for each activity.

PROCEDURE:
More ideas to stimulate children's interest in painting are:

1. Have the children work together on a long piece of paper (computer paper) to produce one large mural.
2. Have the children paint the fence with water and large brushes.
3. Have the children draw firmly on paper with crayons and paint over it to produce "crayon resistant" art.
4. Use all pastel colors (start with white and add color a bit at a time when mixing).
5. Set up a table with many colors of paint and encourage the children to select the colors they prefer.

VARIATION:
Have the children paint to music.

ACTIVITIES FOR CHILDREN — Painting with Soft Objects

GOALS: To encourage children's development in art

To stimulate children's interest in painting

To encourage creative thinking

MATERIALS: Cotton balls, shallow dish of wet paint, shallow dish of dry paint, and paper

PREPARATION: Cover the painting area with newspapers. Have the children wear smocks or painting shirts.

PROCEDURE:

1. Have the child dip a cotton ball in a shallow dish of wet paint.
2. Have the child smear it or squish it on paper.
3. Have the child dip the cotton ball into dry powdered paint.
4. Have the child rub it across dry paper to create an interesting soft effect.

VARIATION: Dip cotton swabs into paint, and use them as a brush.

ACTIVITIES FOR CHILDREN

More Painting Ideas

GOALS: To encourage children's development in art
To stimulate children's interest in painting
To encourage creative thinking

MATERIALS: Sponges cut into different shapes, liquid tempera paints in shallow dishes, and paper

PREPARATION: Cover the painting area with newspapers. Have the children wear smocks or painting shirts. Place tempera paint and sponges within easy reach of the children.

PROCEDURE:

1. Have the child dip each sponge shape in paint.
2. Have the child dab, press, or rub the sponge onto paper.

ACTIVITIES FOR CHILDREN

Creative Crayoning

GOALS: To encourage children's development in art
To stimulate children's interest in using crayons
To encourage children's creativity

MATERIALS: Crayons, paper, and materials specific for each activity

PREPARATION: Gather materials together. Have them within easy reach of children.

PROCEDURE:

1. Have the children try a variety of surfaces for crayon drawings.
2. Have the children draw with crayons on these surfaces for variety:
   - fabric
   - egg cartons
   - paper towel rolls
   - sandpaper
   - wood scraps
   - sticks and stones
   - cardboard
   - Styrofoam trays

ACTIVITIES FOR CHILDREN

All Kinds of Printing!

GOALS: To encourage children's development in art
To stimulate interest in printing
To encourage children's creativity

MATERIALS: Shallow dishes or pans with several colors of liquid tempera paint, paper, and miscellaneous materials specific to the activities listed below: combs, old small wheel toys, clay, paper cups, plastic alphabet letters and numbers

PREPARATION: Cover the work area with newspapers. Have the children wear smocks or painting shirts.

PROCEDURE:
Try one or several of these printing ideas:

1. Toy Prints—Dip the wheels of an old toy car, truck, or other toy in paint. Have the children make tracks on the paper.
2. Plastic Alphabet Letters and Numbers—Dip plastic alphabet letters and numbers in paint and print them on paper.
3. Paper Cup Printing—Dip the rim of a paper cup into paint. Press the rim on the paper to make a design.
4. Comb Printing—Dip the teeth of a comb into paint. Print with it by drawing it along the paper.
5. Printing with Clay—Have the children pound clay into small flat cakes about an inch thick. Then have them carve a design on the flat surface with a bobby pin or popsicle stick. If desired, the design may be either brushed with paint or dipped in paint and pressed onto paper to print the design.

VARIATION: Roll whole or pieces of pinecones in paint. The large ones with flat bottoms can be dipped into paint and used to print images and designs.

ACTIVITIES FOR CHILDREN

Combination Painting

GOALS: To encourage children's development in art
To stimulate children's interest in painting
To encourage children's creativity

MATERIALS: Dry tempera paint; liquid starch; miscellaneous materials to sprinkle such as: salt, coffee grounds, eggshells, glitter, tiny Styrofoam balls, seeds, cornmeal, sequins, and tiny beads; paintbrushes; and paper

PREPARATION: Thicken tempera paint with liquid starch. Divide the paint up into individual portions. Cover the work area with newspapers. Have the children wear smocks or paint shirts.

PROCEDURE:
1. Have the children use the paint in their paintings.
2. While the paint is still wet, have the children sprinkle the painting with any of the above materials for attractive combination paintings. As the material dries in the paint, interesting effects occur.

VARIATION:
Have the child paint an area of paper with either a white glue mixture or liquid starch. Then, have the child shake on any small-grained media such as sand, salt, flour, or cornmeal. These can be put into shakers with large or small holes. (Dry tempera can also be added to granular material.)

ACTIVITIES FOR OLDER CHILDREN Artful Science
(Grades 4–5)

GOALS: To encourage children's development in art
To develop an understanding or relationship between art and science
To develop children's creativity

MATERIALS: Science books, large sheets of paper, pencils, crayons, and markers

PREPARATION: Have the students look through science books for illustrations of structures with lines (snowflakes, bones, blood circulation, plants, geological forms, and so on).

PROCEDURE:

1. Have each child select a small section of one of the illustrations.

2. Have the child draw a similar structure on a large sheet of paper.

3. After the drawing is completed, have the child use dark colors, crayons, or markers to increase the width of lines, making an abstract design.

4. Have the children color in the shapes between the lines.

5. Display the work.

6. Discuss the relationships between the "artistic structure" and the structure shown in the science book illustration.

ACTIVITIES FOR OLDER CHILDREN Colorful Words
(Grades 4–5)

GOALS: To encourage children's development in art
To encourage aesthetic awareness

MATERIALS: Blackboard, chalk, paper, crayons, and markers

PREPARATION: Discuss with the children phrases such as "the blues," or "I'm feeling blue," "green with envy," and the like.

PROCEDURE:

1. Ask the children to give more examples of the use of color-related words to describe moods or feelings.

2. Write the phrases on the blackboard, in two columns: one for phrases with warm colors and one for phrases with cool colors.

3. Have each child select one of these phrases.

4. Have the child create an artwork that uses the phrases as a title and is dominated by variations on the color in the title.

ACTIVITIES FOR OLDER CHILDREN
Aesthetic Awareness
(Grades 4–5)

GOALS: To develop children's aesthetic sense

To develop an understanding of the concept of color and contrast

MATERIALS: Collection of old magazines, newspapers, and some black and white photographs.

PREPARATION: Provide each child with a viewfinder made out of a 4″ × 6″ index card rolled up into a tube.

PROCEDURE:

1. Have the child place the viewfinder over the picture or photograph.
2. Have the child look for the darkest area of the picture or photograph.
3. Show the child how to trace around the edges of the hole of the viewfinder to mark the place on the photograph.
4. Cut out and save the piece.
5. Continue to identify and cut out four or five other pieces that differ from each other in darkness (value).
6. Arrange the pieces in a light to dark sequence.

VARIATION:
Glue the pieces onto a sheet of paper. Make a drawing around the pieces.

REFERENCE

Feeney, S., Christensen, D., & Maravcik, E. (1995). Who am I in the lives of children? *An introduction to teaching young children* (5th ed.). Upper Saddle River, NJ: Prentice Hall.

SECTION 3

The Early Childhood
Art Program

CHAPTER **7**

TWO-DIMENSIONAL ACTIVITIES

sing as a framework the basic information presented thus far on developmental levels, creativity, aesthetics, and planning and implementing creative activities, let us now take a closer look at the general processes of picture making, printmaking, and collage.

A variety of brush sizes needs to be available for children's use.

PICTURE MAKING

The term **picture making** in this chapter refers to any and all forms of purposeful visual expressions, beginning with controlled scribbling. A common error associated with picture making is to equate it with artwork that contains recognizable objects or figures. Yet children's pictures (artwork) may take any form, just as long as the child is expressing herself visually in a nonrandom way.

PAINTING WITH A BRUSH

Painting with a brush is an excellent form of picture making.

Materials. Basic materials for painting with brushes include the following:

■ Watercolor paint sets. These are actually dehydrated tempera colors in concentrated cakes. They provide easy and convenient paint for individual use or group activity in the classroom. *To use paints in cakes:* Place a few drops of water on the surface of each cake of color to moisten the paint. Dip brush in water and brush surface of moistened cake of paint to obtain smooth, creamy paint. *To use powder paint*

(**tempera**): Fill a can one-fourth full of dry paint. Add water slowly, stirring constantly until the paint has the consistency of thin cream. A small amount of liquid starch or liquid detergent may be added to the mixture as a binder. Use enough paint to make good rich colors. For best results, prepare paint when needed; large amounts kept over a period of time have a tendency to sour. Containers for use with powder paint include milk cartons, juice cans, baby food jars, coffee cans, plastic cups, and cut-down plastic bottles. A set of paints can be carried easily if containers are placed in tomato baskets, soft-drink carriers, boxes, or trays (see Figure 7–1).

■ Individual pieces of paper, at least 12″ × 18″: roll paper, manila paper, newspaper, wallpaper, newsprint, or freezer paper.

■ Water containers for painting and rinsing brushes: coffee cans, milk cartons, juice cans, cut-down plastic bottles. Half-gallon plastic containers with handles (the kind used for liquid bleach) are light and can be filled to carry water during the painting lesson.

■ Paper towels or scrap paper for blotting brushes while painting.

■ Newspapers to protect the painting area. Painting may be done on paper-covered tables, desks, pinned to a bulletin board, fastened to a chalkboard, or on the floor if protected with newspaper.

■ A bucket of child-sized moist sponges for cleanup. Figure 7–1 has more hints on painting materials.

PAINTING HINTS

■ Thicken easel paint with liquid starch to cut down on drips.

■ To help paint stick better to slick surfaces such as foil, waxed paper, styrofoam, or plastic, mix dry tempera with liquid soap.

■ To keep paints smelling fresh and sweet, add a few drops of mint extract or oil of wintergreen or cloves.

■ For an added sensory experience, try adding lemon flavoring to yellow paint, mint to green, vanilla to white, and peppermint to red paint. You might want to caution the children not to taste the paint, especially with younger children.

FINGER PAINTING

Paint. The quickest, simplest way to make finger paint is to combine liquid starch with dry tempera. This may be done by pouring a generous dollop of starch onto the paper and then sprinkling it with dry tempera. Alternatively, some teachers like to stir the dry pigment into an entire container of starch base. No matter how

---

Art Tool Holder
Heavy paper, folded several times, will make a holder that keeps tools from rolling. It is also good for drying cleaned paintbrushes.

Drying Rack
Drying racks for wet artwork are ideal if space is at a premium. A number of wooden sticks of the same size tacked or stapled to pieces of corrugated cardboard of the same size will make a drying rack. If pieces of wood are not available, substitute two, three, or four pieces of corrugated cardboard taped together. Tape stacked pieces to the cardboard base.

Paint Container
Paper milk cartons stapled together (with tops removed) and with a cardboard handle make an ideal container for colored paint and water.

Paint Dispensers
Plastic mustard or ketchup containers make good paint dispensers. An aluminum nail in the top of each will keep the paint fresh. In some cases the plastic containers can be used for painting directly from the container. Syrup pitchers make good paint dispensers and are ideal for storing paint.

Plastic Spoons
Keep plastic spoons in cans of powdered tempera for easy paint dispensing.

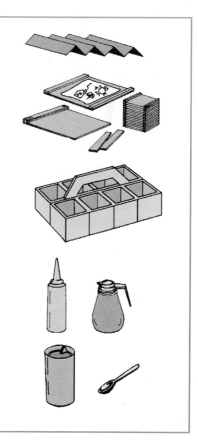

FIGURE 7–1 | Some helpful hints for storing and handling painting materials.

the paint is originally prepared, you need to be ready to add more ingredients as the children work. The results to strive for in mixing are rich, brilliant color and sufficient paint to fill the paper completely if the child wishes. Children must be allowed to experiment with the paint as they wish, using their fingers, the palms of the hands, wrists, and arms.

Prepared finger paints may be used, or the children may help mix a recipe from Appendix C. If the recipe is used, the mixture may be separated into three or four parts and coloring added—either food color or the powdered tempera used for easel painting. Children like to add their own color; they may use salt shakers containing powdered paint and mix in the color with their fingers. Adding soap flakes (not detergents) to the paint mixture increases variety.

Paper. The best type of paper for finger painting is:

1. Paper that has a shiny surface. This can be butcher paper, shelf paper, special finger paint paper, freezer wrap, or glossy gift wrap paper.
2. A water supply to make the paper damp. A damp sponge or rag works best. Water may also be sprinkled directly onto the paper.
3. Finger paint. This can be special finger paint or dry tempera paint mixed with liquid starch or liquid detergent to make a thick mixture.
4. Racks to dry the finished work. Cake-cooling racks work well for this.
5. A smock for each painter.
6. A nearby sink and running water for washing hands and cleaning up or a bucket of soapy water, sponges and paper towels.

Finger Painting Hints. Another method of finger painting is to cover a table with white oilcloth and let the children work on the oilcloth. The mixture can later be washed off with a hose or under a faucet. This activity is good for all ages.

Use waxed paper for a change, instead of regular finger painting paper, because of its transparent quality. A combination of any liquid dishwashing detergent and a dark-colored tempera paint (one part paint, one part soap) can be applied onto waxed paper. Cover the surface evenly so the painter can make a simple design with his fingers.

Finger painting without paper is another variation. The children finger paint directly onto plastic trays. When each child finishes, place a piece of paper on top of the finger painting and rub across the back of the paper. Lift the paper from the tray and a print of the finger painting is made. The trays are easily rinsed off in the sink.

Crayon drawings are one of the most popular two-dimensional art activities.

CRAYONS

Most young children are introduced to using crayons before starting school.

Materials. Crayon drawings may be done on a wide assortment of surfaces, such as newsprint, wrapping paper, newspaper, construction paper, corrugated board, cloth, and wood. This is an ideal medium for all children; it is bold, colorful, clean, and inexpensive. Crayons work well on most papers. They do not blend well; when attempts are made to do this, the wax often "tears." Crayons can be applied thinly to produce semitransparent layers of subtle color, and these layers can be coated with black crayon and scratched through for crayon etchings.

Crayon Hints. The crayon offers new areas of creative interpretation when used in combination with other materials:

■ Use crayon and white chalk on colored construction paper.
■ Make a crayon rubbing by placing shapes or textures under paper and rubbing over the surface.
■ Make a crayon resist by first drawing in brilliant color, then cover the drawing with watercolor paint.
■ Paint a colorful background, allow to dry, and then draw directly over the painted surface with chalk or crayon.

FOOD FOR THOUGHT

Why Coloring Books?

Many early childhood teachers would have to admit that they use pre-drawn images which they ask the children to either add to or complete by coloring in. One fourth-grade teacher I know requires an intensive book report for his class and then gives them a picture to color in for the cover! Where does creativity enter into that?

Whenever I discuss this "coloring book problem" with colleagues, many of them share their experiences with coloring books and dittos and remark that coloring was, and still is, a very relaxing activity. Why would this be bad for children?

Dittos and coloring books are adult-generated images designed to occupy children's time. There are times when occupying children's time is exactly what we want to do; for example, during long car trips. Coloring in coloring books can be relaxing because children are not required to think to complete the work. In school, do we want children *not to think?* Activities such as these often reduce children's ability to think for themselves and result in dependence on the teacher at a time when children should be learning independence.

Teachers sometimes use these methods so they can accomplish work of their own, such as correcting homework and classroom papers. Children can become so accustomed to seeing adult-generated images that when asked to create drawings of their own, they become frustrated because their work resembles that of a child rather than that of an adult. If children become frustrated, they lose interest in drawing and the creative process.

■ Use white crayon underneath a color to make a brighter color.

■ Use craypas (oil pastel crayons) on colored construction paper. Apply the oil pastels thickly to get rich colors.

PASTING

Pasting is a valuable medium for creative expression. The stickiness, texture, odor, and changes that take place as paste is used provide children many opportunities for creative discoveries.

Materials. Basic materials for pasting activities are:

1. Small jars of paste. (Or give each child a square of waxed paper with a spoonful of paste on it. This prevents waste.) A wooden tongue depressor is a good tool for spreading the paste, or paste can be spread with the fingers.

2. Sheets of plain or colored manila or construction paper in many sizes.

3. Collage materials. Some of these can be paper shapes in different colors, scraps of cloth, feathers, yarn, tinfoil, string, beans, sawdust, bottle caps, buttons, styrofoam packing pieces, rock salt, bits of bark, and any other things that look interesting.

4. Blunt scissors, for both left- and right-handed children.

Scissoring is a developmental skill.

Pasting Hints.

■ Pasting should be done away from climbing toys, building blocks, and similar large motor activities.

■ Materials for pasting should be on a shelf at child level.

■ Place collage and pasting materials on a separate table and sort them into shallow containers, such as baskets or clear plastic boxes, so that children can easily see the kinds of things that are available.

- Keep paste in small plastic containers or jars.
- Show children how to rinse out paste brushes and where to return all pasting materials.
- Set up a place to put finished work to dry.
- Using common recycled household disposables will make cleanup easier:
  - Aluminum pie tins and frozen food trays are both excellent for holding paint, paste, or glue for table activities.
  - At the end of the activity, you may want to recycle the aluminum.
  - Another way to make cleanup easier is to fold over the top edges of a large paper bag, then tape the bag to one end of your work table.
  - When the children have finished their projects, scraps can easily be swept off the table into the bag. Then, just toss the bag in the trash.

Avoid instructing children on the uses of paste and allow them to make their own discoveries. Eventually a child will begin to create a collage, arranging random shapes of varied colors on large paper.

By adult standards, it may appear that the amount of paste children use is exorbitant, but their explorations are limited if they cannot have as much paste as they need. Although most paste for children is nontoxic, a teacher should be certain that the commercial paste used in the classroom is safe, because children put paste in their mouths. Paste can also be child and/or teacher-made. (See Appendix C for paste recipes.)

CHALK

Chalk is an inexpensive material for picture making that comes in a variety of colors.

Materials.

1. Stack of wet or dry (or both) paper.
2. Sticks of white and colored chalk in a container.

Chalking Hints. Chalk drawing is best done on a paper with a slightly coarse, abrasive surface. This texture helps the paper trap and hold the chalk particles. Many papers have this quality, including inexpensive manila paper.

Chalks are brittle and easily broken. They are also impermanent, smearing very easily. Completed works should be sprayed with a "fixative" (ordinary hairspray works well); this should be done with proper ventilation.

Chalk strokes can be strengthened by wetting the chalk or paper. Various liquids have also been used with chalks for interesting results. These include dipping the chalk sticks in buttermilk, starch, and sugar water. Liquid tends to seal the chalk, so teachers must occasionally rub a piece of old sandpaper on the end of the chalk in order to break this seal and allow the color to come off again.

FOOD FOR THOUGHT　　Using Chalk in Picture Making

Here are more ideas for using chalk as a medium for young children's drawing and picture making.

- **Texture:** Place thin paper, such as copy paper or tracing paper, over a surface with a unique texture like sandpaper, bricks, or corrugated cardboard. Then rub over the paper with the side of the chalk so that the texture of the model appears. Numerous textures can be used for many interesting effects.
- **Chalk on wet paper:** Using colored chalk on wet paper (construction paper or toweling), glide the chalk over the damp surface to give a flowing motion to the drawing. This process provides bold and colorful pictures.
- **Starch and chalk:** Pour a small amount of liquid starch on a sheet of paper. Dip the colored chalk in the starch and create a unique art experience.
- **Wet chalk:** Soak chalk in water for several minutes before using it on a dry surface. The wet chalk can be used on windows, paper, ceramic surfaces, and numerous other slick areas. This chalk medium reacts much like a finger painting activity and provides a leaded glass appearance.
- **Chalk sand painting:** Place sawdust or sand with chalk shavings mixed with tempera paint in a bowl of water (just enough water to cover), stir, and allow to dry overnight. The following day apply liquid glue, paste, or starch on construction paper, posterboard, or cardboard. Sprinkle colored sand or sawdust over the glued or starched areas to create a sand painting. Outlining the details of the picture creates interesting effects.

See "Food for Thought: Using Chalk in Picture Making" for more ideas on using chalk for picture drawing.

MURALS

A storytelling picture or panel intended for a large wall space is called a **mural,** another form of picture making. A suitable topic for a mural may come from children's personal experiences at home, at school, or at play, or it may relate to other school subjects. In the classroom, mural making is a versatile art activity; it may involve a large group or just a few children, depending on the size of the mural. It may require a variety of materials or just one or two. With young children, it should be a simple, informal, spontaneous expression with a minimum of preplanning. Tedious planning destroys much of the intuitive quality and reduces interest. In contrast, older children will enjoy planning a group mural almost as much as making it.

Materials

kraft paper	paste
roll paper	newspapers
wallpaper	collage materials
crayons	brushes
paint	scissors
water and container	colored construction paper

Mural Hints.

- Watercolor paint allows for spontaneous bold design and brilliant color, ideal for murals.
- Cut or torn paper is a flexible medium suitable for murals, permitting many changes and parts as the mural progresses.
- Other techniques for manipulating paper are folding, curling, pleating, twisting, fringing, and overlapping.
- Place background paper on a bulletin board, then plan, pin, and move parts before attaching.
- Various papers such as tissue, wallpaper, illustrated magazine pages, and metallic paper add interest.

 PRINTMAKING

Long before they enter the classroom, most children have already discovered their footprints or handprints, made as they walk or play in snow or wet sand. *Relief prints* are created in a similar manner. An object is pressed against a flat surface to create a design that may be repeated over and over again. Generally, the process of relief printing consists of applying paint to an object and pressing it onto the paper. Techniques range from a simple fingertip printing to carving a styrofoam plate and printing with it. Emphasis should be on the free ma-

Finger painting is a popular two-dimensional activity for young children.

nipulation of objects and experimentation with color, design, and techniques.

MATERIALS

Materials for printmaking may include the following:

- *Paint.* Any of the following are suitable: tempera paint in sets of eight colors, powder paint in a thin mixture, food coloring, or water-soluble printing ink.
- *Stamp pad.* Discarded pieces of felt or cotton cloth inside a jar lid, cut-down milk carton, frozen food tin, or similar waterproof container saturated with color.
- *Paper.* Absorbent papers suitable for printing include newsprint, manila paper, wallpaper, tissue, construction paper, classified pages of the newspaper, plain wrapping paper, or paper towels. Avoid using paper with a hard slick finish because it does not absorb paint and ink well.
- *Cloth.* Absorbent pieces of discarded cloth can also be used to print on, such as pillow cases, sheets, men's handkerchiefs, old shirts, and napkins.
- *Other items.* Newspaper for covering tables, brushes for applying paint when not using a stamp pad, or cans for water.

ONE'S FOR YOU

Creative Budgeting

Painting supplies can eat up a large part of your budget. The following ideas may help your budget (and maybe your creativity, too):

1. Individual watercolor sets can be made by pouring leftover tempera paint into egg carton cups. Set them aside to dry and harden. Use the paints with water and brushes just as you would ordinary paint sets.

2. Paint containers need to be sturdy and inexpensive. Here are some ideas for different types of paint containers:

   ■ Cupcake or muffin tins are excellent for painting with several colors at a time.

   ■ Egg cartons work well when children are painting with cotton swabs. Cut cartons in thirds to make four-part containers, and pour small amounts of paint into each egg cup.

   ■ Store liquid tempera in recycled glue or dishwashing liquid bottles. Paint can be squirted quickly and neatly into paint cups from these bottles.

   ■ Use baby food jars as paint containers. Make a holder for them by cutting circles out of an egg carton lid. An empty six-pack soft drink carton makes a great tote for baby food jars of paint.

   ■ When using paint cups, make a nontipping cup holder from an empty half-gallon milk or juice carton. Cut holes along the length of the carton and pop in the cups.

   ■ Sponges can be good paint holders, too. Cut a hole the exact size of the paint jar or cup in the center of the sponge, then fit the jar/cup in the hole. Besides keeping paint containers upright, the sponges also catch drips.

   ■ Cotton-ball painting is more fun (and neater) when you clip spring-type clothespins to the cotton balls. Children use the clothespins like handles. The same clothespins can be used when printing with small sponge pieces.

PRINTMAKING HINTS

The following are some hints on printmaking activities suitable for young children.

With color.

■ Alternate thin transparent watercolor with thick, opaque tempera paint.

■ Use a light color to print on dark paper or vice versa.

■ Use transparent paint on colored paper or cloth so that the color of the background shows through.

■ Combine two sizes of objects of the same shape.

■ Combine objects of different sizes and shapes.

■ Use one object in various positions.

■ Try overlapping and grouping objects.

With texture.

■ Vary the amount of paint used in printing.

■ Use objects that create different textures, such as sponges, corrugated paper, wadded paper or cloth, stones, vegetables, and sandpaper.

With background paper.

■ Try using a variety of shapes and sizes of paper.

■ Paint background paper and allow to dry before printing.

■ Paste pieces of tissue or colored construction paper onto background paper, allow to dry, then print.

■ Print a stippled design on background with a sponge, allow to dry, then print with a solid object.

With pattern.

■ Print a shape in straight rows or zigzag. Repeat the design to create an all-over pattern.

■ Use a different shape for each row and add a second color in alternate rows.

■ Print in a border design with a single shape or group of shapes.

 COLLAGE

Collage, a French word meaning "to paste," is the product of selecting, organizing, and arranging materials of

THIS ONE'S FOR YOU   Teacher Tips

The way a teacher sets up her own materials, supplies, and space can make or break the children's and teacher's successful experiences in art. The following are suggestions on how to arrange teacher supplies for art experiences, as well as how to organize children's supplies.

1. *Scissors Holders.* Holders can be made from gallon milk or bleach containers. Simply punch holes in the container and place scissors in holes with the points to the inside. Egg cartons turned upside down with slits in each mound also make excellent holders.

2. *Paint Containers.* Containers can range from muffin tins and plastic egg cartons to plastic soft drink cartons with baby food jars in them. These work especially well outdoors as well as indoors because they are large and not easily tipped over. Place one brush in each container; this prevents colors from getting mixed and makes cleanup easier.

3. *Crayon Containers.* Juice and vegetable cans painted or covered with contact paper work very well.

4. Crayon pieces may be melted down in muffin trays in a warm oven. These, when cooled down, are nice for rubbings or drawings.

5. Printing with tempera is easier if the tray is lined with a sponge or paper towel.

6. A card file for art activities helps organize the program.

7. *Clay Containers.* Airtight coffee cans and plastic food containers are excellent ways to keep clay moist and always ready for use.

8. *Paper Scrap Boxes.* By keeping two or more boxes of scrap paper, children will be able to choose the size paper they want more easily.

9. To color rice or macaroni, put two tablespoons each of rubbing alcohol and food coloring into a jar. Cap and shake well. Add rice and macaroni and shake again. Turn out onto towels and let dry approximately 10 to 15 minutes.

10. Cover a wall area with pegboard and suspend heavy shopping bags or transparent plastic bags from hooks inserted in the pegboard. Hang smocks in the same way on the pegboard (at child level, of course).

11. Use the back of a piano or bookcase for hanging a shoe bag. Its pockets can hold many small items.

12. Use divided frozen food trays or a revolving lazy Susan to hold miscellaneous small items.

Working with two-dimensional materials can be fun in a new space.

contrasting color and texture and attaching them to a flat surface.

One way children become aware of things around them is by touching. Through manipulation of everyday objects, they grow in sensitivity to shapes and textures and discover ways to use them in creating new forms and images. With added experience, the tactile sense becomes an instrument of knowledge and a tool of expression. Unlike the *imitation of texture* in drawing and painting, the textural materials in collage are *real*.

Materials.

■ *Background:* Manila paper, construction paper, cardboard, and shirtboard.

■ *Collage materials:* Paper and cloth scraps, magazine pages, yarn, string, ribbon, lace, and any other items the children and teacher collect.

THIS ONE'S FOR YOU

So You Think You Know About Pencils . . .

The humble pencil may seem boring to you. But there are a lot of interesting things about pencils. A few of them follow:

THE HISTORY OF THE PENCIL

Lead pencils do *not* have any lead in them. They are made from clay and graphite. We still call the pencil core the "lead" because the ancient Greeks and Romans drew with thin sticks of lead. Also, the people who first discovered graphite thought it was a kind of lead.

Graphite was discovered about 600 years ago in what is now Germany. It gets its name from the Greek word "graphos," meaning "to write." About 500 years ago the English wrapped graphite in string to make an early pencil. In 1765 a German, Kasper Faber, began making some of the first modern pencils. He put his mixture of clay and graphite into a wooden container to make this now-common tool. Eberhard Faber, Kasper's great-grandson, was the first person to mass produce pencils in the United States in 1861. His name might be stamped on some of your pencils.

MAKING THE LEAD

Clay and graphite are crushed and mixed together. The hardness of the lead depends on how much clay is put in the mixture. The higher number on a pencil, the harder the lead. Most people use a No. 2 pencil. The clay-graphite mixture is poured into wooden forms. The wood in pencils is usually from cedar tree logs. Finally, did you know that . . .

- Every year in the United States two billion pencils are sold.
- You can write 45,000 words with an average pencil.
- You can draw a line 35 miles long with the average pencil.
- You now know more about pencils than the average teacher!

- *Natural materials:* Leaves, twigs, bark, seed pods, dried weeds, feathers, beans, ferns, sands, small stones, and shells.
- Scissors, brushes, paste, stapler, and staples.

Sort and keep materials of a similar nature in boxes to facilitate selection.

Collage Hints.

- When working with beginners, limit the number of collage materials; this lessens the confusion in selection.
- Encourage children to use materials in their own way. Instead of giving exact directions, suggest ways of selecting materials for a variety of shape, size, color, and texture.
- Materials may be cut, torn, or left in their original shapes.
- As children arrange and rearrange the shapes on the background, they may form a representational picture or compose an abstract design.

- Throughout the work period, emphasize thoughtful use of space by overlapping and grouping shapes, trying different combinations of colors and textural surfaces.
- Create three-dimensional effects by crumpling flat pieces of material and attaching them to the background in two or three places. Other techniques include overlapping, bending, folding, rolling, curling, and twisting paper.
- Include buttons, braids, tissue, or yarn for added interest and accent.
- Use glue or staples to fasten heavy materials and plastics.
- A collage may be displayed in a shadow box, using a box lid as a frame; it can also be mounted in an old picture frame or on a sheet of colored construction paper.
- Create a nature collage using all natural materials.

ACTIVITIES FOR CHILDREN   Crayons and T-shirts

You will note in this activity section that activities for older children are not listed separately. This is because all of the activities are designed to be springboards for art experiences and are not strictly limited to certain age groups.

GOALS: To encourage children's drawing with crayons

To develop children's creativity

MATERIALS: Wax crayons, light-colored t-shirts, and newspapers

PREPARATION: Set up an iron and ironing board away from the children's reach.

PROCEDURE:

1. Give each child a t-shirt to color a picture on.
2. Have the child make a design or picture on the t-shirt.
3. Press the shirt, with newspaper over the picture, on the ironing board. The picture will stay indefinitely on the t-shirt.

VARIATION:
Have the children bring in t-shirts for this activity.

CAUTION: Only an adult should use the iron in this activity.

ACTIVITIES FOR CHILDREN   Watercolors and Salt

GOALS: To encourage children's painting

To develop children's creativity

MATERIALS: Watercolors, table salt, brushes, and paper

PREPARATION: Set out watercolor sets, water, brushes, and paper for the children's use.

PROCEDURE:

1. Have the children paint a picture with watercolors, using enough water to make a moist picture.

2. Sprinkle a little table salt over the picture while it is still wet. The salt causes the paint to separate, and gives the painting a completely new look.

VARIATION:
Use this activity to talk about *change* in objects and to discuss what the child *sees* as a change.

ADDITIONAL INFORMATION:
Children love to paint with watercolors, but sometimes the colors seem too quiet and dull. This activity livens up their painting experience with watercolors.

ACTIVITIES FOR CHILDREN

Fun with Chalk

GOAL: To encourage children's chalk drawings

MATERIALS: Fat, soft chalk of different colors, paper, and brown paper bags

PREPARATION: Cover each piece of chalk with a piece of aluminum foil, leaving about half an inch of chalk exposed. This prevents colors from smearing and transferring from one piece of chalk to another while they are stored.

PROCEDURE:

1. Wet the paper and brown paper bags.
2. Have the child draw on the wet paper with dry chalk. The colors will be bright and almost fluorescent.

VARIATION:

■ If a slippery surface is desired, liquid starch may be applied to the paper before the dry chalk. There will be less friction with starch, and the paper will be less likely to tear.

■ Soaking pieces of large chalk in sugar water (one part sugar and two parts water) for about 15 minutes and then using the chalk on dry paper is another method of application. Sugar gives the chalk a shiny look when dry.

ACTIVITIES FOR CHILDREN

Crayon Resists

GOALS: To encourage children's drawing with crayons
To develop children's creativity

MATERIALS: Crayons, paper, tempera paint diluted with water (a dark color is best), and a brush

PREPARATION: Have the child make a drawing or design on paper with crayons, pressing hard.

PROCEDURE:

Have the child paint over and around the crayon drawing with the thinned paint. A dark-colored paint works best, as the dark color fills in all the areas that the crayon has not covered. In the areas covered with crayon, the crayon "resists," or is not covered by the paint.

ADDITIONAL INFORMATION:
Crayon resist gives the feeling of a night picture. It is a thrilling experience for the child to see the changes that come when the paint crosses the paper.

ACTIVITIES FOR CHILDREN

Crayon Rubbings

GOALS: To encourage children's crayon drawings
To encourage children's creativity

MATERIALS: Crayons; objects with textured surfaces, such as bark, leaves, bricks, corrugated cardboard, sandpaper, bumpy paper food trays, and so on; and paper

PREPARATION: Peel the paper off the crayons so children can use the sides of the crayon.

PROCEDURE:

1. Have the child put a piece of paper over a textured surface.

2. Have the child rub the sides of the peeled crayon over the paper. The crayon picks up the texture on the paper in a design.

VARIATION:
Perform this activity outdoors on a nice day. The sidewalk, trees, and rocks all make great things for crayon rubbings.

ACTIVITIES FOR CHILDREN

Crayon Waves

GOALS: To encourage children's drawing with crayons
To develop children's creativity

MATERIALS: Crayons, paper

PREPARATION: Have the children select one of their favorite CDs or tapes. Play the tape.

PROCEDURE:

1. Ask the children to imagine the sound waves they hear in the song.

2. Have them listen to the sound again.

3. Have the children use crayons to draw the sounds they hear.

VARIATION:
Perform the same activity with painting, chalking, collage, and printing.

ACTIVITIES FOR CHILDREN

Splatter Printing

GOALS: To encourage children's printing activities
To develop children's creativity

MATERIALS: Old toothbrushes, watercolor paint, paper, ruler, emery board or tongue depressor, shapes cut out of paper, and other small flat objects

PREPARATION:
Show the children how to dip the toothbrush in paint and how to pull the straight-edged object across the brush. Give each child a toothbrush, a piece of paper, and a straight-edged object.

PROCEDURE:
1. Have the child dip the toothbrush in paint.
2. Have the child gently pull a straight-edged object (ruler, emery board, tongue depressor) across the ends of the bristles. This causes the bristles to snap forward, throwing small particles of paint onto the paper.
3. Have the child create designs by placing small, flat objects on the paper. When the bristles snap the small particles of paint forward, the object prevents the spray from striking the paper directly under the object. This leaves the shapes free of paint spray while the rest of the paper is covered with small flecks of paint.

VARIATION:
- A variety of shapes can be used for this activity.
- A variety of colors of paint can also be put one on top of the other.
- Natural forms such as twigs, leaves, and grass are excellent for this activity.
- Several forms can be combined, leading to interesting arrangements.
- A field trip is a good way to find new print forms and shapes.

ACTIVITIES FOR CHILDREN

Paper Stencils

GOALS: To encourage children's printing activities
To encourage children's use of chalk
To develop children's creativity

MATERIALS: 4–5 pieces of drawing paper (about four inches square) per child, scissors, sheets of regular drawing paper, tissue, small pieces of cotton or patches of cloth, and colored chalk

PREPARATION:
Have the child cut holes of various sizes and shapes in the center of each piece of paper. These pieces with holes in them are the stencils.

PROCEDURE:
1. When the holes have been cut, give each child a tissue, small piece of cotton, or patch of cloth.
2. Have the child rub this on a piece of colored chalk to pick up enough dust to stencil.
3. Have the child select a shape and place it on the paper on which the design is to go.
4. Have the child rub the tissue across the hold, making strokes from the stencil paper toward the center of the opening.
5. Have the child continue around the edge of the opening until the paper under the stencil has a clear print. The same shape can be continued across the paper.

VARIATION:
- Have the child choose the shapes and combinations desired.
- Use the same technique with crayons, rubbing them directly on the stencil.
- Use unbleached muslin or cotton material to print on as well.

ACTIVITIES FOR CHILDREN — Styrofoam Prints

GOALS: To develop children's interest in printing
To develop children's creativity

MATERIALS: Flat piece of Styrofoam, permanent markers, brushes, tempera paint, construction paper, and glue

PREPARATION:
Have the children draw pictures or designs onto the piece of Styrofoam, using permanent markers. Permanent markers will dissolve the foam.

PROCEDURE:
1. Have the child use a brush or sponge to apply a thin layer of tempera to the surface of the styrofoam.
2. Have the child place a piece of construction paper over the tempera.
3. Have the child rub the paper. A print of the design will be made on the construction paper.

VARIATION:
Another way to print with Styrofoam is to make a pattern, picture, or design by squeezing glue onto the Styrofoam. After the glue has dried, brush tempera paint onto the entire surface. Place a piece of construction paper over the paint and rub.

ADDITIONAL INFORMATION: Because this is a two-step process, it is more appropriate for children in kindergarten and elementary grades.

ACTIVITIES FOR CHILDREN — Vegetable Printing

GOALS: To develop children's interest in printing
To develop children's creativity

MATERIALS: Potato, carrot, or other firm vegetables; brushes; and tempera paint in small, shallow containers

PREPARATION: Cut a potato, carrot, or other firm vegetable into sections for ease of handling. Cut a design into the section. Keep the design simple, avoiding thin lines.

PROCEDURE:
1. Have the child paint the raised part of the design in the vegetable piece.
2. Have the child press it onto paper or cloth.

VARIATION:
Older children can draw the design on the flat cut surface and carve the design about 1/4-inch deep, leaving the area desired to be printed.

CAUTION: Never allow children to use a sharp, pointed knife for carving their designs. A plastic serrated knife or a table knife works well for carving.

ACTIVITIES FOR CHILDREN — Fingerprint Printing

GOALS: To develop children's interest in printing
To develop children's creativity

MATERIALS: Sheets of newsprint paper, inked stamp pad or tray filled with thickened tempera paint

PREPARATION: Discuss fingerprints, especially how they are unique to each person.

PROCEDURE:

1. Have the child press one finger onto a stamp pad or onto a tray filled with thickened tempera paint.
2. Have the child press the finger onto newsprint.

VARIATION:

- Experiment using different fingers, singly or in combination, and so on.
- Add details with markers and crayons.

ADDITIONAL INFORMATION:
A stamp pad can be made by putting discarded pieces of felt or cotton cloth inside a jar lid, cut-down milk carton, or similar waterproof container saturated with paint.

ACTIVITIES FOR CHILDREN — Found Object Printing

GOALS: To develop children's interest in printing
To develop children's creativity

MATERIALS: Collection of familiar objects, such as forks, spools, sticks, buttons, bottle tops, some paper, paint, and brushes

PREPARATION:
Provide children easy access to the collection of objects for printing.

PROCEDURE:

1. Show the children how to dip objects into paint and press them onto paper to make a print.
2. Show the children how they can print across the paper, up and down the paper, and so on.

VARIATION:

- Use objects of nature such as leaves, weeds, seeds, and stones in a similar manner.
- Use absorbent pieces of discarded cloth to print on, such as pillow cases, sheets, men's handkerchiefs, old shirts, and napkins.

ADDITIONAL INFORMATION:
Papers suitable for printing include newsprint, manila paper, wallpaper, tissue, construction paper, classified pages of the newspaper, plain wrapping paper, and paper towels. Avoid using paper with a hard slick finish because it does not absorb paint and ink well.

ACTIVITIES FOR CHILDREN — Seed Collage

GOALS: To develop children's interest in collage
To develop children's creativity

MATERIALS: Play dough or clay, plastic lids, and an assortment of seeds, beans, and other grains.

PREPARATION: Roll play dough or clay into balls.

PROCEDURE:
1. Have the child press a ball into the plastic lid.
2. Have the child arrange seeds, beans, and other grains on top of the dough/clay.
3. Have the child press the seeds into the dough, and allow the dough to dry.

ACTIVITIES FOR CHILDREN — Patchwork Collage

GOALS: To develop children's interest in collage
To develop children's creativity

MATERIALS: Piece of cardboard, collection of beautiful "junk," such as beads, pieces of cloth or various textures, feathers, pieces of trim, wrapping paper pieces, buttons, and so on.

PREPARATION: Divide the piece of cardboard into several rectangle spaces using a pencil and ruler.

PROCEDURE:
1. Have the children fill each rectangle with one type of "beautiful junk."
2. Have the child glue the objects on with white glue.

VARIATION:
- Use a theme such as the seasons, and glue items that relate to that season in each rectangle.
- Use a color for each rectangle and glue objects of that color in that space.

ACTIVITIES FOR CHILDREN

Texture Collage

GOALS: To develop children's interest in collage
To develop children's creativity

MATERIALS: Objects with texture, cardboard or heavy construction paper, glue or paste

PREPARATION:
Select a texture theme (soft, hard, smooth, rough, and so on). Find objects at home and in the classroom that have that texture.

PROCEDURE:

1. Have the children glue the collection onto cardboard or heavy construction paper.

2. Discuss the colors, textures, lines, and designs in the collection.

3. Display the texture collection in the classroom.

ADDITIONAL INFORMATION:
Discuss the qualities of materials and how they are related to ideas to be expressed: Gold paper is bright and "shiny like the sun"; cotton is soft and white "like snow."

More Ideas for Collages

Collage is a two-dimensional art activity that has endless possibilities. Here are a few more of them to try with your children:

■ Encourage children to use materials in their own way. Instead of giving exact directions, suggest ways of selecting materials for a variety of shapes, sizes, colors, and textures.

■ Materials may be cut, torn, or left in their original shapes.

■ Children may form a picture or an abstract design.

■ Encourage thoughtful use of space by overlapping and grouping shapes, or trying different combinations of colors and textural surfaces.

■ Create three-dimensional effects by crumpling flat pieces of material and attaching them to the background in two or three places. Other techniques include overlapping, bending, folding, rolling, curling, and twisting paper.

■ Include buttons, braids, tissue, or yarn for added interest and accent.

■ Use glue or staples to fasten heavy materials and plastics.

■ A collage may be displayed in a shadow box (using a box lid as a frame), mounted in an old picture frame, or mounted on a sheet of colored construction paper.

■ Make a paper or cloth collage, exploring a variety of one kind of material. Do the same with leaves, buttons, or any one kind of material children enjoy.

ACTIVITIES FOR CHILDREN

Cut Paper Collage

GOALS: To develop children's interest in collage
To practice cutting skills
To develop children's creativity

MATERIALS: Scissors (left and right handed), paper, and paste

PREPARATION: Review the ideas in the chart on page 24 (More Ideas for Collages). Choose one or several.

PROCEDURE:

1. Have the child cut paper into shapes.
2. Have the child manipulate paper by twisting, curling, and fringing.
3. Have the child arrange (and re-arrange) pieces on a sheet of paper.
4. When the design is complete to the child's liking, have him or her glue shapes onto the sheet of paper.

Some Suggestions for Working with Cut Paper Artwork

Children who have mastered scissoring skills will enjoy cut paper activities. Some suggestions for working with cut paper artwork are:

■ Encourage children to think about the shape of an object and its edge before cutting.

■ Plan the composition. Cut the big, important shapes first. Cut details, patterns, and textures later. Glue last.

■ Use a variety of shapes. Repeat shapes and change their size for variety. Repeat colors by changing their intensity or value for variety.

■ Create textured areas by folding, fringing, pleating, curling, and weaving the paper.

■ Overlap shapes to give depth and distance to a cut paper design. Create distance in cut paper by working from the background forward.

■ Glue small shapes, details, patterns, and textures to larger shapes before gluing the larger shapes to the background.

■ Glue around the outside edge of the shapes, not over the entire back of the shape.

■ Use positive and negative shapes in the design. The positive shape is the cut shape. The remaining paper is the negative shape.

■ Use the lightest colors first when creating with tissue paper. Cut and arrange all the big important shapes before gluing. Change the arrangement of the shapes until a pleasing composition is found.

ACTIVITIES FOR CHILDREN

Litter Collage

GOALS: To encourage children's interest in collage
To develop children's creativity

MATERIALS: Magazines, crayons, markers, paste, and scissors

PREPARATION:
Discuss how litter pollutes the school grounds and the environment. Talk about the types of items that are litter.

PROCEDURE:

1. Have the students cut pictures of things from magazines that could litter the playground or cause environmental pollution.

2. Have the students draw objects for the collage.

3. Give the collage a title that reinforces the message of the artwork.

VARIATION:
Have the students write about their artwork, or dictate a story about it.

CHAPTER 8

THREE-DIMENSIONAL ACTIVITIES

The term **three-dimensional art** refers to any art form that has at least three sides. Three-dimensional art is "in the round," which means that one can look at it from many sides. Modeling with clay, working with play dough, making creations with paper boxes, and creating other sculpture forms are examples of three-dimensional art activities.

Just as in drawing, there are basic stages of development in working with three-dimensional material, much the same as for two-dimensional media. While the names of stages in two-dimensional art do not apply (a child does not "scribble" with clay), the same process of growth and basic ideas for each stage apply.

See Figure 8–1 for a summary of the stages of development with three-dimensional media.

Modeling with clay is a relaxing and social activity.

 ## THE VALUE OF CLAY AND PLAY DOUGH

At all ages, work with clay and play dough gives the child many chances for creative experiences. Most children like the damp feel of play dough or clay. They like to pound it, roll it, poke holes in it, and pull it apart. Just as in drawing, it is the fun of working with the clay that counts. The end product is not as important as using it; a child becomes really involved in the process.

Children who perceive clay as "messy" or "slimy," however, may not want to work with it. Never force the issue! Be patient and give these children lots of time and plenty of opportunities to see the fun others have with clay. Some teachers find that involving timid children first in a "cleaner" aspect of clay work, such as mixing up play dough, helps involve them on a gradual basis.

CLAY AND PLAY DOUGH MATERIALS

1. Potter's clay or play dough (mixed from the recipe in Appendix C) kept in an airtight container. See Figures 8–2 and 8–3 for more information on using clay and making play dough.
2. Clay or play dough table. Use a table with a formica top or any table that is easy to clean. (Or use large pieces of plastic spread out on the table, or cut one for each child's use.)
3. Tools for clay work, like toy rolling pins, cookie cutters, spoons, and blunt plastic knives.

Stage	Characteristics	Muscle Control
Random manipulation	Clay squeezed in uncontrolled manner for no special purpose other than physical enjoyment	Minimum, little control over hand movements
Patting and Rolling	Clay used with purpose. Child enjoys seeing the effects of his movements	Beginning of muscle control
Circles and Rectangles	Clay shaped into basic forms	More developed motor control allows purposeful movements
Clay figures	Basic forms combined to build objects like figures in drawings	Increased motor control allows selective movements to form shapes
Clay figures with details	Clay figures formed with more complex details such as arms, legs, feet, and fingers	Most developed motor control, allowing increased small details

FIGURE 8-1 | Summary of the stages of development with three-dimensional media.

Making play dough.

■ Children should participate in making dough whenever possible. If allowed to help make the dough, children learn about measuring, blending, and cause and effect, and also have the chance to work together.

■ The doughs that require no cooking are best mixed two batches at a time in separate deep dishpans. Using deep pans keeps the flour within bounds, and making two batches at a time relieves congestion and provides better participation opportunities.

■ Tempera powder is the most effective coloring agent to add because it makes such intense shades of dough; adding it to the flour before pouring in the liquid works best.

■ Dough can be kept in the refrigerator and reused several times. Removing it at the beginning of the day allows it to come to room temperature before being offered to the children—otherwise it can be discouragingly stiff and unappealing.

■ The addition of flour or cornstarch on the second day is usually necessary to reduce stickiness.

Dough variations.

■ All the dough recipes in Appendix C have been carefully tested and are suitable for various purposes. In preschool centers where process, not product, is emphasized, the dough and clay are generally used again and again rather than the objects made by the children being allowed to dry and then sent home.

■ For special occasions, however, it is nice to allow the pieces to harden and then to paint or color them. Two recipes included in Appendix C serve this purpose particularly well: ornamental clay and baker's dough.

■ For dough to be truly satisfying, children need an abundance of it rather than meager little handfuls, and they should be encouraged to use it in a manipulative, expressive way rather than in a product-oriented way.

FIGURE 8-2 | More information on making play dough.

- Potter's clay may be purchased at any art supply store in moist form. This is much easier to deal with than starting from dry powder.
- Potter's clay is available in two colors: gray and terra cotta. Terra cotta looks pretty but stains clothing and is harder to clean up.
- Clay requires careful storage in a watertight, airtight container.
- When children are through for the day, form the clay into large balls, press a thumb into it, and then fill that hole with water and replace it in the container.
- If oilcloth table covers are used with potter's clay, they can simply be hung up to dry, shaken well, and put away until next time.

FIGURE 8–3 | More information on potter's clay.

HINTS FOR WORKING WITH CLAY AND PLAY DOUGH

Some tips for set up are:

- The tables used for working with clay should be placed away from wheel and climbing toys. They should be covered with linoleum or formica to make cleaning easier. If the tables in the room are formica-topped, additional covering is not usually needed.
- The number of children at a table at one time should be limited, allowing each child enough room to spread out and use as much arm and hand movement as he or she needs.
- Each child should be given a lump of clay at least the size of a large apple or a small grapefruit. The clay may be worked with in any way the child wants. These basic guidelines help: the clay may not be thrown on the floor, and no child may interfere with another child's work.
- The teacher may sit at the table and play with clay, too; this adds to the social feeling. But the teacher should avoid making objects for the child to copy. This discourages the child's creative use of the clay.
- When the children are done, clay needs to be stored until its next use. It is best to form it into balls, each about the size of an apple. A hole filled with water in each ball helps keep the clay just right for use the next time. Keep the clay in a container with a wet cloth or sponge on top of the clay. The container should be covered with a tight-fitting lid. (Margarine

tubs with plastic lids work well.) Clay becomes moldy if it is too wet and hard to handle if it becomes very dry. If clay should dry out, it can be restored to a proper consistency by placing the dried-out clay in a cloth bag and pounding it with a hammer until it is broken into small pieces. After soaking this clay in water, it can be kneaded until it is the proper consistency again. If clay does become moldy, there is no need to throw it away. Simply scrape off the moldy area and drain off any water collected in the bottom of the container.

 PAPER PULP (PAPIER-MÂCHÉ)

Paper pulp (papier-mâché), is another type of three-dimensional material which is easy to work with, does not crack or break readily, and is inexpensive.

This modeling material is made from mixing either paper pulp of paper strips with wheat paste or glue. It can be molded into various three-dimensional shapes when it is wet and painted when it is dry. This medium is not appropriate for very young children, since it is a two-step process and involves a sustained span of interest.

MATERIALS

1. Wheat paste or glue.
2. Pieces of soft paper such as newsprint, newspapers, paper towel, or facial tissue shredded into small bits or thin strips.
3. Pan of water.

HINTS FOR WORKING WITH PAPER PULP

To prepare paper pulp. Shred pieces of soft paper, such as newsprint, paper towels, or facial tissue, into small bits or thin strips. Soak several hours in water, then drain, squeeze out the extra water, and mix the pulp with prepared wheat paste to the consistency of soft clay. Let the mixture stand for an hour before beginning to work with it. Use the pulp to form shapes.

To prepare paper strips. Tear newspaper or newsprint into long, thin strips about 1/2″ wide. Dip the strips into a wheat paste or starch and white glue mixture, and then put down a layer of wet strips over the shape to be covered. Continue putting strips on the form until there are five or six layers. This thickness is strong enough to support most papier-mâché projects.

Creating three-dimensional objects can be done with many objects.

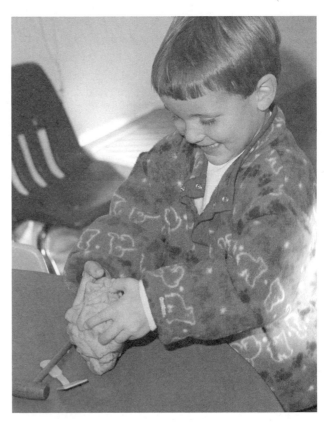

Pounding clay is a good exercise as well as a three-dimensional activity.

Foundations. Good forms that can be used as foundations for papier-mâché include the following: rolled newspapers secured with string or tape, blown-up balloons, plastic bottles, paper sacks stuffed with newspapers and tied with string, and wire or wooden armatures used as skeletal forms.

 ## ASSEMBLAGE

As an art form, **assemblage** refers to placing a number of three-dimensional objects, natural or manmade, in combinations to create a unified composition.

There are many ways to make an assemblage. One way is to put things together. Matchboxes, a paper cup, a cardboard roll, and an egg carton can be glued together. Another way to make an assemblage is to build *up* a form, using materials you can shape yourself. For older children, cardboard is a good material for shaping an assemblage by building up a form. Cardboard can be found anywhere and it is easy to work with. All the children need are scissors and glue to cut and stick the cardboard shapes together. You can bend, twist, fold, cut, or glue shapes to make a sculpture.

MATERIALS

Some materials for an assemblage are:

■ *Containers:* Wooden boxes, cardboard boxes, cigar boxes, matchboxes, suitcases, egg cartons and crates,

and packing cartons. These may be painted or decorated if the children desire.
■ *Mounting boards:* Pasteboard, corrugated cardboard, wood, crates, and picture frames.
■ *Objects:* Wooden forms or scrap lumber, driftwood, screening, corks, cardboard boxes, discarded toys, household items, or articles of nature such as seeds, weeds, stones, twigs, and any other interesting items.
■ *Adhesives:* Paste, glue, staples, or tape.
■ *Tools:* Scissors, stapler, hammer, nails, or pliers.

HINTS ON ASSEMBLAGE ACTIVITIES

Encourage children to collect objects that are meaningful to them. Almost any area of interest or everyday experience is a possible theme for assemblage.

■ Objects may be selected according to an idea, topic, size of container, or variation in line, form, color, and texture; use multiple items for repetition of shapes.
■ Three-dimensional forms may be altered or transformed so that they lose their original identity and take on a new meaning. They can be bent, twisted, stretched, crumpled, or painted.

THIS ONE'S FOR YOU — More Sculpture Ideas

Here are some more ideas to encourage young children's experiments with three-dimensional media. You will probably have many more of your own.

FOIL SCULPTURE

Supplies: Foil, gummed tape, brush, liquid detergent, tempera paint.
Procedure: Crumple the foil into individual forms, shapes, or creations that when assembled will create a piece of sculpture. Join these forms together, if desired, with tape. Color can be added to the surface by painting with a drop or two of liquid detergent mixed in the tempera paint.

NATURAL OBJECT SCULPTURE

Supplies: Natural materials (seeds, twigs, pinecones, seed pods, stones, driftwood, and so on), quick-drying glue, clear quick-drying spray, paint, construction paper, and felt.
Procedure: Collect a number of natural objects of various sizes and colors. Arrange several of these items to create a small piece of sculpture. When satisfied with the creation, glue it together. Paint or colored paper can be added to enhance the design. Spray with clear spray to preserve the finish. Spray with optimum ventilation, preferably outdoors. Glue a piece of felt to the bottom to prevent scratching.

SPOOL SCULPTURE

Supplies: Spools (a variety of sizes are useful), assorted fabric pieces, glue, and anything that will serve to stimulate children's imaginations as decorations.
Procedure: There is no prescribed procedure in this project, as each of the spool sculptures is made differently, according to the imagination of the artist. Basically, the procedure involves "dressing" the spool, which serves as a body. The materials are contrived to serve as clothing and are glued onto the spool. If desired, a child may use the spool purely as a base; it does not have to be a figure to dress. Details can be made with drawing materials, and bits and pieces of yarn, ribbon, and so forth can be glued on for interest.

- Objects also can be made by cutting out pictures or illustrations and pasting them over cardboard, wood, or other substantial material.
- Objects can be glued, stapled, taped, or even nailed together or onto a mounting board.
- Arrange and rearrange objects until the desired effect is achieved. Distribute paste and other fastening materials *after* the arrangement is satisfactory in the child's opinion.

CARDBOARD CONSTRUCTION

Cardboard, an indispensable material for construction projects, stimulates and challenges the imagination of children on all levels. It is readily available in various forms. Such commonplace objects as milk and egg cartons, apple-crate dividers, toweling tubes, and assorted sizes of boxes offer unlimited possibilities for creative art projects.

MATERIALS

Gather together an assortment of cardboard materials. Some suggestions are:

- Assorted cardboard boxes, cartons, corrugated cardboard, paper cups, and plates of all sizes.
- Recycled materials: paper bags, yarn, string, buttons, feathers, cloth, tissue paper, scraps of construction paper, and wrapping paper.
- Paste, glue, tape, crayons, colored markers, paint, brushes, scissors, stapler, and staples.

THOUGHT **Cornstarch**

Believe it or ... ascinating modeling medium is plain old cornstarch. Use the following recipe to mix up cornstarch for children's three-dimensional play.

CORNSTARCH AND WATER

2 cups warm water
3 cups cornstarch
Put ingredients in a bowl and mix with your hands. This mixture will solidify when left alone, but turns to liquid from the heat of your hands. Magic!

Involve the children in making the above cornstarch recipe. Have them feel the dry cornstarch. Encourage their reactions to it, using their senses of sight, smell, touch, and even taste. Add a little water, and then let the children mix it and feel it again. It is lumpy. After this lumpy stage, you can add a little more water until it's all moist. Wet cornstarch forms an unstable material, which is fun because of its unexpected behavior—it breaks, but it also melts. It doesn't behave like glue, or like milk, or like wood; it's a liquid, and it's a solid, too. If you rest your fingers lightly on the surface of the cornstarch-water mix, it will let your fingers drift down to the bottom of the container. If you try to punch your way to the bottom, it will resist.

Cornstarch works well in a baby bathtub set on a table, with a limit of two or three children using the entire recipe. If you leave it in its tub overnight, by morning it's dry. Add some water, and it becomes that wonderful "stuff" again. Be sure to invite the children to watch this event.

It's a clean sort of play: the white, powdery mess on the floor can be picked up easily with a dustpan and brush or a vacuum cleaner.

Children come back to this cornstarch and water mix again and again, because it feels good and behaves in an interesting way (Clemens, 1991).

HINTS FOR CARDBOARD CONSTRUCTION

Most topics of interest to young children can be adapted to cardboard construction projects. Creations are as endless as the imaginations of young children. Some possibilities for creative construction projects include using boxes for making various buildings, houses, cities, and even neighborhoods. Young children also enjoy making such things as imaginary animals, people, and favorite characters from a story out of various cardboard rolls and containers. Some children have even made costumes out of boxes large enough to fit over a child's body. Cars, trucks, and trains are some other favorite construction projects with young children. Cardboard construction provides a wealth of possibilities for creative expression in arts and crafts projects as well. More ideas on cardboard construction include the following:

■ Have the cardboard construction materials out and available for the children to explore on their own. Encourage the children to stack materials or combine them in different ways. Encourage children to explore the possibilities for creating they may discover while playing with the materials.

■ Discuss with the children and demonstrate (if needed) ways of fastening boxes together, covering them with paint or paper, and how to add other parts or features.

■ Encourage the children to select as many objects as they need for their construction.

■ Boxes with waxed surfaces can be covered with a layer of newspaper and wheat paste and allowed to dry before painting. Powder paint mixed with starch adheres well to box surfaces.

■ Textured surfaces can be created by using corrugated cardboard, shredded packing tissue, or crinkled newspaper.

■ Shapes and sizes of cardboard objects may suggest ideas for a project, such as using an oatmeal box for the body of an elephant or a milk carton for a tall building.

■ Use a variety of materials to complete the design, such as pieces of ribbon, buttons, sequins, spools, and so on.

■ Older children are able to appreciate lessons combining three-dimensional assemblage projects with architectural ideas. For example, after drawing their plans for a building or structure, the students might like to use boxes, cardboard, or cut-and-fold paper techniques to make three-dimensional models of their buildings. Students who are particularly excited by such projects may wish to create realistic settings for their structures as well, using sand, pebbles, dried moss, and the like to create their own miniature scene.

 ## WOODWORKING

Woodworking involves a range of activities from hammering nails to sanding, gluing, and painting wood. As with other three-dimensional activities, woodworking can be an excellent medium for fostering a child's creativity if the *process,* and not the product, is emphasized.

MATERIALS

1. A bin of soft lumber pieces (leftover scraps of lumber).
2. Supply of nails with large heads.
3. Wooden spools, corks, and twigs.
4. Wooden buttons, string, and ribbons to be nailed to wood or tied to heads of nails already hammered into the wood.
5. Bottle caps.
6. Small-sized real tools. Hammer and nails are best to start with. Saws, screwdrivers, a vise, and a drill may be added later.
7. Workbench.
8. Sandpaper.
9. A vise or C-clamp placed near the corner of the workbench, flush with the table top.
10. Safety goggles.

For older children:

11. Screws and screwdrivers—standard and Phillips.
12. Pencils, rulers, and tape measures.
13. Files, planes, and levels.
14. Crowbars.

HINTS FOR WOODWORKING

Woodworking needs to be done in a special area away from other activities. Provide children plenty of good wood and satisfactory tools. A sturdy workbench of the right height is helpful.

The most basic woodworking tools are hammers and saws. The hammers should be good, solid ones—*not* tack hammers. The saws should be crosscut ones so that they can cut with or across the grain of the wood, and they should be as short as possible. A well-made vise in which to place wood securely while sawing is invaluable. Preferably, there should be two of these, one at each end of the table. (C-clamps can also be used for this purpose and are less expensive.)

Very young children enjoy sawing up the large pieces of styrofoam that come as packing for electronic equipment. Hammering into such material or into plasterboard is also quick and easy and does not require more force than two- and three-year-olds can muster. Older children need plentiful amounts of soft wood to work with.

Woodworking needs careful adult supervision, since children can easily hurt themselves or each other with a hammer and saw. General guidelines for adult supervision include the following:

■ Stay very close to the woodworking activity. Be within the reach of each child.

■ There should be no more than three or four children for one adult to supervise. Only one child at a time should use a saw.

■ Show the children how to saw away from their own fingers and from other children. Show them how to avoid hitting their fingers with the hammer.

■ Hand out nails a few at a time.

■ Never turn your back on the activity for even a few seconds.

■ Make a wall-mounted toolboard to store frequently used tools. (Less-used tools can be stored in a cupboard.) The outline of each tool can be marked on the board so children can figure out where to hang each tool.

■ Remember to vary the tools the children use as their skill (and self-control) increases.

■ Purchase a variety of nails by the pound, not by the little box, from a hardware store. Children love an assortment of these. They can be set out in small foil pie plates to keep them from getting mixed up. These pie plates can be nailed to a long board to prevent spilling.

■ Offer various kinds of trims to go with woodworking, such as wire, thick colorful yarn, and wooden spools (with nails long enough to go through the spool).

■ Offer round things for wheels, such as bottle caps, buttons, or the lids of 35 mm film containers.

■ Provide dowels of various sizes that will fit the holes made by the different sizes of bits.

SAFETY

For all the activities in this chapter and in any art activities for young children, be sure that you are not using any unsafe art supplies. Potentially unsafe art supplies include the following:

■ Powdered clay, which is easily inhaled and contains silica, which is harmful to the lungs. Instead, use wet clay, which cannot be inhaled.

■ Paints that require solvents such as turpentine to clean brushes. Use only water-based paints.

■ Cold water or commercial dyes that contain chemical additives. Use only natural vegetable dyes, made from beets, onion skins, and so on.

■ Permanent markers, which may contain toxic solvents. Use only water-based markers.

■ Instant papier-mâché, which may contain lead or asbestos. Use only black-and-white newspaper and library paste or liquid starch.

■ Epoxy, instant glues, or other solvent-based glues. Use only water-based white glue (Clemens, 1991).

THE TEACHER SHOULD:

■ **Read labels.**

■ Check for age-appropriateness. The Art and Craft Material Institute labels art materials AP (approved product) and CP (certified product) when they are

THIS ONE'S FOR YOU

Me Be Creative? . . . Artistic? But I Can't Even Draw!

Many teachers rely on ready made art "recipes" for their early childhood art program because they feel they are not "creative" enough without them. An art recipe is comfortable for the teacher because she knows exactly what to expect; she knows what the product will look like. Materials can be organized ahead of time and remain neat and tidy. It is unfortunate for the child, however, because without any input the activity is not self-expressive or creative.

We want children to be able to think for themselves, to be able to make decisions, and to act on them. By providing a step-by-step art activity, we are not allowing young children to make decisions, nor are we teaching them to become independent.

A creative art opportunity allows the young child to begin choosing and seeking knowledge on her own, giving her more and more confidence in her own abilities. Think about the art activities you offer children and see if they allow children this creative freedom.

Teachers often feel inadequate when it comes to art and may fall back on what they did in school as a child. Many of those activities were craft oriented, pattern determined, and teacher controlled.

Teachers are often not given enough training in the area of planning expressive art activities for children. Teacher preparation in this area is often minimal at best. This is why it's not fair to fault teachers who feel timid about letting children leap into art, when it is the teacher preparation programs that in many cases are lacking.

Many teachers feel that being creative is a talent that you either have or do not have. Research shows, however, that being creative, as well as being able to draw, are learnable skills (Edwards, 1979). It is unfortunate for a child to hear a teacher say, "I can't draw," when the teacher really should say, "I never *learned* to draw." There is a big difference between these two remarks, and children are perceptive enough to notice it. If their teacher believes that artistic ability is an unteachable talent, then children will believe that. But if the teacher believes people can *learn* how to create with art materials, the children will believe that, too (Szyba, 1999).

safe for young children, even if ingested. These labels are round. A product bearing the square "Health Label" is safe only for children over twelve.

■ Check for ventilation requirements. In most cases, one open window or door is not sufficient ventilation.

■ A list of materials safe for young children is available from the Art and Craft Material Institute, Inc., 715 Boylston Street, Boston, MA 02116. Write to the National Art Education Association, 1916 Association Drive, Reston, VA 22091 for an updated, detailed list of safety guidelines.

■ **Know your students.**

■ Be aware of students' allergies. Children with allergies to wheat, for example, may be irritated by wheat paste used in papier mâché. Other art materials that may cause allergic reactions include chalk or other dusty substances, water-based clay, and any material that contains petroleum products.

■ Be aware of students' habits. Some students put everything in their mouths. (This can be the case at any age.) Others act out or behave aggressively. Use your knowledge of individual students' tendencies to help you plan art activities that will be safe for all students.

ACTIVITIES FOR CHILDREN — Clay Work and Story Books

GOALS: To develop children's interest in clay work
To encourage children's creativity

MATERIALS: Clay, prepared area for clay work

PREPARATION: Read an exciting story to the children before they work with clay. For example, try M. Sendak's *Where the Wild Things Are* or Dr. Seuss' *To Think It Happened on Mulberry Street.*

PROCEDURE:

1. Give the children time and materials for clay work.

2. Do not tell the children what to make.

3. See if their work with clay shows any influence from the story regarding the following: type of figures made, size of figures made, or details of figures made.

VARIATION: Use a book about science or read poetry to the children. Then see if there is any influence on the children's work in clay after these readings.

ACTIVITIES FOR CHILDREN

Play Dough Variations

GOALS: To encourage children's work with play dough

To encourage children's creativity

MATERIALS: Ingredients for play dough (see Appendix C), mint flavoring, green food coloring, yellow food coloring, and lemon flavoring

PREPARATION: Discuss colors and flavors with the children (examples include green and mint flavor; yellow and lemon flavor).

PROCEDURE:

1. Make play dough with the children.

2. Work a drop of food flavoring and a drop of food coloring into your play dough recipe.

3. Have the children match scents with colors, such as mint flavoring with green and lemon flavoring with yellow.

VARIATION:

■ Use a tasty mixture of peanut butter and powdered milk as play dough for another three-dimensional taste treat.

■ Make your play dough recipe slippery by adding a little vegetable oil.

ACTIVITIES FOR CHILDREN

Bread Dough Sculptures

GOALS: To encourage children's use of play dough

To develop children's creativity

MATERIALS: White glue, bread, lemon juice, paint (water color, tempera), brush, plastic bag

PREPARATION:

1. Remove the crusts from four slices of bread.

2. Tear the bread into small pieces, mixing them thoroughly with three tablespoons of white glue and one or two drops of lemon juice.

PROCEDURE:

1. Have the children model or cut the bread dough as desired.

2. Allow one or two days for complete drying.

3. Have the children paint the pieces with watercolor or tempera paint.

VARIATION: Various materials may be added for details or designs. Some examples include beads, bits of straw, yarn, trip pieces, and so on.

ADDITIONAL INFORMATION: Bread dough clay can be preserved by wrapping it in plastic and placing it in a refrigerator.

ACTIVITIES FOR CHILDREN — Foil Sculpture

GOALS: To encourage children's use of a three-dimensional material

To encourage children's creativity

MATERIALS: Foil, gummed or transparent tape, brush, liquid detergent, and tempera paint

PREPARATION: Show children how to crumble foil. Suggest they can make objects from the crumbled foil.

PROCEDURE:

1. Have the children crumble foil into various forms.
2. Join these forms together with tape.
3. Add color to the surface by painting with a drop or two of liquid detergent mixed in the tempera paint.

ACTIVITIES FOR CHILDREN — Natural Object Sculpture

GOALS: To encourage children's interest in three-dimensional media

To develop children's creativity

MATERIALS: Collection of natural objects of various sizes and colors, such as seeds, twigs, pine cones, seed pods, stones, driftwood, and so on; quick-drying glue; clear, quick-drying spray; paint; construction paper; and felt.

PREPARATION: Provide children with the natural objects and art supplies listed above in an easily reached area.

PROCEDURE:

1. Have the children arrange several natural objects to create a small piece of sculpture.
2. When satisfied with the creation, have the children glue it together.
3. Add paint or colored paper to enhance the sculpture.
4. Spray the sculpture with clear spray to preserve the finish. Use optimum ventilation when spraying.
5. Glue a piece of felt to the bottom to prevent scratching.

ACTIVITIES FOR CHILDREN

Salt and Flour Sculpture

GOALS: To encourage children's use of three-dimensional material

To develop children's creativity

MATERIALS: One cup of salt, one cup of flour, one tablespoon of powdered alum, mixing bowl, food coloring or dry tempera (if color is desired), shellac and brush, and alcohol for cleaning the brush

PREPARATION: Mix one cup of salt, one cup of flour, and one tablespoon of alum to the consistency of putty. Add color, if desired.

PROCEDURE:

1. Have the child make animals, figures, and any object he desires from this mixture.
2. Allow the pieces to dry and harden (one to two days).
3. Use shellac on the pieces for permanence.

CAUTION: Use shellac in a well-ventilated area.

ACTIVITIES FOR CHILDREN

Stuffed Newspaper Sculpture

GOALS: To encourage children's interest in three-dimensional materials

To develop children's creativity

MATERIALS: Newspaper or newsprint, glue or rubber cement, paint (tempera, watercolor), brush, and container for water

PREPARATION: Provide each child with at least four pages of newspaper.

PROCEDURE:

1. Have the child cut the shape of her intended design from at least four pages of newspaper.
2. Have the child glue two of the shapes together.
3. Have the child glue the remaining two pieces together.
4. Have the child glue the edges of these two sets together, leaving a space approximately four inches unglued somewhere along the edge.
5. Allow the glue to dry thoroughly.
6. Have the child stuff crumpled paper through the four-inch opening until the design takes a three-dimensional form. Be careful not to tear the design by stuffing it too tightly.
7. Have the child glue the opening together.
8. Have the child paint the stuffed sculpture, if desired.

ACTIVITIES FOR CHILDREN

Cardboard Construction— Buildings

GOALS: To encourage children's interest in three-dimensional material

To develop children's creativity

MATERIALS: Collection of round and rectangular cartons, paste, scissors, crayons, markers, and construction paper

PREPARATION: Discuss the buildings children see in their neighborhood. Discuss the shapes and sizes of these buildings.

PROCEDURE:

1. Have the children use the round and rectangular cartons to make buildings.

2. Have the children glue the pieces of paper on for windows, doors, chimneys, and balconies.

3. Have the children color the buildings or cover them with colored construction paper.

VARIATION:

■ Arrange buildings to create a city, small town, or farm.

■ Create store windows that can have merchandise painted on, or cut out and pasted on.

ACTIVITIES FOR CHILDREN

Cardboard Construction— Box Characters

GOALS: To encourage children's interest in three-dimensional materials

To develop children's creativity

MATERIALS: Cardboard boxes of assorted sizes, paste, scissors, crayons, markers, and scraps of material

PREPARATION: Discuss the shapes of the boxes. Discuss how they can be made into a character, an animal, or a person special to the child.

PROCEDURE:

1. Have the children use the cardboard box to form the body of the figure.

2. Have the children attach arms made of paper strips to either side of the box.

3. Have the children add costumes with cup-paper or cloth scraps.

VARIATION:

■ Add bits of cloth, rickrack, feathers, yarn, string, or ribbon for color and texture.

■ Create facial features with buttons, beads, and sequins.

ACTIVITIES FOR CHILDREN

Cardboard Construction— Imaginary Animals

GOALS: To encourage children's interest in three-dimensional materials

To develop children's creativity

MATERIALS: Collection of boxes of various sizes and shapes, glue, masking tape, stapler, paint, crayons, and markers

PREPARATION: Discuss animals, specifically the different kinds, their sizes, their appearance, and so on. Discuss how the shapes and sizes of boxes may suggest certain animals, such as an oatmeal box for an elephant, or a long narrow box for a giraffe's neck.

PROCEDURE:

1. Have the children stack boxes one on another, rearranging them until they are satisfied with their "animal" shape.
2. Use smaller boxes or toweling rolls for legs or a head.
3. Have the children fasten boxes together with glue, masking tape, or a stapler.
4. Have the children decorate the animal with markers, crayons, or paint.

VARIATION:

■ Glue wood shavings, bark, or wrinkled-paper scraps to boxes to create interesting textures.

■ Make exaggerated features with large buttons for eyes, frayed string or rope for a mane or tail, or pieces of cloth for ears.

■ Create textured surfaces by using corrugated paper or egg cartons for the bodies of animals.

ADDITIONAL INFORMATION: Boxes with waxed surfaces can be covered with a layer of newspaper and wheat paste, and then allowed to dry before painting.

ACTIVITIES FOR OLDER CHILDREN

(Grades 4–5)

Dioramas (Shadow Box)

GOALS: To encourage children's interest in three-dimensional materials

To develop children's creativity

MATERIALS: Shallow boxes, paint, paper, paste, pipe cleaners, and soda straws

PREPARATION: Discuss dioramas, which are three-dimensional boxes (also called shadow boxes) which are like a miniature stage setting.

PROCEDURE:

1. Provide each child with a shallow box.
2. Have the child draw or paint a background in the bottom of the box or use cut-paper objects.
3. Have the child make paper or cardboard figures stand by folding the lower part for a base.
4. Have the child make other figures with pipe cleaners or soda straws.
5. Make smaller objects of clay to add to the scene.

VARIATION: Add painted bits of sponges or twigs for trees, small gravel for rocks, cotton for snow, or a mirror for water.

ADDITIONAL INFORMATION: Children should experiment with the arrangement of the objects before fastening them with glue, tape, or staples.

ACTIVITIES FOR OLDER CHILDREN Soft Wire Sculptures
(Grades 4–5)

GOALS: To encourage children's interest in three-dimensional materials

To develop children's creativity

MATERIALS: Pipe cleaners, paper, pencils, and markers

PREPARATION: Discuss skeletons, the bones underneath the body.

PROCEDURE:

1. Have the children use three pipe cleaners to create a simple "skeleton" of a person.
2. Have the children wrap other pipe cleaners around the skeleton figure to suggest the form of muscles.
3. Have the children bend their sculptures into different poses.
4. Have the children draw each pose on paper.
5. Have the children draw in the details—clothes, faces, and the like.

VARIATION:

■ Plan the poses to create an action picture of a group of people.

■ Plan the poses to show a favorite sport, game, dance, or another activity such as a family watching television or going on a picnic.

ACTIVITIES FOR OLDER CHILDREN Assemblage—Memory
(Grades 4–5) Boxes

GOALS: To encourage children's interest in three-dimensional materials

To develop children's creativity

MATERIALS: Cardboard boxes, collection of objects from each student

PREPARATION: Have the children paint the inside and outside of their boxes. Using a dark color, such as black or brown, works best since objects stand out more on these colors.

PROCEDURE:

1. After the boxes have dried, have the children compose their assemblages.
2. Have the children look through their memorabilia collections and select objects they want to use.
3. Advise students to select objects with contrasting qualities (i.e., objects with different sizes, colors, shapes, and textures).
4. Have the children use white glue to attach all the parts of the assemblage.
5. When the glue has dried overnight, set up a display of all the memory boxes.

VARIATION: Use boxes with interior divisions, such as boxes used to package various kinds of fruit or Christmas tree ornaments, for this activity. The cardboard divisions work like tiny interior shelves for displaying objects.

ADDITIONAL INFORMATION: Do not pass out glue until everyone has had a chance to explore different combinations of their objects in their memory box. Remind the children that they should place objects so that they can be seen as the box stands upright or hangs on a wall. They should not arrange the box to be viewed from above.

ACTIVITIES FOR OLDER CHILDREN Toothpick Sculpture
(Grades 4–5)

GOALS: To encourage children's interest in three-dimensional materials

To develop children's creativity

MATERIALS: Quick-drying glue, such as household cement, toothpicks, paint, and brushes

PREPARATION: Have one box of toothpicks per child.

PROCEDURE:

1. Have the children glue the toothpicks together to form various three-dimensional structures.
2. Let the toothpick creations dry thoroughly.
3. Have the children paint the structures.

VARIATION: Add colored paper areas as an experience in color and design.

ACTIVITIES FOR OLDER CHILDREN Wood Scrap Sculpture
(Grades 4–5)

GOALS: To encourage children's interest in three-dimensional materials

To develop children's creativity

MATERIALS: Scrap pieces of wood, glue, paints or crayons, and brushes

PREPARATION: Gather a generous supply of scrap wood of various sizes and colors.

PROCEDURE:

1. Have the children choose pieces of wood that will work well together in creating a piece of sculpture.
2. When satisfied with the arrangement, have the children glue all the components together.
3. Add paint or crayon decorations to finish the sculpture.

ADDITIONAL INFORMATION: Be sure to remind the children that a piece of sculpture should present interesting views from all sides.

ACTIVITIES FOR OLDER CHILDREN Spool Sculpture
(Grades 4–5)

GOALS: To encourage children's use of three-dimensional materials

To develop children's creativity

MATERIALS: Spools (a variety of sizes are useful), assorted fabrics, needle and thread, glue, and any other pieces of trims, beads, and so on to stimulate clothing accessories

PREPARATION: Discuss how spools can be little people. Encourage children to use their imaginations to think about how they would look.

PROCEDURE:

1. Have the child "dress" the spool, which serves as a body.
2. Have the child glue materials on as clothing.
3. Have the child sew materials on the spool as well.
4. Have the child add facial features with drawing materials such as pens, pencils, crayons, and so on.

VARIATION: Use doll hair to crown the figure, or use hair made from thread, string, or anything suitable.

REFERENCES

Clemens, S. C. (1991, Jan.). Art in the classroom: Making every day special. *Young Children,* 4–11.

Edwards, B. (1979). *Drawing on the right side of the brain.* Los Angeles: Jeremy P. Archer.

Szyba, C. (1999). Why do some teachers resist offering open-ended art activities for young children? *Young Children, 54*(1), 16–20.

PART 2

CREATIVE ACTIVITIES IN THE EARLY CHILDHOOD PROGRAM

Using a creative approach in every area of early childhood curriculum is the focus of Part 2. These curricular areas include dramatic play and puppetry, movement, music, language arts, science, math, food experiences, social studies, and health and safety.

All of the activities presented in Part 2 are based in developmental theory, yet are simple to reproduce and expand upon. All are presented in the hope that they will be adapted to children's individual needs, abilities, and interest levels.

In all chapters in Part 2 the teacher should *always* consider the developmental level of a child or a group of children before initiating any activity. Activities are included for children from preschool through grade 5. Appropriate age and/or grade levels are indicated on these activities.

Finally, while guidance of a child's activities is appropriate, *each child should be given the freedom to adapt these activities and the processes used to his or her own creative needs.* Most important, emphasis in all activities should be on the *process* and not the end product. The beginning, middle, and end of every activity is *the child*—unique and singular in his or her own way.

SECTION 4
Creative Activities in Other Curricular Areas

SECTION 4

Creative Activities in Other Curricular Areas

CHAPTER 9

DRAMATIC PLAY AND PUPPETRY

 ## IMPORTANCE OF DRAMATIC PLAY

Dramatic play is an excellent means for developing the creativity and imagination of young children. One of the best ways children have to express themselves is through creative **dramatic play.** Here, they are free to express their inner feelings. Often, teachers find out how children feel about themselves and others by listening to them as they carry out dramatic play. The pretending involved in such dramatic experiences, whether planned or totally spontaneous, is a necessary part of development. In the home center with dramatic kits and in other such activities, children can act out feelings that often cannot be expressed directly. For example, the child who is afraid of the doctor can express this fear by giving shots to dolls or stuffed animals in the home center. Children can learn to deal with their anxieties as well as act out their fantasies through creative dramatic play.

Through the imitation and make-believe of dramatic play, children sort out what they understand and gain a measure of mastery and control over events they've witnessed or taken part in—making breakfast, going to work, taking care of a baby, and going to the doctor. The logic and meaning of these events often escapes young children, but dramatic play helps them enter and begin to make sense of the world of adults.

THE DEVELOPMENT OF DRAMATIC PLAY

The beginning of dramatic play is visible in the actions of children as young as one year, who put a comb to

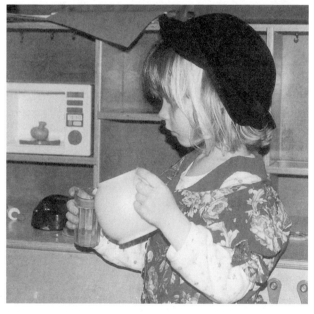

For young children, dramatic play might involve toys and equipment or just the power of their imaginations.

their hair, for example, and pull it along the side of their face, imitating the activity that has been performed on them with the same "prop." Given the right prop, the baby will imitate the behavior associated with that prop. For example, if offered a cup, the baby drinks; if offered a hat, the baby puts it on his head; or if offered a sleeping pillow, the baby puts his head on it.

As children grow and develop, so does their dramatic play. From simple imitative movement, children move on to more complex dramatic play.

Many times creative dramatics begins with one child, and others soon join in. Playing store with a storekeeper and a number of customers is a form of creative dramatic play. Speaking on a toy telephone to a friend is another form. Puppet shows in which children use finger puppets and make up a story as they go along is still another form (see Figure 9–1).

As they develop in their dramatic play, children become involved in more complex make-believe. In this dramatic play, they learn to listen and respond to each other.

In the development of their dramatic play, children repeat words and phrases they have learned and enjoy saying them. They name objects, talk about what they are doing, and plan as they go along. They begin to recognize the importance of planning and take time to formulate more detailed plans for their dramatizations.

In contrast to younger children two to four years old, children five years and older are involved in dramatic play for a much longer period of time. Their dramatic play may also reach into other areas of the room. For example, a child who needs some pretend money to put in her purse may decide to make some in the art area. She also might go to the manipulative area to gather beads, chips, or even puzzle pieces to use as money. This later development of dramatic play is a definite contrast to the brief dramatic play of a two-year-old who plays with a purse for a few minutes and then moves on to something else.

Teachers of young children encourage children's dramatic play by providing kits containing "props" for them to use. Dramatic play kits are created by assembling a variety of available everyday items into groups that have a common use or theme. Children select the props and use them in groups or alone to play roles or create dramatic play experiences. Just letting the children know about the use of these kits is often enough to get them started. Materials for these dramatic kits can be kept together in shoe boxes or other containers. Some common types of dramatic play kits are:

Post Office and Mail Carrier

Index card file, stamp pads, stampers, crayons, pencils, Christmas seals, envelopes, hats, badges, mail satchel, supply of "resident," or other third-class mail

Firefighter

Hats, raincoats, badge, boots, and short lengths of garden hose

Cooking

Pots, pans, eggbeaters, spoons, pitchers, flour sifter, metal or plastic bowls, salt and pepper shakers, aprons, measuring spoons and cups, and egg timer

Cleaning

Small brooms, mops, feather duster, cakes of soap, sponges, bucket, toweling, plastic spray bottles, clothesline, clothespins, and doll clothes to wash

Doctor

Tongue depressors, old stethoscope, satchel, bandages, cotton balls, and uniforms

Beauty Salon

Small hand mirrors, plastic combs and brushes, cotton balls, towels, scarves, clip-on rollers, colored water in nail polish bottles, empty hair spray containers, wigs, play money, and blow-dryer

Grocery Store

Old cash register or adding machine, play money, paper pads, pencils or crayons, paper bags, empty food cartons, wax fruit, grocery boxes, and cans with smooth edges

Plumber

Wrenches, sections of plastic pipes, tool kit, hats, and shirts

Painter

Paint cans full of water, brushes of different sizes, drop cloth, and painter's hat

Mechanic

Tire pump, tool kit, boxes to become "cars," shirt, and hat

Entertainer

Records, cassette tapes, record player, cassette tape player, musical instruments, and costumes

Many more dramatic play kits can be added to this list. It is important to encourage both boys and girls to assume a variety of roles. Imagination can also be used to transform regular classroom items into "new materials." Chairs can become trains, cars, boats, or houses. A table covered with a blanket or bedspread becomes a cave or special hiding place. Large cardboard cartons that children can decorate become houses, forts, fire stations, and telephone booths.

FIGURE 9–1 | Dramatic play kits.

FOOD FOR THOUGHT

Developmentally Appropriate Dramatic Activities

The following personal story of a first-year teacher provides an excellent example of a developmentally inappropriate dramatic activity. Teachers can benefit greatly from reading, rereading, and sharing this story with other teachers and parents, too!

It was time for the annual Christmas program. Because I doubled as the music teacher, my principal appointed me chair of the program committee. I was excited! This was my first year teaching, my first class of five-year-olds, and the principal wanted me to be in charge of the Christmas program. I decided that the whole school would do *The Nutcracker Suite,* complete with costumes, music, props, and all the embellishments. I was eager to impress the parents and the other teachers, so I decided to teach my kindergarten boys "Dance of the Toy Soldiers." For weeks, I taught these children perfect steps, perfect timing, turn right, stand still, curtsy, and step-and-turn. At first, the children seemed to enjoy it, but as the days and weeks went on, they started resisting going to practice or would actually beg not to have to do "the program" again. On several occasions, some complained of being tired and some were discipline problems . . . disrupting, acting out, hitting, and being generally unhappy; however, we did make it to the big night. The parents loved the performance. We all congratulated ourselves on a wonderful program. I remember talking with a first-grade teacher about how much the children loved it and what a good time they had. The truth is that the children were exhausted. They were fidgety and irritable, tired and pouty.

After a long weekend, the children returned to school and seemed to be the happy, well-adjusted children they had been before I had had this brilliant idea of performing. Young children, as you know, are so resilient. In the weeks that followed, they didn't want me to play music during center time. I would put on a Hap Palmer album, and they would argue about the right and wrong way to "march around the alphabet." Why would kindergartners turn against the sacred Hap Palmer? They didn't want to hear the music from the ballet. Just the mention of the words "dance" or "costume" or "program" would change them into terrors.

It wasn't until years later that I came to know that I had forced these little children to perform (under the name of "creative arts"—specifically, "dance") in ways that were totally inappropriate for children their age. Not only had I involved them in a developmentally inappropriate practice, I had imposed my own ideas of how to be a flower and a toy soldier without regard as to how *they* might interpret or create their own ideas, thoughts, fantasies, or forms of expression (Edwards & Nabors, 1993, p. 78).

DRAMATIC PLAY IN THE HOME (OR HOUSEKEEPING) CENTER

One of the best places for children to express themselves in creative, dramatic play is the housekeeping or home center. Here, in a child-sized version of the world, children are free and safe to express how they feel about themselves and others. While they carry out dramatic play in the housekeeping center, they can pretend to be many different kinds of people, "trying on," so to speak, many social roles. (Figure 9–2 presents a summary of basic home center experiences and equipment.)

The home (housekeeping) and creative dramatics center provides endless opportunities for the teacher, as

a facilitator of learning, to broaden the children's horizons. The center can be decorated and rearranged to represent an area that pertains to a specific content. Possibilities include creating a home, hospital, post office, grocery store, and more. The change of seasons as well as certain holidays can be easily incorporated in this center. For example, during fall, a child's rake, sweaters, and pumpkins might be included in the center. During the winter months, mufflers, mittens, a child's shovel, a holiday apron, and bells may be additions to the center. For spring, the teacher may add plastic or silk flowers, and a variety of hats. Be sure to include clothing, dishes, and dolls that are familiar and represent each of the ethnic groups in your classroom. Figure 9–1 gives more ideas for props in the home center.

Activities in this center provide the child experiences in the following:

- clarifying adult roles
- trying out social skills
- getting along with others
- sharing responsibilities
- making group decisions
- controlling impulsive behavior

- recognizing cause and effect
- developing positive attitudes about one's self and others
- enjoying the fantasy of the grown-up world
- using oral language spontaneously
- practicing the use of symbols, which are subskills in reading
- learning social ease and confidence in his own strengths

Materials:*

Full-length mirror
Stove
Refrigerator
Sink
Closet or rack of clothes
Cooking/eating utensils
Table and chairs
Tea set
Telephone
Stethoscope
Props for cleaning (broom, mop, dustpan, pail, sponge, rags, duster)

Play dough
Doll bed, doll carriage, baby highchair
Rocking chair
Empty cans, food boxes— multicultural foods
Mirror/hand mirror
Carriage
Dolls/doll clothes—multicultural
Iron/ironing board
Puppets

A variety of hats, dresses, shirts, ties, belts, scarves, shoes, pocketbooks, and jewelry
An old suitcase (for "trips")
A nurse's cap (hypodermic needles—minus needles— pill bottles, a play thermometer)
Play money
An old briefcase
Dress-up gloves, rubber gloves, baseball gloves, garden gloves

*Add objects as needed for special emphasis.

FIGURE 9–2 | Experiences and equipment in the home center.

It is also important to emphasize a nonsexist approach in the housekeeping area. Boys' dramatic play must be encouraged in the early childhood program as much as the girls' dramatic play. A good tactic to encourage boys' participation is to change the themes of the dramatic play corner to topics that interest the boys, such as garage, doctor, boat, and so on.

CREATIVE DRAMATICS IN THE ELEMENTARY GRADES

Dramatic play is the free play of very young children. It is their earliest expression in dramatic form, but it is *not* the same as creative dramatics.

Dramatic play is fragmented, existing only for the moment. It may last for a few minutes or go on for some time. It even may be played repeatedly, but it is a repetition for the pure joy of doing. It has no clear beginning, no end, and no development in the dramatic sense.

Creative drama refers to informal drama that is created by the participants. It goes beyond dramatic play in scope and intent. It may make use of a story with a beginning, a middle, and an end. It may, however, explore, develop, and express ideas and feelings through dramatic enactment. (See "This One's for You!" box in this chapter for examples of creative dramatic experiences.) It is, however, always improvised drama. Dialogue is created by the players. Lines are not written down or memorized. With each playing, the story becomes more detailed and better organized, but it remains improvised. It is at no time designed for an audience. Participants are guided by a leader rather than a director; the leader's goal is the optimal growth and development of the players.

The term *creative drama* is generally used to describe the improvised drama of children from age six and older. Creative drama offers elementary children the opportunity to develop their creativity and imagination. Few activities have greater potential for developing the imagination than creative dramatics.

THIS ONE'S FOR YOU

Creative Dramatics in the Elementary Grades

While adults rely on reason and knowledge, children use play and imagination to explore and understand their world. It makes sense, then, for teachers to use these two resources—play and imagination—as a learning tool. Creative dramatics links the world of play to the world of knowledge and reason.

Dramatic play is an accepted part of the preschool and kindergarten curricula. Yet, elementary teachers of young children often neglect this important learning tool for the elementary child.

Creative dramatics is a form of imaginative play that helps students learn and uses no written dialogue. This makes it different from performing a play. Actors in a play read or memorize lines written by somebody else. In creative dramatics, actors create their own words to convey meaning. Some examples of a creative dramatics experience would be:

- In a third-grade classroom, students using creative dramatics "become" metal containers, expanding with heat and contracting with cold. These expanding and contracting movements are put into a drama and eventually accompanied by a dance.

- In a first-grade classroom, children become clouds releasing raindrops, shimmery rays of sunshine, and seeds that grow roots, sprout, and squeeze their faces through the dirt.

- A fourth-grade teacher introduces a dramatic activity having individuals or small groups of students repeat the same line while portraying different qualities or characters. Say in a very mysterious way, "Are you going to wear the red hat to the fair?" Say in a very angry way, "Are you going to wear the red cap to the fair?" How might a mouse ask the same question? How might a spoiled rich kid ask the same question? The teacher repeats this using different lines, qualities, and characters. After five minutes, students are thinking creatively and are ready to move into a dramatic activity.

- In a third-grade class students are performing *The Three Billy Goats Gruff* with a twist. The teacher tells the actors before they begin that they can only use dog language. That is, they will have to do the whole drama using only barks, yips, and pants. This forces the children to convey meaning and develop characterization using only their faces and bodies, while watching and reacting to other actors.

In all of these examples, teachers are using creative dramatics to reinforce concepts in the curriculum. In the process, these teachers are creating an active learning experience that is fun, allowing the students to work together to achieve a common goal, and allowing everyone to be successful.

This is the essence of creative dramatics. Creative dramatics is a form of imaginative play that helps elementary students learn in an active, enjoyable way.

Figure 9–3 gives information on specific steps involved in setting up creative dramatic experiences for elementary children.

PUPPETS*

Puppets can be used for almost any of the dramatic experiences that have been described here. They offer the child two ways to express creativity: (1) the creative experience of making the puppet and (2) the imaginative experience of making the puppet come to life.

Puppets fascinate and involve children in a way that few other art forms can because they allow children to enter the world of fantasy and drama so easily. In this magic world, children are free to create whatever is needed right then in their lives.

USING PUPPETS

The use of puppets usually begins in the nursery or preschool, where they are invaluable for dramatic play. Teachers can teach fingerplays with simple finger puppets; hand puppets can act out familiar nursery rhymes. Music time is enhanced by a puppet leading the singing and other puppets joining in. The shy child who is

*Portions of this section adapted from the book *The Magic of Puppetry: A Guide for Those Working with Young Children,* by Peggy Davison Jenkins. © 1980 by Prentice-Hall, Inc. Published by Prentice-Hall, Inc., Englewood Cliffs, NJ 07632. Used with permission.

The following guidelines should assist you in getting started on creative dramatics for elementary students:

■ **Provide a structure.** While pretending is very natural for children, improvising a short drama can be an abstract process. Children will need structure to guide their actions and dialogue during the initial stages. The teacher can provide this structure by modeling and demonstrating the basic story, as well as possible actions, dialogue, and characterizations. It is best to keep early dramas short and simple, using only two to four characters. Older students and those with experience in creative dramatics will need less structure.

■ **Encourage open-endedness.** Creative dramatics is spontaneous and changeable. Although it works best when teachers provide a beginning structure, this structure should be flexible and open-ended. As students become more comfortable with creative dramatics, they will begin to use ideas and experiences from their own lives to create unique variations on the original themes. Using a prepared script would prevent this kind of creativity and individualization. It is a good rule not to use written dialogue.

■ **Promote a safe environment.** Creativity is enhanced when the teacher creates a fun, safe environment. Closing the classroom door during the initial learning stages of creative dramatics can help to develop a sense of safety and community. A teacher who is willing to take creative risks by modeling and participating in creative dramatics encourages the children's participation. Positive, specific feedback that acknowledges actors and their efforts will put students at ease to continue acting creatively. Finally, a teacher should never force students to participate in creative dramatics; rather, she should always ask for volunteers.

■ **Provide feedback.** Students like to receive feedback, both formal and informal. Informal feedback is best when a teacher responds in a way that is appropriate to the dramatic experience; for example, laughing at the comedic parts. Once a drama is over, the teacher can give more formal feedback by processing the experience with students, recognizing those things that were done well.

■ **Take your time.** Allow students to slowly become comfortable with creative dramatics. Remember, creative dramatics is meant to be an enjoyable learning experience. Make having fun your number one priority.

FIGURE 9–3 | Steps to creative dramatics in elementary grades.

A hand puppet is one of the most basic puppet forms.

reluctant to sing often will participate through a puppet. Puppets are also excellent for concept teaching and can help clarify abstract concepts and demonstrate concrete concepts. For instance, in the preschool the concepts of "above," "below," "behind," "in front of," and so on can be clearly shown with the puppet.

Puppetry, as a form of dramatic play, is a sure means of stimulating creative storytelling in younger children. Some teachers tape-record spontaneous puppet skits and, by writing them down, show the children how they have created a story.

HINTS FOR USING PUPPETS

■ Put together a puppet center—puppet materials, props, and theater for children to use during the day.

■ Recycle small plastic detergent bottles for a hand puppet rack. Bolt these small detergent bottles to scrap lumber and your puppets will have a "home." See Figure 9–4 for a diagram of this puppet rack.

Detergent Bottle Puppet Rack

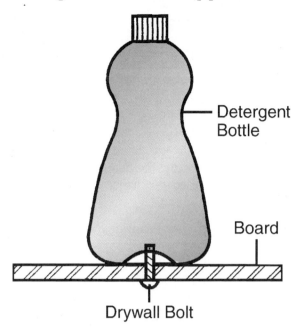

Detergent
Bottle

Board

Drywall Bolt

FIGURE
9–4 | Detergent bottle puppet rack.

Finger-Leg

Finger-Cap

Finger-Face

FIGURE
9–5 | There are many different kinds of finger puppets.

■ Consider having a specific puppet for each center area. This puppet could remind the class that it is music time, for instance, and be used to give directions and explain new concepts.

■ Felt boards and puppets work well together. A puppet with hands can help the adult or child put pieces on or take them off the felt board.

■ In music experiences, puppets help young children develop a feeling for rhythm and music interpretation by moving the puppets to the beat. They also encourage reluctant children to sing, since the puppet does the singing for the child.

■ Social studies is a natural area for puppets; it presents countless opportunities to represent particular ethnic customs, or portray the roles of various community helpers.

These suggestions are simply intended to be idea starters. The use of puppets in the classroom is limited only by imagination—yours and the children's. (See Appendix G for puppet patterns.)

ACTIVITIES FOR CHILDREN   Stick Puppets

The following puppets can be made by the children for use in dramatic play. For very young children, the teacher may want to make the puppet for the children's use, if they are unable to do so.

GOALS: To encourage children's dramatic play
      To develop children's creativity

MATERIALS: Sticks of various types. Examples may include large twigs, wood popsicle sticks, sticks from the lumber yard, paper bags, pieces of cloth, newspaper, and cotton balls

PREPARATION: Assemble all materials within easy reach for children's use.

PROCEDURE:

1. Have the child put a bag or piece of cloth over the stick.
2. Have the child stuff the bag or cloth with wads of newspaper or cotton.
3. Have the child then tie the top of the bag to the stick, making a head.
4. Have the child use a rubber band instead of string to form a head.
5. Have the child paint the head or make a face with crayons or colored paper and paste.

VARIATION:

■ Use scrap yarn, wood shavings, and buttons for the puppet's face.
■ Use scrap pieces of fabric to "dress" the puppet. Wallpaper samples are an inexpensive material for puppets' clothes.

ADDITIONAL INFORMATION: With the stick, move the puppet around or turn it from side to side. The stick puppet is a good first puppet for preschoolers, since a stick can be attached to any little doll, toy animal, cutout figure, fruit, or vegetable, making the puppet easy to operate.

ACTIVITIES FOR CHILDREN   Bag Puppets

GOALS: To encourage children's dramatic play
      To develop children's creativity

MATERIALS: Common paper bags (lunch bag size), newspaper, staples, glue, paint, crayons, colored paper, and paste

PREPARATION: Give each child two paper bags. Show the children how two bags can become a puppet: one for the head and the other for the body.

PROCEDURE:

1. Have the child stuff one bag with wads of newspaper and staple or glue it shut.
2. Have the child make a body with the second bag by stapling it to the first bag. Leave room in the second bag for the child's hand to slip in and work the puppet.

VARIATION:

■ Make a face with paint, crayons, or bits of colored paper and paste.
■ Use odds and ends for the face, too. Buttons make eyes, crumpled tissue makes a nose, and yarn makes hair.

ACTIVITIES FOR CHILDREN

Finger Puppets (see Figure 9–5)

GOALS: To encourage children's dramatic play
To develop children's creativity

MATERIALS: Felt tip markers, paper, and crayons

PREPARATION: Show children how fingers can be a puppet's legs, or how fingers can be a puppet's face.

PROCEDURE:

1. Have the child draw a face on a finger(s) with a felt pen. This becomes a puppet's face.
2. Have the child draw a face on each finger. This makes a group of finger puppets.
3. Have the child draw the puppet's body on a piece of paper.
4. Have the child cut out the puppet body.

5. Have the child paste the puppet body over the index and middle finger to make a finger-leg puppet (see Figure 9–5) .

VARIATION:

■ Have one child put on a performance with an "entire cast" of five finger puppets on one hand.
■ Use finger puppets when doing fingerplays.

ADDITIONAL INFORMATION: Finger puppets are easy to manipulate, even by a toddler. They maintain interest because they are always easy and quick to make. They can be made in spare moments, since materials are small and mobile.

ACTIVITIES FOR CHILDREN

Wooden Spoon Puppets

GOALS: To encourage children's dramatic play
To develop children's creativity

MATERIALS: Wooden spoons, yarn, string, material scraps, glue, and construction paper

PREPARATION: "Walk" the spoon around, showing how it can be a puppet.

PROCEDURE:

1. Have the child draw a face on the wooden spoon.
2. Have the child glue on yarn or string for hair, and scraps of material for clothing.

VARIATION: Use plastic spoons. They can be decorated with markers and glued-on scrap materials.

ACTIVITIES FOR CHILDREN

Two-Faced (Paper Plate) Puppets

GOALS: To encourage children's dramatic play
To develop children's creativity

MATERIALS: Paper plates, wood popsicle sticks, glue, crayons, markers, stapler, yarn, scraps of material, and miscellaneous materials for decoration

PREPARATION: Give each child two paper plates.

PROCEDURE:

1. Have the child draw a face on the back of each paper plate.

2. Have the child add features with various types of materials.

3. Have the child insert a stick between the paper plates and glue it into place.

4. Have the child staple the edges together.

VARIATION: Make paper plate animals—real or imaginary.

ACTIVITIES FOR CHILDREN

Play Dough Puppets

GOALS: To encourage children's dramatic play
To develop children's creativity

MATERIALS: Play dough, toothpicks, small pebbles, and bits of cereal

PREPARATION: Give each child a small amount of play dough.

PROCEDURE:

1. Have the child place a small amount of play dough onto a finger.

2. Have the child mold play dough into a face shape covering the finger, making a finger puppet.

3. Have the child add bits of cereal, small pebbles, toothpicks, and so on for facial features and added emphasis.

ACTIVITIES FOR CHILDREN

Styrofoam Ball Puppets

GOALS: To encourage children's dramatic play
To develop children's creativity

MATERIALS: Sticks, styrofoam balls, bits of fabric, rubber bands, string, glue, buttons, and felt scraps

PREPARATION: Give each child a styrofoam ball and one stick.

PROCEDURE:

1. Have the child insert stick into the styrofoam ball.

2. Have the child cover the styrofoam ball with fabric.

3. Have the child fasten the fabric around the stick with a rubber band (or tie it with a string).

4. Have the child glue on buttons and felt scraps for facial features.

VARIATION: Use white muslin fabric and draw on features with markers.

ACTIVITIES FOR CHILDREN

Ping-Pong Ball Puppets

GOALS: To encourage children's dramatic play
To develop children's creativity

MATERIALS: Ping-pong balls, lightweight fabric, glue, markers, and crayons

PREPARATION: Cut X shapes out of ping-pong balls.

PROCEDURE:

1. Have the child place a piece of lightweight fabric on the finger.

2. Have the child cover the X-out area of the ball with glue.

3. Have the child force the ball at the X onto the fabric on the finger.

4. While the glue is drying, draw or paste a face onto the puppet.

ACTIVITIES FOR CHILDREN — Sock Puppet

GOALS: To encourage children's dramatic play
To develop children's creativity

MATERIALS: Old socks, buttons, pieces of trim, rickrack, glue, paint, brushes, and markers

PREPARATION: Have each child choose a sock.

PROCEDURE:

1. Have the child pull the sock over his hand.
2. Have the child glue or paint facial features onto the toe of the sock.
3. Have the child decorate as desired.

ACTIVITIES FOR CHILDREN — Finger Puppets from Gloves (see Figure 9–6)

GOALS: To encourage children's dramatic play
To develop children's creativity

MATERIALS: Old gloves, such as garden gloves, rubber gloves, driving gloves, and so on; markers; pompoms; glue; bits of felt; and fabric scraps

PREPARATION: Give each child a glove.

PROCEDURE:

1. Recycle stray gloves and use them for finger puppets.
2. Have the child draw features on the glove fingers with markers.
3. Have the child glue pompoms on each finger for the "head."
4. Have the child glue bits of cloth or felt for facial or character details.

VARIATION: Use old mittens for puppets. Have the child slip his hand into the mitten and make the puppet "talk" by moving his thumb up and down against his four fingers.

FIGURE 9–6 | Garden glove puppets.

ACTIVITIES FOR CHILDREN

Cardboard Cylinder Puppet

GOALS: To encourage children's dramatic play
To develop children's creativity

MATERIALS: Cardboard cylinders from paper towels or toilet tissue, styrofoam balls, ping-pong balls, markers, bits of cloth, and paste

PREPARATION: Give each child a cardboard cylinder.

PROCEDURE:

1. Have the children place a cardboard cylinder over their fingers.
2. Have the children decorate with desired features.
3. As an alternative, use a cylinder for the body, with a styrofoam ball or ping-pong ball placed on top for the head.
4. Have the children add facial features.

ACTIVITIES FOR CHILDREN

People Puppets

GOALS: To encourage children's dramatic play
To develop children's creativity

MATERIALS: Paper grocery bags, scissors, paint, brushes, construction paper, paste, markers, and crayons

PREPARATION: Give each child a large paper sack to put over his or her head.

PROCEDURE:

1. Have the children cut out holes for the eyes, nose, and mouth.
2. Have the children add facial features and decorations with paint or paper and paste.
3. Turn the bags up slightly above the shoulder, or cut away on the sides, for arm holes.

ADDITIONAL INFORMATION: People puppets make a natural transition from puppetry to creative drama. Shy children generally feel more protected behind this kind of puppet than all the other types.

CAUTION: Be sure not to force a child to use this type of puppet if he does not like his head covered.

ACTIVITIES FOR OLDER CHILDREN Aesthetic Awareness
(Grades 4–5)

GOALS: To encourage children's creativity
To encourage children's dramatic play

MATERIALS: None required

PREPARATION: Discuss how terms for movement in dance relate to terms in the visual arts. Examples include glide, dart, slide, pivot, hop, sway, and twirl.

PROCEDURE:
1. Have the students create pantomimes or dances based on motions in nature such as a bird flying, a fish swimming, a leaf falling, and so on.

VARIATION:
■ Have students invent vocal or instrumental sounds that seem to fit the above list of motions.
■ Put the sounds together in different ways.

ACTIVITIES FOR OLDER CHILDREN Creative Drama
(Grades 4–5) Exercises

GOALS: To encourage children's interest in drama activities
To develop children's creativity

MATERIALS: None required

PREPARATION: Refer to the guidelines presented in this chapter to help you use this activity.

PROCEDURE: Ask the children to act out one or more of the following: elephant, feather, grasshopper, cooked spaghetti, uncooked spaghetti, a very quiet mouse, or a very careful chicken.

VARIATION: More activities to act out are:
■ Blow a bubble, catch it in the air, then set it down very carefully on a table.
■ Walk into the kitchen, take a jar of pickles out of the refrigerator, open the jar, and eat one. It is very sour.
■ Prepare and eat ice cream with spinach on top.
■ Walk through a room where your foot gets stuck on some glue. As you sit down to think, other parts of you get stuck, too.
■ You are a mouse looking at some cheese on a mouse trap. Can you take it?
■ Lift something heavy, light, smelly, gooey, small, big, wiggly, or shaky.
■ Tell a story without using your voice.
■ Using only your face, show anger, surprise, sleepiness, pain, fear, being funny, being silly, or someone who just heard a very loud noise.

REFERENCE

Edwards, L. C., & Nabors, M. I. (1993 March). The creative arts process: What it is and what it is not. *Young Children*, 78.

CHAPTER 10

CREATIVE MOVEMENT

Y oung children learn by doing. They are immensely active and energetic. Movement activities are natural avenues for this energy.

This chapter addresses the importance of creative movement and provides some guidelines for adults working with young children.

Creative movement activities concern the whole child and not just physical fitness and recreation. Through **creative movement activities** a child is able to express her creative self in a very natural way.

THE IMPORTANCE OF MOVEMENT ACTIVITIES FOR YOUNG CHILDREN

To adults, the word "exercise" calls to mind visions of doing sit-ups and other unpleasant actions. Yet to a child, physical exercise is one of the activities nearest and dearest to his heart.

This is because the young child is busy acquiring all sorts of large and small motor skills during the early years of life. His main learning strategy is through physical manipulation of his world. Movement activities, more than any other type of activity, offer children many opportunities for the development of their total selves.

CREATIVE MOVEMENT

Creative movement is movement that reflects the mood or inner state of a child. In creative movement, children are free to express their own personalities in their own style. They do not have an example to follow

Movement activities contribute to the total physical, mental, social, and emotional growth and development of the child.

or an adult to imitate. Creative movement can occur in any situation where children feel free and want to move their bodies. It can be done to poetry, music, rhythm, or even silence. By feeling a pulse, beat, idea, or emotion, children's bodies become instruments of expression. They are anything they want to be. Their movement is an expression of that being.

CREATIVE MOVEMENT ACTIVITIES FOR YOUNG CHILDREN

Let us now consider the different ways creative movement can be incorporated into the early childhood classroom.

CREATIVE MOVEMENT ACTIVITIES WITH POETRY AND MUSIC

Music and poetry can encourage children's creative movement in the classroom.

Music. Listening to music is a natural way to introduce creative movement. Distinctive types of music or rhythm should be chosen for beginning movement experiences.

Only a few items are necessary to provide the music or rhythm for creative movement. A tape or CD player and some tapes or CDs, sticks, and bells may be more than enough.

Hints for using music with creative movement. Some basic ideas for the teacher to remember when using music for creative movement are:

■ Make it clear that anything the children want to do is all right, as long as it does not harm them or others.

■ Be sure the children understand that they do not have to do anything anyone else does. They can do anything the music or an idea "tells" them to do.

■ The child is allowed to "copy" someone for a start.

■ Children are encouraged to respect each other as different and able to move in different ways.

The teacher may begin the experience by playing a CD or tape. Music that has a strong and easily recognized beat or rhythm is a good start. The children should not be told what to listen for. Let them listen first and then ask them to think about what the music is "saying" to them.

While the children are listening, the teacher may turn the music down a bit lower. The teacher might talk with each child about what the music is saying. Some of the children probably may already be moving to the music by this time, and the teacher may join in. The children may go anywhere in the room and do anything that the music "tells" them to do. For this exercise, clapping, stomping, and even shouting are all

Outdoor play equipment offers children many possibilities for creative play activities.

possible. When appropriate, a quieter piece of music may be played to allow the children to rest and to give them a sense of contrast.

As children become involved in movement explorations, try to redirect, challenge, and stimulate their discoveries by suggestions such as, "Do what you are doing now in a slower way," "Try moving in a different direction or at a different level," or "Try the same thing you were doing but make it smoother or lighter."

Older children may begin to be a bit self-conscious and need other kinds of ways to encourage their creative movements. They often enjoy working in small groups for this reason. A small group activity involving mirror movements, copying, and shadowing movements is appropriate for older children. For example, working together in groups of three or more, children perform movements matching the leader of the group. The leader leads the group in a sequence of movements that the rest of the group copies as closely as possible. A second member takes over as leader, moving in a different sequence. Then, the third member leads the group in yet another sequence of movements. In this type of activity, the small group size helps students overcome the fear of the "whole class looking at me." It is also easier for children of this age to participate in a group when they know everyone else will be participating along with them in the activity.

Poetry and prose.   For creative movement, poetry has rhythm as well as the power of language. It is not necessary to use rhyming verses at all times. In the beginning, poems that rhyme may help to start a feeling of pulse and rhythm. Poems should be chosen that fit the young child's level of appreciation.

Start by asking the children to listen to a poem. After they have heard it, they may pick out their favorite characters in it. Discuss who these characters are and what they do. Read the poem a second time; suggest that the children act out their characters as they listen to the poem. Anything goes—the children may hop like bunnies, fly like planes, or do whatever they feel.

Encourage each child to move in his own way, and encourage as many variations as you see!

THIS ONE'S FOR YOU

More Possibilities: Suggested Movement Interpretations

The following are some suggested movement interpretations. Movement explorations and creative movement experiences can be used to interpret nearly every experience, thing, or phenomenon. This list can be expanded with endless possibilities.

1. Life cycle of butterfly
   a. caterpillar crawling
   b. caterpillar eating grass
   c. caterpillar hanging very still from branch or twig
   d. chrysalis hanging very still
   e. butterfly emerging from chrysalis
   f. butterfly drying its wings
   g. butterfly flying

2. Piece of cellophane or lightweight plastic
   a. item is put into teacher's hands without children seeing; children encouraged to guess what item might be, interpreting their guesses through movement.
   b. teacher's hands are opened, children watch plastic move, and then interpret what they see through movement.
   c. piece of plastic is used for movement exploration.

3. Shaving cream
   a. spurting from aerosol can
   b. foaming up
   c. spreading on face
   d. being used for shaving

4. Airplane sequence
   a. starting motor
   b. taking off
   c. flying
   d. arriving
   e. landing safely

5. Popcorn
   a. butter melting
   b. popping
   c. everyone ending in a ball shape on the floor, all "popped"

6. Water
   a. dripping
   b. flooding
   c. flowing in a fountain
   d. freezing
   e. melting
   f. spilling
   g. sprinkler

7. Laundry
   a. inside washing machine
   b. inside dryer
   c. being scrubbed on a washboard
   d. being pinned to a clothesline
   e. drying in a breeze

8. Fishing
   a. casting out
   b. reeling in
   c. pretending to be a fish
   d. fly fishing
   e. pretending to be a hooked line
   f. frying and eating fish

As readings continue, more complex poems may be selected, containing a series of movements or simple plots. The same general idea can also be carried through with prose.

Older children are able to sustain their interest for a longer period of time and enjoy the procedure of listening, picking out roles, and acting out what is read. They also enjoy adding costumes and props to their creative movements.

Fingerplays and creative movement. Fingerplays provide an endless supply of creative movement opportunities. You might encourage children to invent movements when learning a new fingerplay or ask them to suggest variations to revitalize a well-loved rhyme you've repeated often. Don't forget that it isn't necessary for all children to make the same motions during fingerplays. Always accept individual interpretations.

A child's book can be inspiration for later dramatic and creative movement.

FOOD FOR THOUGHT

Creative Movement for Transition Times

Whenever young children move from activity to activity (in transitional times), they often lose their focus and may even get a bit confused and disruptive. The following hints may help children move more easily from one activity to another.

■ Pretend you are a train, with the teacher as the engine and each child as a car in the train. Assign one child to be the caboose, to turn off the lights and close the door.

■ Turn your jump rope into a dragon, worm, caterpillar, or other animal by attaching a head at one end of the rope and a tail at the other end. Have the children make the body and legs by holding onto the rope with one hand and walking down the hall and out to the playground.

■ Imagine you are a tired puppy; yawn and stretch and roll on the floor. Then lie very still. (Suggested for the beginning of rest time.)

■ Construct a "feel" box or bag or a "look" box or bag. Place an item in the bag or box that will suggest the next activity or topic for each child to feel or look at.

■ To help children quiet down between activities, clap a rhythm for them to copy. Start by clapping loudly, then gradually clap more softly until your hands are resting in your lap.

■ Pretend to be a bowl of gelatin and shake all over.

■ Pretend to lock your lips and put the key in a pocket.

■ Pretend to put on "magic" ears for listening.

■ Pretend to walk in tiptoe boots, Indian moccasins, or Santa's-elf shoes.

■ To make lining up more fun and to enhance motor skills, make a balance-beam "bridge" for the children to cross. Cut two 5″ wide strips from a carpet sample and tape them together end to end with duct tape. Place the "bridge" on the floor alongside a smiling paper alligator for children to walk across, being careful not to let the alligator "nip" their toes (Church, 1993; Hohmann, 1993).

ACTIVITIES FOR CHILDREN — Animal Cracker Game

GOALS: To encourage children's creative movements
To develop children's creativity

MATERIALS: Box of animal crackers, full-length mirror

PREPARATION: Discuss all the kinds of animal crackers that might be in the box. Talk about how they look, sound, and move.

PROCEDURE:

1. Have the child stand before the full-length mirror.
2. Without looking, have the child take one of the crackers from the box.
3. Have the child look at the cracker, then eat the cracker. By eating the cracker, the child "becomes" that animal.
4. Allow the child to act like that animal for at least 30 seconds.
5. Have another child select a cracker and repeat the activity.
6. End the activity when all the crackers are gone.

VARIATION: Have the children draw, paint, or make their animals out of play dough after acting them out.

ACTIVITIES FOR CHILDREN — Be A . . . Tree!

GOALS: To encourage children's creative movements
To develop children's creativity

MATERIALS: None required

PREPARATION: Gather children in an area large enough so they will not bump into each other.

PROCEDURE:

1. Seat the children on the floor with their eyes closed.
2. Have them think about different trees they've seen.
3. Have them stand up.
4. Have the children raise their arms to look like a tree.
5. Have the children breathe slowly in and out.
6. Have the children try to hold the pose for about ten seconds.

VARIATIONS:

■ Show the tree in a big windstorm.
■ Show the tree losing its leaves in autumn.
■ Show the tree loaded with snow after a blizzard.
■ Show the tree in the summer when the sun is very hot.

ACTIVITIES FOR CHILDREN

Be A . . . Mountain!

GOALS: To encourage children's creative movements
To develop children's creativity

MATERIALS: None required

PREPARATION: Have children seated on the floor with enough room between them so they don't bump into each other.

PROCEDURE:

1. Have the children cross legs, or sit in any position that's comfortable.
2. Have the children slowly raise their arms to create a mountain peak.
3. As they hold the position, ask the children to pretend they are a huge, quiet mountain.
4. Have someone in the group, or the teacher, describe the peaceful scenes you might see below.

ACTIVITIES FOR CHILDREN

Be A . . . Cat!

GOALS: To encourage children's creative movements
To develop children's creativity

MATERIALS: None required

PREPARATION: Discuss cats, how they move, and how they look.

PROCEDURE:

1. Have the child curl up like a cat.
2. Have the child pretend to be sleeping in a warm, comfy place like near a fireplace or in a sunny place.
3. Have the child wake up and stretch.

VARIATION: Act like a cat that's angry, afraid, or curious . . . and be other animals.

ACTIVITIES FOR CHILDREN

Movement with Music and Partners

GOALS: To encourage children's creative movement to music

To develop children's creativity

MATERIALS: CD or tape of music with a good beat

PREPARATION: Play the music. Let the children move to it as they desire.

PROCEDURE:

1. Pair up the children.
2. Have the children face each other to do a "mirror dance" with their hands and arms. This involves one partner doing exactly what the other partner does, just like a mirror image.
3. Have the children do a mirror dance using feet and legs.
4. Have the children do a mirror dance using facial expressions.

VARIATIONS:

■ Hold hands with your partner and slide, leap, gallop, and so on until you hear the signal; then find a new partner and continue to move to the music.

■ What interesting body shapes can you and your partner make? Can the two of you create an interesting design in the space you share?

ACTIVITIES FOR CHILDREN

Stop and Go

GOALS: To encourage children's creative movements

To develop children's creativity

MATERIALS: None required

PREPARATION: Do this activity in an area large enough so children don't bump into each other.

PROCEDURE:

1. Have the children walk around to music, doing whatever they want to with their arms and bodies.
2. When the teacher says "stop," have the children "freeze."
3. Have the children hold their position until the teacher says "go."
4. Encourage all children's movements.

VARIATION: Have a child be the leader and give the "freeze" and "go" directions.

ACTIVITIES FOR CHILDREN

Jump Over the River

GOALS: To encourage children's creative movements

To develop children's creativity

MATERIALS: Two long sticks

PREPARATION: Tell the children the two long sticks are the banks of a river. Place the sticks parallel to each other in an area large enough so children don't bump into each other.

PROCEDURE:

1. Have the children jump from one bank to another.
2. Move the sticks further apart at times to make a wider river.
3. Encourage children to find creative attempts to "cross."

VARIATION: Cross the river by sliding, crawling, rolling, and so on.

ACTIVITIES FOR CHILDREN

Line Challenges

GOALS: To encourage children's creative movements

To develop children's creativity

MATERIALS: Tape or chalk

PREPARATION: Mark a line on the floor with either tape or chalk.

PROCEDURE:

1. Have the children see how many things they can do.
2. Have the children jump over the line.
3. Have the children walk on the line.
4. Have the children hop along the line.
5. Have the children slide on the line.
6. Have the children tiptoe across the line.
7. Have the children roll over the line.
8. Have the children lie beside the line.
9. Have the children run around the line.
10. Have the children skip round and round the line.

VARIATION:

■ Have the children make up their own challenges.

■ Do the above activity to music.

ACTIVITIES FOR CHILDREN Jet Planes

GOALS: To encourage children's creative movements

To develop children's creativity

MATERIALS: None required

PREPARATION: Use a large, open area for this activity.

PROCEDURE:

1. Have the children pretend to be jet planes.
2. Have the children be the jet on the ground.
3. Have the children be the jet in the air.
4. Have the children be the jet climbing up into the clouds.
5. Have the children be the jet nose diving.
6. Have the children be the jet coming in for a landing.
7. Have the children be the jet on the ground again.

VARIATIONS:

- Pretend your jet is a stunt plane that can write in the sky.
- Pretend your jet can make loops and turn upside-down. Make a number 2. Make a 3. Now make a 5.
- Can you make an S? How about a P?
- Make the shape of a funny animal. How about a wiggly worm?
- Do any and all of these movements to music.

ACTIVITIES FOR CHILDREN Unwinding

GOALS: To encourage children's creative movements

To develop children's creativity

MATERIALS: None required

PREPARATION: Discuss windup toys, such as how they are wound up, how they act, and how they wind down. If possible, have a windup toy to accompany this discussion.

PROCEDURE:

1. Have the children pretend they are windup toys.
2. Have the teacher "wind up" each toy.
3. Have the children begin moving at a quick pace.
4. Have the children gradually get slower and slower.
5. Have the children completely "run down," stop, and collapse to the floor.

VARIATION: Have a child "wind up" the other children and the teacher, too!

ACTIVITIES FOR OLDER CHILDREN **Collapsing**
(Grades 4–5)

GOALS: To encourage children's creative movements

To encourage children's creativity

MATERIALS: None required

PREPARATION: Discuss what "collapsing" means, such as relaxing a body part or the whole body, allowing gravity to pull it down to earth.

PROCEDURE:

1. Have the children stand and stretch tall.
2. Have the children slowly collapse (relax) one body part at a time. First the fingertips, then the wrists, elbows, arms, head and shoulders, and so on.
3. Allow the children to collapse to the floor.

VARIATION: Play soft music during this activity.

ACTIVITIES FOR OLDER CHILDREN **Rope Skills**
(Grades 4–5)

GOALS: To encourage children's creative movements

To develop children's creativity

MATERIALS: Various lengths of rope

PREPARATION: Lay out various lengths of rope in a straight line on the floor as if it were a tightrope.

PROCEDURE:

1. Challenge the children to walk the "tightrope" in these ways:
   - With eyes shut
   - While moving backward
2. Have the children jump from side to side across the rope without touching the rope.
3. Have the children hop from side to side without touching the rope.
4. Have the children lay your rope in the pattern of a circle.
5. Have the children get inside the circle, taking up as much space as possible, without hanging over the edges.

VARIATION:

■ Make up a design on your own. See if you can walk in it. Can your friend?

■ Can you walk in your friend's design?

■ Do any and all of the movements to music of the children's choice.

ACTIVITIES FOR OLDER CHILDREN
(Grades 4–5) **Moving in So Many Ways—With Partners**

GOALS: To encourage children's creative movements
To develop children's creativity
To share creative movements with others

MATERIALS: Yarn

PREPARATION: Divide the group into pairs. Conduct this activity in a large open area.

PROCEDURE: Challenge children to use their bodies in the following ways:

1. Working with a partner, do the same movement your partner does. Then do the same movement with another body part.

2. Create a dance with your partner using two different movements suggested by each person.

3. Attach a piece of yarn loosely to a body part (not around the neck) and to the same body part of the partner. Have one begin the movement with the attached body part following the movement. Try moving in different ways.

4. Create a dance with each person initiating a movement in turn, which is followed by a repeated movement from the attached body part of the partner.

ACTIVITIES FOR OLDER CHILDREN
(Grades 4–5) **Moving in So Many Ways—Alone**

GOALS: To encourage children's creative movements
To develop children's creativity

MATERIALS: None required

PREPARATION: Conduct this activity in a large open area

PROCEDURE: Challenge children to use their bodies in the following ways:

1. Begin a movement in one body part and gradually move it to other body parts. Try moving in different ways.

2. Create a dance in which the movement flows from one dancer to another.

3. Explore moving different body parts in unison.

4. Combine two or three movements and move in sequence.

VARIATION:

▪ Have the children make up challenges for each other.

▪ Do any and all of the activities to music of the children's choice.

REFERENCES

Church, E. B. (1993, Feb.). Moving small, moving quiet. *Scholastic Pre-K Today,* 42–44.
Hohmann, M. (1993). *Young children in action.* Ypsilanti, MI: High/Scope Press.

CHAPTER 11

CREATIVE MUSIC

Lisa sang to herself in a sing-song way while drawing with crayons: "One purple, two purple, three purple, four purple." Next to her, William was humming the jingle for a fast-food restaurant advertisement and keeping rhythm with his coloring strokes.

Out on the playground, Drew chanted, "I-am-going-to-be-a-lawn-mo-wer." And as he slid down the slide, he made a sound like a lawn mower. Picking up his cue, Claire and Christy slid down after him, each on their stomach making motor-growling sounds.

Musical experiences like these are a common occurrence in a young child's life. Making up original chants and songs while moving rhythmically to musical beats is quite natural to a young child. Music is a natural avenue for creative expression for young children. In contrast, an adult finds it more difficult to be as spontaneous as children in the inclusion of music in everyday life. Consider how your friends would react to your chanting as you read this paragraph, "One paragraph, two paragraph, three to go—yeah, yeah, yeah." Unlike William's humming in our opening scenario, your musical monologue probably would not go unnoticed by your friends as they hummed to themselves!

This is the challenge—overcoming an "adult" approach to music so you can share musical experiences with young children in a way that preserves and encourages their natural spontaneous and open attitude. You are challenged in this chapter to put aside any self-consciousness and fears about your own musical talents and to try returning to the openness of a young child experiencing music. You don't need to know how to play a musical instrument or even be able to read music to plan and conduct creative music experiences for children.

As with other areas of the curriculum, **appropriate music activities** can be planned only if the teacher understands the developmental levels of the children involved. Although individual rates of development vary widely, the sequence of development follows a particular pattern. Figure 11–1 shows some important behavioral characteristics for each stage of development, along with their effect on a child's experiences with music. Figure 11–1 may be used as a guide for choosing from the musical activities for children listed at the end of this chapter.

YOUNG CHILDREN'S MUSIC EXPERIENCES

Music activities in the early childhood program should build on the child's natural appreciation of music. Focusing and then building on this natural enjoyment of music will help you produce the most successful and joyous music program for young children. As in all early childhood activities, it is the *process* that teaches and enriches a young child and not the finished *product*.

INFANTS AND TODDLERS

Infants and very young toddlers experience music by hearing it, by feeling it, and by experimenting with pitch and timbre as they vocalize. Adults can provide infants and toddlers music experiences daily while giving children caring, physical contact. Singing to children during changing and feeding times is a basic way to provide music experiences for very young children.

Playing music during periods of the day is another. Adults can further encourage the musical development of infants and toddlers by exposing them to a wide variety of vocal, instrumental, and environmental sounds. Simple things like talking about the sounds children hear on their walks outside, if they are loud sounds or soft, or if they are near or far away are basic beginning music experiences for very young children.

In the classroom, infants and toddlers need to hear all kinds of music. Adults need to talk about this music and

Age	Behavioral Characteristics	Music Experiences
Newborn to 1 month	Responds to stimuli by moving entire body.	Quiet singing and rocking soothe the baby. Scary sounds avoided. Sound stimuli important.
1 to 4 months	Changes from hearing to listening. Turns head toward stimulus. Follows moving objects with eyes.	Same as for newborn.
4 to 8 months	Involved in purposeful activity. Reproduces interesting events. Develops hand–eye coordination.	Hits suspended bells again and again to reproduce the sound.
8 to 12 months	Anticipates events, shows intention. Knows that objects have functions. Imitates actions.	Hits drum or xylophone with stick. Claps hands to music. Hits instrument to produce a sound. Understands purpose of instrument.
12 to 18 months	Invents new actions. Uses trial and error to solve problems.	Experiments by hitting instrument in different ways with different objects.
18 to 24 months	Creates new actions through prior thought. Imitates actions after person leaves.	Continues music activity after adult stops. Listens to radio, dances to it.
2 years	Steps in place. Pats. Runs. Increases language. Has limited attention span. Attends to spoken words a few at a time. Develops independence, is very curious. Tendency to tire easily.	Enjoys action songs and moving to music. Can learn short, simple songs. Enjoys activities with short, simple directions. Many opportunities to experiment with instruments and sound. Likes record player because he can watch it turn. Opportunity for frequent rest breaks in strenuous rhythmic experiences. Avoid prolonged activities.
3 years	Jumps, runs, and walks to music. Has self-control. Attentive, has longer attention span. Uses more words. Compares two objects. Participates in planning. Initiative emerges.	Special music for special movements. Can wait for a turn. Longer songs or small group experiences can be planned. Experiments with sound comparisons. Suggests words for songs or additional activities. Can recognize several melodies and may have several favorites. Choices important along with an opportunity to try out own ideas.

FIGURE 11–1 Developmental characteristics and music experiences.

(continued)

Age	Behavioral Characteristics	Music Experiences
4 years	Has better motor control. Interested in rules. Plans ahead with adults. Likes to imagine.	May begin skipping. Rule songs and games appropriate. Can make suggestions for music activities. Adds words to songs. Creates songs on instruments. Dramatic movements. Likes to experiment with the piano. Likes to play records over and over. Can identify simple melodies.
5 to 6 years	Has good motor control. Likes to have rules. Vision not yet fully developed; eye movements slow; likely to have trouble seeing small print or making fine linear distinctions when music staff is not enlarged. Heart in stage of rapid growth.	Able to sit longer. Enjoys songs and dances with rules. Can follow specific rhythm patterns. May pick out tunes on the piano. Likes musical movies but may become restless. Strenuous activity periods should be brief.
7 to 8 years	Begins to read written symbols. Concerned with rules. Cooperation and competition. Logical thought processes emerge. Can compare more than two objects after first object removed (seriation). Thoroughly enjoys group play, but groups tend to be small. Boys and girls play together.	May be able to read words to songs. Rule dances and songs especially valued. Better able to tell reality from fantasy. Can compare three or more sounds or pitches. Likes duets and doing anything musical with a friend. May want to take piano or dancing lessons. Likes group activities including singing games, playing informal instruments, phrase games.
9 to 11 years	Has more developed language arts skills. Understands rules and strategies of games. Peer group assumes greater importance. Logical thought processes are present. Has more flexible thought. Enjoys play with peer group. Boys and girls prefer same-sex play. Begins to see other's opinions and ideas as unique.	Can read words to songs, can create original lyrics. Enjoys dances with varied steps and patterns. Begins to enjoy small group singing experiences, such as duets, trios, chorale. Can compare sounds, pitch, rhythms in music. Can understand elements of music such as tone, basic notations, styles, and forms of music. Introduce harmony and part singing for small groups. Provide duet singing experiences, all boy, all girl singing groups. Enjoys multicultural music and dance.

FIGURE 11–1 | Developmental characteristics and music experiences. (Continued)

how it expresses feelings. Rocking, patting, touching, and moving with the children to the beat, rhythm patterns, and melodic direction of the music are all appropriate musical experiences for infants and toddlers.

PRESCHOOLERS

When children enter the preschool program, music continues to be an important part of their lives.

Listen to the sounds of young children playing in the housekeeping corner, on the playground, in the sandbox, and in the building block area—you will often hear young children in these everyday situations singing, humming, or chanting familiar songs. Songs and singing are a common occurrence in the everyday life of a young child. Therefore, teaching songs and singing are a natural part of the early childhood program. The way in which you teach songs and singing to young children reflects the same natural and enjoyable place music holds in a young child's life.

HINTS FOR MUSIC ACTIVITIES

The two keys to success in all creative music activities are **flexibility** and **acceptance.** Accept more than one kind of response to a music activity and adapt the activity accordingly. If, for example, the child in a planned clapping activity chooses to pat the rug or his leg, accept the response and imitate it as you continue the activity. Or if the child is more interested in just listening to music than in dancing to it, accept that too. Try to catch him for your dancing activity at another time when he is in a dancing mood. In other words, take your cues from the children and build enjoyment and learning on what they already find enjoyable.

Singing is probably the most common music activity in the early childhood program. The following are some hints on making singing experiences fun for both you and the children.

■ Choose songs that have a natural appeal for young children. Popular topics include the children themselves, family members, animals, seasons, toys, holidays, and so on. Be sure to include songs for all ethnic and cultural groups represented in the class, as well as in the larger community group.

■ Choose songs with a clear, strong melody. If the melody is easy to hear, it will be easier to remember.

■ Try out all songs yourself first.

■ Once you've chosen a song, learn it yourself—and learn it *well*. Nothing is less inspiring to eager songsters than a teacher who has to check notes while teaching a song.

■ Based on the length of a song, you may want to teach it in sections, by verses, or even in short phrases. Often, a song's wording may be a bit tricky, and you may want to practice key words a bit more. Whatever method you choose, remember to be light on practice and heavy on praise.

Musical activities with simple instruments are appropriate for young children.

■ In the first stages of teaching a song, use a record, tape, or CD. But be careful not to use them too often in the process of teaching songs, to avoid causing a dependence on equipment over the human voice. You and the children can sing without them!

■ Add movements, gestures, and props when appropriate for the song and for the children. A too-heavy emphasis on gimmicks to teach a song is unnecessary if you have chosen a song that interests the children and is of an appropriate level of difficulty for them to learn. Added devices need to be thought of as "spices" and used as such: a few appropriately placed hand gestures in a song is like a dash of cinnamon in the applesauce. An entire routine of cute gestures and too many props adds too much "spice" to the recipe.

■ Include the new song in other areas of the curriculum by playing the song softly during center time or rest periods.

■ Introduce new books related to the song's topic in the language-arts area.

■ Include art activities related to the song's topic throughout the week's activities.

RHYTHM ACTIVITIES

In an early childhood program, one of a child's earliest musical experiences is clapping and moving to rhythmic music. The addition of **rhythm instruments** is

Each child approaches musical activities in his own way.

Leading the marching "band" is great fun.

another traditional practice in early childhood music programs. Young children, who love movement and motion in general, are naturally drawn to the use of rhythm instruments. Listening first to the music for its rhythmic pattern and then matching the beat with rhythm instruments is the most familiar method of introducing rhythm instruments. Having young children listen to the music and clap out the beat with their hands or tap it out with their feet is another appropriate, traditional rhythm activity.

Whenever rhythm instruments are added, they should have a specific purpose. Instruments are not used just to make "noise," but rather to enhance the activity. Instruments should be in good condition. Be sure children know the proper use of rhythm instruments before beginning any activities. Instruments may be hung on a pegboard or placed on a shelf within the child's easy reach.

Using rhythm instruments, children learn to listen for a pattern of sounds in the music. In beginning rhythm activities, it's a good idea to choose music with a clear, easy-to-hear beat or rhythm. Marches and many types of ethnic music are excellent choices for this strong beat.

Some children may have difficulty hearing rhythms and/or reproducing them. This can be handled in the same way you would handle a reluctant singer. Specifically, never force the child to copy your pattern or to use a rhythm instrument or practice this activity. Your emphasis should be on the child's natural enjoyment of music. Rhythm instruments may be made by the children as well as by the teacher. Using recycled materials, such as toweling rolls, pebbles, and spools can be yet another creative outlet for young children. (See Appendix E for suggestions on how to create rhythm instruments from recycled materials.)

MUSIC EXPERIENCES FOR OLDER CHILDREN

With children in the middle and upper elementary grades, teachers are able to offer a broader array of musical experiences for children.

One of the most basic experiences children of this age need to have is a broader experience with a variety of forms and styles of music. Students in this age group need to have even more listening experiences with the world's finest music including the classics, multi-cultural folk, and composed music. By the end of fifth grade, students should have been exposed to the main periods of music history and acquainted with composers and repertoire from each period.

Singing is an important classroom activity for children in the middle and upper elementary grades. Opportunities to sing in parts (harmony) or in rounds (like "Row, row, row your boat") are enjoyable musical experiences for children of this age. They are also able to sing simple melodies while reading a musical score. They are learning more about musical notation as well. For example, they can begin to recognize and understand what a whole note, half-note, and rest notations mean.

ACTIVITIES FOR CHILDREN

Musical Imaginations

GOALS: To help sharpen musical listening skills
To develop children's creativity

MATERIALS: Music on CD or tape

PREPARATION: Have children think of a small animal and a large animal. Divide the group into two smaller groups.

PROCEDURE:

1. Have one group be the small animals.
2. Have the other group be the large animals.
3. When you play music with high notes, have the small animals move and dance.
4. When you play music with low notes, have the large animals move and dance.

VARIATION:

■ Have the children draw or paint a picture of the large or small animals they played in the exercise above.

■ Have a child go to the piano or some other instrument and hit a high or low note. The children can show with their hands, arms, or body whether the note is high or low.

■ Reverse the groups, letting the small animal group become the large animal group and vice versa.

ACTIVITIES FOR CHILDREN

Name That Instrument!

GOALS: To encourage children's interest in music activities

To develop children's creativity

MATERIALS: Several rhythm instruments, pictures of these instruments

PREPARATION: Set up the music center with two chairs and tables separated by a divider that children can't see over.

PROCEDURE:

1. On one side of the divider, place several rhythm instruments on the table.
2. On the other side, place pictures of the instruments.
3. Have the child on one side play an instrument.
4. Have the child on the other side hold up a picture of the identified instrument.

VARIATION:

■ Have a child play a rhythm instrument such as a bell, tambourine, drum, triangle, or wood block. Have another child close his eyes and identify the object played.

■ Play two sounds, and have the children identify them. The number of sounds can gradually be increased to see how many can be identified at once.

■ Listen for the sound of a bell, drum, and so on from some specific position in the room. Have the children close their eyes and identify where the sound came from. They might also identify the instrument and tell whether the tone was loud or soft.

ACTIVITIES FOR CHILDREN

Games with Music

GOALS: To encourage children's interest in music activities

To develop children's creativity

MATERIALS: Chairs for "Musical Chairs," one less than the number in the group playing, and a CD or tape of music to play

PREPARATION: Arrange chairs in a line.

PROCEDURE:

1. Have the children walk around the chairs while the music is playing.
2. When the music stops, have the children sit down in chairs.
3. Identify the child without a chair as "out."
4. Remove one chair, and start the music again.
5. Continue playing until only one child is left for the remaining one chair.

VARIATION:

■ Musical games can focus on voice recognition. Challenge children to guess who is humming the song or who sang the last verse.

■ Let the children who are "out" accompany the musical with rhythm instruments or by clapping to the beat.

ACTIVITIES FOR CHILDREN

Where Is the Bell?

GOALS: To develop children's musical listening skills

To encourage children's interest in music activities

MATERIALS: Two or three little bells

PREPARATION: Seat the children in a circle. Have one child leave the room. This child is "it."

PROCEDURE:

1. Give one of the children in the room a bell which is small enough to hide in his hand.

2. Ask the child who left the room to come back in.

3. When the child has returned, have all of the children stand and shake their fists above their heads.

4. Give the child who is "it" three chances to locate the child holding the bell.

5. Have the child holding the bell who is correctly identified become "it."

VARIATION: Use more than one bell when the children become accustomed to the game.

ACTIVITIES FOR CHILDREN

Mime and Music

GOALS: To encourage children's interest in music activities

To develop children's creativity

MATERIALS: Flash cards with words for objects, actions, sensations, and emotions, CD or tape of music

PREPARATION: Make flash cards. Some examples are "wash a dog," "hot," and "spaghetti." If children are not reading yet, use pictures instead.

PROCEDURE:

1. Play some music.

2. After 30 seconds or so, hold up one of the cards.

3. Have the children do whatever movements the words and music suggest to them.

VARIATION:

■ Have the children make up their own flash cards for this activity.

■ Have the children draw or make a painting or three-dimensional object of their experience with this activity.

ACTIVITIES FOR CHILDREN Making Tambourines

GOALS: To encourage children's interest in music activities
To tie in art with music activities

MATERIALS: Egg cartons, bottle caps, tape, crayons, markers, paint, and brushes

PREPARATION: Discuss what a tambourine is. Show the children one and let them shake it.

PROCEDURE:

1. Put a few bottle caps in each egg carton space.

2. Tape the carton closed.

3. Have the children decorate the egg carton as desired.

VARIATION:

■ Use a margarine tube or yogurt container to make tambourines.

■ Have the children use their tambourines in rhythm activities.

ACTIVITIES FOR CHILDREN Visual Aids and Music Activities

GOALS: To encourage children's interest in music activities
To tie in language arts with music activities

MATERIALS: Pictures of key characters for flannel board, puppets

PREPARATION: Choose a song such as "Farmer in the Dell" that has several familiar characters. Draw or cut out pictures of key characters. Glue pieces of felt to the back of the characters to use on the felt board.

PROCEDURE:

1. As children sing the song, have one child put up the character they are singing about.

2. Continue singing the song.

3. Have the children continue putting up the characters until the song is finished.

VARIATION:

■ Use puppets to accompany a song. If you're shy, this will help you, as children can't help but focus on the puppet and not you!

■ Make finger puppets to use with a song. Have the children use their puppets as they sing the song.

ADDITIONAL INFORMATION: Keep a list of songs on hand you have taught the children, as they really enjoy singing old favorites, and it's easy to forget which songs they know. You may want to post the list with some associated picture words so that the children can choose their favorites.

ACTIVITIES FOR CHILDREN

Music—Your Servant

GOALS: To use music throughout the day

To encourage children's musical listening skills

MATERIALS: None required

PREPARATION: Make a list of children's favorite songs.

PROCEDURE:

1. Use music throughout the day.

2. When children are waiting in the classroom for your turn to join the cafeteria line, sing one of the children's favorite songs.

3. When children are waiting for each other to get their coats on, sing one of their favorite songs.

4. When children are waiting for others to finish cleanup, sing a favorite song.

VARIATION: Have the children choose the songs they want to sing in the "waiting" times of the day.

ACTIVITIES FOR CHILDREN

Paper Towel Flutes

GOALS: To encourage children's interest in music activities

To use recycled materials for music activities

To develop children's creativity

MATERIALS: Paper towel or tissue paper rolls, crayons, markers, and stickers

PREPARATION: Give each child a paper towel or tissue roll.

PROCEDURE:

1. Have the children decorate a roll with crayons, markers, and stickers.

2. Have the children use their "flutes" to "hum along" to a song.

VARIATION: Make a "hummer" from a cardboard roll. Fasten a piece of waxed paper over one end of the tube. Humming through the waxed paper is fun. Be sure to change the paper after each use.

ACTIVITIES FOR CHILDREN

Taping Children's Singing

GOALS: To encourage children's singing
To develop children's interest in music activities

MATERIALS: Tape recorder, cassette tape

PREPARATION: Tape the children singing a song.

PROCEDURE:

1. Put the tape in the listening center for the children to enjoy (with earphones or without).

2. Play the tape during your next musical activity session.

3. Re-tape the next version—with rhythm instruments.

VARIATION:

■ Re-tape another version with a "solo" performance by one of the children.

■ Re-tape with a version of the children's choice.

ACTIVITIES FOR OLDER CHILDREN

Weather and Music
(Grades 4–5)

GOALS: To encourage children's interest in music
To develop children's creativity

MATERIALS: None required

PREPARATION: Discuss weather, especially thunderstorms.

PROCEDURE:

1. Plan and perform a thunderstorm using different dynamic levels.

2. Use voices (choral reading).

3. Select instruments to create the storm.

4. Have students perform "the storm" as it was created and then gradually fade the sounds away.

VARIATION:

■ Make masks to accompany "the storm."

■ Draw or paint a picture of the storm.

ACTIVITIES FOR OLDER CHILDREN Musical Creations
(Grades 4–5)

GOALS: To tie in art with music activities

MATERIALS: Art supplies to create works of arts, such as crayons, markers, paint, brushes, clay, and play dough

PREPARATION: Have the children create their own works of art—drawings, paintings, collages, sculptures, or whatever they wish.

PROCEDURE:
1. Have each child select sounds for his or her work of art.
2. Let the children serve as composers/conductors for their own pieces.
3. Have each child share the sounds related to his or her artwork.

VARIATION:
- Allow children to make up orchestras with their classmates. Then have them perform their works of art.
- Use artwork that the children have already created in another activity or in another art activity.

ADDITIONAL INFORMATION: Student's musical interpretations may require sounds that can't be created with normal means. Rather than suggesting that they abandon their ideas, ask them to describe in detail the sounds that they have in mind. Discuss how these sounds might be produced. With today's technology, many sounds can be manufactured electronically.

ACTIVITIES FOR OLDER CHILDREN What-Not Box
(Grades 4–5)

GOALS: To encourage children's interest in music activities
To develop children's creativity

MATERIALS: Box, collection of unrelated objects of teacher's or students' choice

PREPARATION: Place the unrelated objects in the box.

PROCEDURE:
1. Using the objects and the children's imagination, improvise a brief musical performance.
2. Have the children work in groups of five or six.
3. Have the children select objects from the What-Not Box and think of a plot that includes one familiar song with a sung conversation.
4. Have the children include dancing or creative movement in their performance. The challenge is for the children to weave each object chosen from the What-Not Box into the story line.
5. Allow the performance to be about five minutes in length.

VARIATION:
- Have the students use improvised sounds to accompany the vocal lines.
- Tape the performances. Listen to the tapes, then draw a picture or make a painting representing one of the performances.

ACTIVITIES FOR OLDER CHILDREN Musical Mural
(Grades 4–5)

GOALS: To develop children's thoughts and feelings about music
To develop children's musical imaginations

MATERIALS: CD or tape of *Peter and the Wolf,* large pieces of paper, crayons, markers, paint, brushes, paste, construction paper, and scissors

PREPARATION: Play the music of *Peter and the Wolf.* Discuss major episodes of the music, such as Peter in the woods, Peter seeing the wolf, and so on.

PROCEDURE:

1. Assign children particular scenes of the story to use for making panels of the mural.
2. Have the children flesh out the details of the story through visual elements (color, shape, perspective, and line).

3. Draw their attention to musical aspects which help tell the story (volume, speed, and use of instruments).

VARIATION: Divide the class into groups. Have each group paint a picture based on another piece of music, such as *Pinocchio, Pocahontas, Sleeping Beauty Ballet,* or *The Nutcracker Suite.*

ADDITIONAL INFORMATION: This activity encourages active listening. Help the children listen by asking questions like:

■ What story do they hear in the music?
■ Do they all hear similar stories?
■ How does the story they see in their mind match the actual title of the music?
■ What do they think the composer had in mind?

ACTIVITIES FOR OLDER CHILDREN Art and Music
(Grades 4–5)

GOALS: To tie in art with music
To develop children's interest in music activities

MATERIALS: Art prints of your choice

PREPARATION: Give children time to look at the art print

PROCEDURE:

1. Ask the children what they see.
2. If they name things that can move or are shown in motion, let them show the movement(s) with their hands.
3. If they name things that make sounds, let them produce these sound(s) with their hands, mouths, voices, or an instrument.
4. Repeat this procedure for all the things they see.

VARIATION:

■ Play the work of art. Find out which parts children think they should play alone, as solos, and which parts they want to play together, in chorus.
■ Ask them in what order they think they should play the parts.
■ Act as a conductor for the first performance, then allow a series of students to take that role.
■ Have the conductor choose from all of the sounds the ones he wants to use to represent each visual element.
■ Conduct the piece more than once if necessary to achieve the effects they desire.

CHAPTER 12

CREATIVE LANGUAGE EXPERIENCES

DEVELOPMENT OF LANGUAGE

Language is part of a child's total development. As with physical growth, there is a definite developmental pattern to a child's use of language. There are four distinct skills involved in the development of language: speaking, listening, writing, and reading. Each of these, in turn, has its own pattern of development.

Ability in one language skill is not always directly related to competence in another. For example, many young children are far better speakers than listeners!

In the early childhood program, language experiences must take into consideration the developmental levels of children in each of these four distinct parts of language development. Emphasis in the early childhood program, however, is *not* on teaching writing and reading. Developing skills that are *related* to reading and writing help prepare a child for more formal instruction in these skills in later years. While this chapter focuses on the development of language skills in the early years, activities and resources are provided for older children where appropriate.

LANGUAGE DEVELOPMENT DURING PLAY

When children move freely to activities of their choice in a child-centered environment, more language is used with greater richness of speech than when children are in classrooms where formal instruction dominates the program. When children discover they can satisfy their needs by speaking, they gain confidence in their abilities to speak and begin to value language.

Interaction is an important part of communication. Children speak and listen as they play with clay, dough, paint, pegs, blocks, sand, and water. If they feel comfortable when they talk, they are more likely to experiment with language. In a housekeeping area, children talk to each other as they re-enact familiar roles. Formal or informal midday snack arrangements provide natural settings for conversations. Such activities as playing with blocks, pounding and rolling clay, experimenting with magnets, all offer children rich opportunities to speak, listen, and exchange ideas with others.

LANGUAGE DEVELOPMENT IN SMALL-GROUP PLAY

In small groups children are more likely to talk to each other and to the teacher and have less anxiety than when they are expected to respond in large groups.

Formal discussion periods are neither as interesting nor as meaningful as informal conversations in a small group. A child who takes a treasured item out of his pocket to share with two or three friends is probably enjoying a very personal experience. But when "Show and Tell" time is made into a daily ritual in which many children are expected to participate, the personal excitement may disappear for the speaker.

DEVELOPMENT OF LISTENING

Good listening involves receiving and processing incoming information. Listening is more than simply

High-quality children's books are an integral part of the language arts curriculum.

Acting out the story with a puppet is a fun way for young children to experience a children's book.

hearing because good listeners filter out much of what they hear in order to concentrate on a message.

Children are not the only ones who should listen and teachers are not the only speakers. Rather, children *and* teachers need to be good listeners, and children should listen to one another as carefully as they do to adults.

Young children may *act* as if they understand concepts at a level that they cannot yet express in words. Because young children think in simple, basic ways, they have difficulty understanding adult language that is abstract or too complex. Abstraction is beyond the thinking capabilities of the young child in preschool and early elementary years. The adult who is not aware of these language limitations of young children can easily lose children's attention. A teacher who directs a child pulling another's hair to "be nice" is too general and abstract in her directions. A more appropriate, direct, and less abstract request for a young child would be, "Don't pull Jane's hair."

LANGUAGE EXPERIENCES—POETRY AND CHILDREN'S BOOKS

Poetry is an excellent language experience for young children. Exposure to poetry raises children's level of general language development and vocabulary development and whets their appetite for reading, too!

Some other benefits of including poetry on a regular basis in the early childhood program include:

■ Fingerplays, or poems recited and accompanied by appropriate body movements, help develop coordination and muscle tone. Asking children to invent

their own movements helps them develop their creativity.

■ Acting out poetry can be a fun and beneficial creative activity for children of all ages. By allowing children to organize and act out poems using props and costumes, the teacher encourages the development of creativity and positive self-concept as well as of language.

■ Children can be encouraged to illustrate their favorite poems to display in the classroom or to take home, thus stimulating artistic expression and development while aiding language development.

■ Learning to recite short poems gives children a real sense of competence and self-confidence.

HINTS FOR CHOOSING POEMS

Using poetry in the classroom will, of course, be much more valuable and enjoyable if the poems are chosen with the children's interests and needs in mind. Not all children have the same needs. And by no means are all children at the same developmental level. Choose poetry that meets all developmental levels in the group.

Don't forget that it's also important that the teacher should like the poem, too. A teacher can't generate much enthusiasm for a poem if she doesn't enjoy it herself.

Here are some hints for choosing poems.

■ When selecting poems, think about what the children are likely to find appealing. From approximately three to six years old, young children like things that seem relevant to them. Relevant means it must somehow relate to the world as they know it. Select poetry about familiar objects, events, and feelings.

■ Focus on popular topics. These are some subjects that almost all young children enjoy: self-awareness, the senses, the family, feelings, transportation, seasons, holidays, animals, plants, water, earth, and sky. By selecting poems that deal with these subjects as they are being emphasized in class, you can capitalize on the interest generated by other classroom activities: science, social studies, music, and so on.

CHILDREN'S BOOKS

Children's books are a traditional part of the language arts program in most early childhood programs. These books must be chosen with care for young children's use. They must be right for the developmental level of the child. The pictures should be easily seen; the story easily understood by young listeners.

THIS ONE'S FOR YOU   Mother Goose Is Back in Style

Mother Goose, it seems, really does matter. Buried in the nonsensical couplets chanted by generations of children is the link to understanding syllable and phonemes, the building blocks to literacy.

A slew of studies since the mid-1980s has shown that rhymes directly contribute to a child's vocabulary and understanding of language. To recognize that two words rhyme is to know something about the sounds that make up words. Learning to recognize the word "clean," for example, helps children learn new words like "lean" and "mean."

The better children are at detecting rhymes, the quicker and more successful is their reading progress—a relationship that holds true in dozens of studies despite children's IQs or social backgrounds. Research on children with reading difficulties has found that many struggling readers are strikingly insensitive to rhyme.

"When children rhyme, it really draws attention to the fact that words have parts," said Sally Shaywitz, a professor of pediatrics and a brain researcher at Yale University. "When most of us hear a word, we don't pay attention to the fact that even a simple word like *cat* has three sounds: kkkk/aaaa/tttt. When you rhyme the last part of a word, you are realizing a distinct part of the word and what the sound is. In order to read, you also have to appreciate that words are made up of different sounds. It's really the same ability. It's learning to break the code." (Farrell, 1999)

This deeper understanding of the power of rhymes has prompted a revival among reading experts for Mother Goose, that collection of English childhood rhymes, jingles, songs, and riddles that originated centuries ago.

It's why rhymes are dubbed "essential" for young children, ages 3 and 4, in a joint statement for parents issued in 1999 by the National Association for the Education of Young Children and the International Reading Association.

What you have to do with Mother Goose is to lift the words off the pages of the book. Just reading a rhyme in a book with a child is not nearly as much fun as when you know the rhymes and use them as part of your daily life. You're diapering a child or riding in the car with your preschooler and doing "one, two, buckle my shoe." Then it's fun, it's alive. If you love it, your child will like it. If you read in a dull, boring way, your child won't relate to it. It's all in the presentation (Farrell).

But how much Mother Goose does anybody truly remember? A recent study by a Pennsylvania researcher suggests that nursery rhymes are part of a dying tradition, with few—if any—passed on to young children.

Beth Goldstone, an assistant professor of education at Beaver College in Glenside, PA, surveyed 150 preschoolers in a Philadelphia suburb and found that more than a third did not know *Jack Be Nimble, Hey Diddle Diddle,* or *Little Miss Muffet,* among others.

Kindergarten teachers often expect children to have that kind of background and too often the children don't. Mother Goose is one of the foundations of our language. She also plays a role in creating a community of knowledge. It's essential for children to hear those rhymes.

So Mother Goose is definitely back in style for young children!

Children learn their alphabet in many different ways.

See the "Food for Thought" box below for guidelines on what to look for in choosing books for children.

HINTS FOR THE BOOK CENTER

Create a place where children can explore the world of books. A library or book center is an important part of every early childhood classroom as well as elementary classrooms. As you use books during circle time, children will realize the "magic" of books, that they have good make-believe stories or are full of facts and have pretty pictures. Children will then want to explore those books on their own, so they need to have a well-organized place where they can go and read.

Here are some hints on organizing the book center.

■ Be sure the book center is away from the more "active" goings-on in the room, a place where the child can quietly explore books.

■ Take time to decorate the nearby bulletin boards or tops of shelves with book jackets, pictures, flowers, and special collections related to the books you have in the book center.

■ Place certain kinds of books on the shelves so that they are readily available at all times—Mother Goose books; poetry books; a children's simple encyclopedia (there are some two- and three-volume sets); "sense" books where children can touch, scratch, and smell as they look; some of the classic stories with

FOOD FOR THOUGHT

What to Look for in Children's Books

Children today live in an exciting media-driven time of television, video games, and computers. Yet, no medium can stir a child's imagination like the pages of a good book. There is an enormous selection of children's books available today. The following are some general guidelines on what to look for in choosing children's books from preschool through grade 5.

BABY BOOKS

There are four basic kinds of baby books.

1. board books which are made with sturdy cardboard pages that can be wiped clean
2. touch and feel books which have cloth, feathers, fur, and familiar "feely" things attached to them for little ones to discover
3. cloth books which are made of safe, washable material
4. bath books which are constructed of soft, durable plastic and can take a lot of abuse

What to look for.

■ Simple text and art.
■ Repetition and bouncy rhymes.

(Continued)

■ Bright and familiar photos or artwork. There should be a connection between baby's surroundings and the book's pictures.

■ A sturdy book that can handle many spills.

■ Rounded corners for safety.

■ A book the right size and shape for little hands.

■ A book you will enjoy as well. Baby will recognize your enjoyment.

PRESCHOOL

Preschool books are on a higher level than baby books, but on a slightly lower level than picture books. In addition to hardcover and paperback, preschool books come in a variety of novelty formats. Among them are

■ lift-the-flap books which have sturdy pages and flaps to lift that reveal hidden words or pictures

■ pop-up books which have paper-engineered pages that make pictures three dimensional

■ pull-tab books which have tabs to pull to change the pictures

Some books combine all of these features. These kinds of books are designed to be played with as much as to be read—yet another way to show that books are fun.

What to look for in preschool books.

■ a book that clearly covers the concept you are trying to teach

■ a book that helps develop the child's sense of humor

■ an easy and fun story line

■ clear and easy-to-read books

■ colorful, high-quality illustrations

■ illustrations that a child can connect with her own life and situation

PICTURE BOOKS

Picture books are one of the most popular forms of children's books, and are appropriate for a wide range of ages and reading levels. Picture books have varying amounts of art and text (some are even wordless). Some story lines are simple, while others are quite complex. Subjects can be beautiful, funny, moving, scary, or just plain silly. What is important is that you find a picture book the children in your life will relate to and enjoy.

What to look for:

■ art or photography the child responds to

■ story lines that elicit questions and discussions

■ stories that develop the child's sense of humor

■ stories that help with children's issues—such as sibling rivalry, or going to school

■ stories you enjoyed as a child and would like to share with children

■ titles recommended by reviewers and award committees

EARLY READERS

These books are designed to supplement a child's reading program at school. As with picture books, early readers cover a wide variety of subjects. They are illustrated, though the emphasis is more on text than on illustrations. Early readers are targeted toward specific reading levels, or by grade. As every child is different, you may wish to judge on your own which reading level is appropriate.

What to look for:

■ a reading level that will challenge but will not intimidate the child

■ clear text (the print size varies with reading levels)

(Continued)

- a topic that will stimulate further interest in reading
- favorite artists the child has enjoyed at an earlier level of reading
- nonfiction subjects the child enjoys, such as sports, history, fantasy, or adventure
- new subjects to introduce the child to, such as fantasy and folklore

FICTION

When we enter the world of fiction, we leave behind colorful pictures and favorite characters, and subject matter becomes more complicated. The early readers are the stepping stones to these more advanced works.

What to look for:

- Books with a reading level that will challenge and stimulate.
- Books with a subject that interests the young reader. Many children want to pick out their own books at this age.
- Some of the more popular and enduring titles are available in different editions. The trim size of the books may vary, and the cover art may vary as well, but almost without exception the text remains the same.
- Some classic tales in abridged formats.

ACTIVITIES FOR CHILDREN Name Games

GOALS: To build sensitivity to the sounds of language

To encourage the development of children's vocabulary

MATERIALS: Rhythm sticks, drums, or triangles

PREPARATION: Show children how you can clap out the rhythm of children's names: Ste'pha'nie', Rich'ard', Al'li'son'.

PROCEDURE:

1. Have the children use rhythm sticks, drums, or triangles to follow the beat of their names.
2. Let the children take turns leading the group in following the beat of names.

VARIATION: Have the children step, jump, hop, or slide to the rhythm of their names.

ACTIVITIES FOR CHILDREN

Outdoor Language Experiences

GOALS: To encourage awareness of the printed word

To develop children's interest in language

MATERIALS: Teacher or commercial-made traffic signs

PREPARATION: Place traffic signs on tricycle paths.

PROCEDURE:

1. Have the children follow traffic signs while riding their trikes.

2. Have the children take turns being a "police person" on the tricycle path.

VARIATION:

■ Encourage children's language experiences by having charts of instructions in the classroom. For example, the work bench can have rebus (picture) charts to describe something to build. Animal cages and insect containers can have picture instructions for care.

■ Seed packages can be used to label plants in the garden, create graphs of plant growth, and gather and label collections of nature objects.

ACTIVITIES FOR CHILDREN

Recycled Materials for Language Experiences— Mail Order Catalogs

GOALS: To encourage children's language development

MATERIALS: Collection of mail order catalogs, paste, paper, and scissors

PREPARATION: Be sure to screen all catalogs first for any inappropriate pictures.

PROCEDURE:

1. Have the children use catalogs to find beginning sounds.

2. Have the children tear (or cut out with scissors) all objects with that beginning sound.

3. Have the children paste objects onto paper in a collage of that beginning sound.

VARIATION: Use catalogs to find categories of colors, objects, or any other basic language concept.

ACTIVITIES FOR CHILDREN

Purse Story

GOALS: To encourage children's language development

To develop children's creativity and imagination

MATERIALS: Old pocketbooks, and assorted items such as tickets, keys, lists, snacks, makeup, combs, and so on

PREPARATION: Have the children examine the contents of the purse.

PROCEDURE:

1. After examining the contents of the purse, have the child tell about the owner.
2. Write down the list of the child's ideas.

VARIATION:

■ Draw pictures of how the owner of the purse might look.

■ Tape stories about the owner.

ACTIVITIES FOR CHILDREN

Original Picture Books

GOALS: To encourage children's interest in books

To encourage children's language development

MATERIALS: Photos from events throughout the year, self-sticking photo album

PREPARATION: Photograph events throughout the year.

PROCEDURE:

1. Have the children use photos to tell stories.
2. Older children may write their stories. Younger children may dictate their stories for the adult to write.
3. Place the photos and the children's stories in the album.
4. Make the album a permanent part of the book corner.

VARIATION: Have the children tape stories about the photos, recalling the events and how they felt about the event. Place these with the album to listen to as they "read" the stories.

ACTIVITIES FOR CHILDREN — Poem of the Week

GOALS: To encourage children's interest in poetry
To encourage children's language development

MATERIALS: Large newsprint, markers, and pictures for the poem chosen

PREPARATION: Choose a poem that the children will enjoy.

PROCEDURE:

1. Use large newsprint to print the poem of your choice.
2. Use illustrations.
3. Use pictures for words in the poem.
4. Have children point to the pictures when you read the poem to them.

VARIATION:

■ Have children draw or paint a picture about the poem.
■ Act out parts of the poem.

ACTIVITIES FOR CHILDREN — Cluster Poems

GOALS: To encourage children's interest in poetry
To encourage children's language development

MATERIALS: Book of poems for children

PREPARATION: Select a subject of interest to the children. Examples include animals, seasons, and weather.

PROCEDURE:

1. Read several poems, each by a different poet.
2. See if the children like one more than another.
3. Have them talk about why.

VARIATION:

■ Have the children draw or paint pictures of their favorite poem.
■ Locate a short piece of music to play as background music while you read poems to the children.

ACTIVITIES FOR CHILDREN

Rhyming Nonsense

GOALS: To encourage children's rhyming of words
To encourage children's interest in poetry

MATERIALS: Paper, markers

PREPARATION: Discuss rhyming words with children. Have them give examples of words that rhyme.

PROCEDURE:

1. Have the children make up a poem using rhyming words of their choice. The words do *not* have to make sense.

2. Write the words on paper for the child.

VARIATION:

■ Have the children draw or paint a picture of their poem.

■ Have the children act out the poem.

ACTIVITIES FOR CHILDREN

Descriptive Poem

GOALS: To encourage children's interest in words
To encourage development of language skills

MATERIALS: Large pieces of paper, markers, and crayons

PREPARATION: Talk with the children about subjects they like. Examples include animals, food, people, and so on.

PROCEDURE:

1. Have the child give two words that tell something about the subject. For example, cat—furry, soft; broccoli—green, yucky.

2. Write down the subject and the words the child used to describe it.

VARIATION:

■ Have the child draw a picture representing the subject and the descriptive words.

■ Make a collage using materials of various textures and colors.

ACTIVITIES FOR CHILDREN

Noisy Story

GOALS: To develop listening skills
To encourage children's language development

MATERIALS: Cards with noisy words on them

PREPARATION: Write a noisy word on each card such as PEEP, BANG, BUZZ, and ROAR.

PROCEDURE:

1. Give each child a card, considering the child's individual reading ability. Or, you may tell the child what the word is.
2. Select one child as leader to begin the noisy story.
3. Have the leader use the noisy word on his or her card.
4. Have the other children take turns in adding to the story, using the words on their cards. The story is complete when all children have had a turn.

VARIATION:

■ Use other groups of words for this activity such as action words, animal words, people words, toy words, and so on.

■ Expand the game to include writing the story, illustrating the story, and acting the story out.

ACTIVITIES FOR CHILDREN

Who Is That?

GOALS: To develop children's listening skills
To encourage children's language development

MATERIALS: Tape recorder

PREPARATION: Tape voices, such as radio and television voices, as well as people the children know.

PROCEDURE:

1. Play the voices for the children.
2. Have the children identify the voices.

VARIATION: Tape singers, news announcers, political figures, comedians, cartoon characters, and movie stars.

ACTIVITIES FOR CHILDREN

Where Is the Bell?

GOALS: To develop children's listening skills

MATERIALS: Bells small enough to hide in a child's hand

PREPARATION: Seat children in a circle.

PROCEDURE:

1. Have one child leave the room.
2. Give one of the children in the circle a bell to hide in one hand.
3. When the child has returned, have all of the children stand and shake their hands above their heads.
4. Give the child three chances to guess who has the bell.

VARIATION: Use more than one bell when the children's listening skills improve.

ACTIVITIES FOR CHILDREN

Are You Listening?

GOALS: To develop children's listening skills
To encourage children's language development

MATERIALS: Eight margarine tubs with plastic lids; different materials, such as flour, buttons, nails, and pins

PREPARATION: Fill two tubs with the same material; for example, fill two with flour, two with buttons, two with nails, and two with pins.

PROCEDURE:

1. Have the child shake one tub.
2. Have the child shake other tubs until he finds a matching sound.

VARIATION: Make a collage with the materials.

ACTIVITIES FOR CHILDREN

Whose Voice Is It?

GOAL: To develop listening skills

MATERIALS: None required

PREPARATION: Form a circle of several children. Blindfold one child or have the child cover her eyes.

PROCEDURE:

1. Have the blindfolded child stand in the middle of the group.

2. Regroup the children so each will be in a different place in the circle.

3. Have each child make a simple statement such as, "I like to play games."

4. Have the child in the center point to one child and identify this child or ask questions (up to three) that must be answered in a sentence.

5. If the child who is "it" guesses correctly or fails to after three times, "it" returns to the circle and another child becomes "it."

ACTIVITIES FOR CHILDREN

Tape That

GOALS: To develop listening skills
 To encourage children's language development

MATERIALS: Tape recorder

PREPARATION: Tape a story all of the children have read, but make some mistakes, such as changing words here and there.

PROCEDURE:

1. Play the tape for the children.

2. Have the children pick out the errors.

3. Have the children give the correct version.

VARIATION: Have the children tape their versions of popular stories with some mistakes. Use their tapes for this exercise.

ACTIVITIES FOR CHILDREN

Character Collage

GOALS: To encourage children's language development

To develop children's creative language skills

MATERIALS: Magazines, catalogs, paper, scissors, paste, or glue

PREPARATION: Talk with the children about a book you have recently read together. Have the children choose their favorite character.

PROCEDURE:

1. Have the children make their favorite character the subject of a picture collage.

2. Have the children think about the character as they go through the magazines, cutting (or tearing as the case may be) out pictures that in some way remind them of the character.

3. After the collage is finished, have the children make up stories about their pictures.

VARIATION: Have the children tape their stories about their favorite character collages.

ADDITIONAL INFORMATION: An example of this activity would be a Winnie-the-Pooh collage, which might include pictures of a honey jar, a teddy bear, and someone looking thoughtful, because Pooh always sits and thinks before he does anything!

ACTIVITIES FOR CHILDREN

I Can Read Pictures

GOALS: To encourage children's language development

To practice looking at pictures for meaning

MATERIALS: Some picture books

PREPARATION: Have the children look at each picture in the book.

PROCEDURE:

1. Ask the children how much they can learn about the characters without reading any of the words to them.

2. Read the story to the children. Do the words and pictures agree?

VARIATION:

■ Have the children make up a different story to go with the pictures.

■ Draw or paint pictures of the story.

■ Make a 3-dimensional model of one of the characters in the story.

ACTIVITIES FOR CHILDREN

Moving to your Name

GOALS: To develop children's understanding of syllables/parts of their names

To encourage children's language development

MATERIALS: None required

PREPARATION: Discuss syllables as parts of names. Use several of the children's names for examples: John-ny is two syllables, Bet-ty Ann is three syllables, and so forth.

PROCEDURE:

1. Seat the children on the floor.
2. Call on one child at a time at first to demonstrate. The other children can be thinking during this time.
3. Ask the child to count the number of syllables/parts in his first name; for example, Johnny would be two: John-ny.
4. Have the child clap his hands to the parts of his first name; for example, John-ny would be two claps, one clap for "John," and another clap for "ny."
5. Continue with the children counting the syllables and then clapping the syllables of their names.

VARIATION:

■ Clap your hands to the parts of your first and last name.

■ Step in place to the parts of your first and last name, taking one step for each syllable.

■ Jump around the room, one jump for every syllable of your name.

■ Make up a movement for each syllable of your name.

ACTIVITIES FOR CHILDREN

What's Happening Here?

GOALS: To encourage children's ability to read pictures

To develop children's creativity

MATERIALS: Paper, markers

PREPARATION: Draw simple stick figures doing something interesting or cut action pictures out of old magazines and newspapers.

PROCEDURE:

1. Give each child one of the pictures and ask, "What's happening here?"
2. After looking at the picture, have the child name what she sees.
3. Have the children go on and make a sentence about the picture.

VARIATION: Have the children draw their own picture describing what they see in their own way.

ACTIVITIES FOR CHILDREN

Nursery Rhyme Activity

GOALS: To develop listening skills

To encourage development of language skills

MATERIALS: Book of simple nursery rhymes with pictures

PREPARATION: Have the children sit on the floor.

PROCEDURE:

1. Begin with a familiar short nursery rhyme, such as *Jack Be Nimble,* or *Old Mother Hubbard.*

2. Have the children help you tell nursery rhymes. "I will tell you a nursery rhyme and then I want you to tell it."

3. Tell the nursery rhyme; then repeat the first word or two ("Jack be . . .") and ask the children to say the rest.

4. Continue stopping and having the children say the rest of the rhyme until it is finished.

5. Let the children choose a nursery rhyme and repeat the process.

ACTIVITIES FOR CHILDREN

Musical Letters

GOALS: To encourage letter recognition

To encourage children's language development

MATERIALS: Squares of paper with large letters written on them, CD or tape of music

PREPARATION: Arrange the letter squares in two large circles.

PROCEDURE:

1. To music, have the children walk around in a circle outside the letters.

2. Have the children stop beside the nearest letter when the music stops.

3. Have the children tell the name of the letter and name a word starting with that letter. Older children can spell the word starting with that letter.

4. Remove a letter each time, so that there will be one fewer letter than the number of children in the game (like musical chairs).

ACTIVITIES FOR OLDER CHILDREN   Fun Book Reports
(Grades 4–5)

GOALS: To encourage development of language skills

MATERIALS: Paper, pencils, crayons, markers, paint, and brushes

PREPARATION: Have the children read the assigned book.

PROCEDURE:
Suggest the following as some fun ways for children to do book reports:

1. Choose a friend who has read the same book. Have a debate about it.
2. Illustrate a mural explaining the sequences of the book.
3. Act out or pantomime scenes from the book.
4. Develop a brochure advertising the book.
5. Give the report in riddle form; have the class guess what book the report is on.
6. Make up comic strips showing the story content.

VARIATION:
■ Write the report as a newspaper article.
■ Write the report as an advertisement for television.

ACTIVITIES FOR OLDER CHILDREN   Reversibles
(Grades 4–5)

GOALS: To develop children's vocabulary
To encourage children's language development

MATERIALS: Paper, pencils

PREPARATION: Explain that reversible words have different meanings when they are turned about; for example "understand" and "stand under."

PROCEDURE:
1. Have the children write or tell sentences for six pairs of reversibles.
2. Use the sentences in a way to show their differences.

VARIATION:
■ Add illustrations of the reversibles.
■ Use spelling words for this activity.
■ Work with a partner to develop lists of reversibles.

ADDITIONAL INFORMATION: Here are some reversibles to begin the activity: understudy, study under; overcome, come over; indoors, doors in; outgoing, going out; overdone, done over; overturn, turn over; withhold, hold with; instill, still in.

ACTIVITIES FOR OLDER CHILDREN Solutions
(Grades 4–5)

GOALS: To encourage children's interest in writing

To encourage children's language development

MATERIALS: Separate strips of paper, marker, paper, and pencils

PREPARATION: On separate paper strips, write a series of problems. Some examples may include: lost my door key, scared to give my book report, came to school late, tore my jeans, and so on.

PROCEDURE:

1. Post one of the problems on a bulletin board.

2. Working in small groups, have the children discuss how to respond to and/or solve the problem.

3. Have the groups present and defend their responses.

4. Guide the groups in considering other responses and solutions.

VARIATION:

■ Write stories about the problem and its solution.

■ Have the children make up other problem situations to solve.

ACTIVITIES FOR OLDER CHILDREN Reading Pictures
(Grades 4–5)

GOALS: To practice writing skills

To encourage children's language development

MATERIALS: Magazines, scissors

PREPARATION: Have students clip magazine photos that show feeling.

PROCEDURE:

1. Show one of the photos to a group.

2. Have them brainstorm the feelings shown in the photo.

3. Write what occurred just before the photo was taken.

4. Write the dialogue when the photo was taken.

5. Write a caption for the photo.

VARIATION: Use photos from *National Geographic*. Have the students describe the weather and location. Tell what happened after the picture was taken, what will happen one day later, or what will happen one week later.

ACTIVITIES FOR OLDER CHILDREN
(Grades 4–5)

Pantomime—Homophones—Can You Believe It?

GOALS: To develop understanding of homophone words

To encourage children's language development

MATERIALS: Large piece of paper, marker

PREPARATION: Design a homophone word list with the children. Explain/review that homophones are words that *sound alike,* but are *spelled differently* and have a *different meaning.*

PROCEDURE:

1. Have the children form a circle.

2. Call out a word and have the children pantomime a meaning for that word.

3. Call out the homophone and have the children pantomime that meaning.

ADDITIONAL INFORMATION: Try using the following words in this exercise: ant/aunt; bear/bare; board/bored; buy/bye; clothes/close; eight/ate; flour/flower; grate/great; hear/here; knight/night; lends/lens; marry/merry; prints/prince; ring/wring; shoe/shoo; tow/toe; we/wee; yolk/yoke.

ACTIVITIES FOR OLDER CHILDREN
(Grades 4–5)

Writing Stories

GOALS: To develop writing skills

To develop children's creativity

MATERIALS: Three to six pictures which may or may not be related; examples may include illustrations from favorite books, pictures of expressive faces, action photos, or art prints; paper, and pencils

PREPARATION: Show the children the three to six pictures in a series.

PROCEDURE:

1. Have the children make up a story based on what they see.

2. Share the stories orally.

3. Change the order of the pictures.

4. Have the children make up a new story to go with the pictures.

VARIATION:

■ Have the children dramatize their stories.

■ Have the children paint a picture or make a drawing of the story.

which children are already familiar, such as *Goldilocks and the Three Bears, The Little Engine That Could, The Three Little Pigs,* and *The Cat in the Hat.* Books reflecting ethnic diversity should always be available for children's use. Books portraying ethnic diversity of children in the group as well as those not represented in the group need to be on the shelves.

Help children understand the rules in the book center related to behavior, care of books, and removal of books from the area.

■ Encourage frequent use of the book center. This means that you need to change the displays and what books are available so that children will want to explore continually to see what is new. It's hard to be interested in a shabby collection of books casually tossed on a table in the corner of the room!

■ Involve the children in decorating the book center. They can help you change the display or make pictures for use on the library corner bulletin board. Then the book center will be a place where they feel they belong.

REFERENCE

Farrell, J. M. (1991, March 31). Literacy experts suggest dusting off Mother Goose. Knight Ridder Newspapers.

CHAPTER **13**

CREATIVE SCIENCE

W hen considering creative activities, it is not possible to skip the area of science. This is because true science is a highly creative activity.

There are twenty young children in a classroom. Each has just been given a small box wrapped in brightly colored gift paper. There is a big ribbon around each box. There are some objects inside each box. Each child is trying to find out what is in a box without taking off the ribbon and paper.

Some children are shaking their gift boxes. Some are holding them up to their ears and listening very carefully. Others are squeezing them.

Is this a game? It may seem so, but it is not. It is a way in which children make creative discoveries. In many ways, it is also the way that scientists make creative discoveries. The little gift box is somewhat like the world in which the children live. The children study their own little worlds by shaking the box, smelling it, squeezing it, and looking at it. Each child makes some discoveries but cannot find out everything because the box cannot be unwrapped. The children may be able to make some good guesses after studying the boxes, however. Some things are open to the children's discovery; some things are not. Scientists are faced with the same problems. They, too, study the world. They, too, can observe some things and only guess about others.

 ## SCIENCE AND THE YOUNG CHILD

There are two things, then, that both the child and the scientist do. They *investigate* (carefully study the world around them) to discover *knowledge* (find answers to questions or problems about that world).

IMPORTANCE OF SCIENCE

In dealing with young children, investigating is much more important than the knowledge that comes from investigating. Young children need a lot of action, not a lot of facts. This does not mean that understanding the world is put aside completely for young children. It just means that learning *how to find* answers is more important than the answers themselves.

Science is important to young children in a number of ways. First, when children are actively involved in investigating their world, they are *learning by doing,* the most effective way for young children to learn.

Second, science activities help young children develop skills in using their senses. Use of these skills is not limited to science. These skills can be used every day throughout a persons lifetime.

Third, science allows children yet another chance to exercise their creative abilities. Science allows young children a chance to play with ideas and materials in an open environment where there is freedom to explore without fear of being "wrong."

TYPES OF SCIENCE ACTIVITIES

There are three types of science experiences for young children: formal, informal, and incidental. All are appropriate in the early childhood program.

FORMAL SCIENCE

Formal science experiences are planned by the teacher to develop particular skills. An example would be planning for fine motor skill development by including pouring and measuring tools in the sand and water area. A teacher would plan to include a specific item, such as hanging a funnel low over the water table or attaching funnels to each end of a length of plastic tubing. These items would be included to serve a specific purpose—the development of fine motor skills.

INFORMAL SCIENCE

Unlike formal science, **informal science** calls for little or no teacher involvement. Children work on their own, at their own rate, and only when they feel like it. They select the kinds of activities that interest them. They spend as much or as little time working at a given activity as they desire. It is when this sort of openness is available to children that creative potential begins to develop.

Most informal science activities occur in the discovery (science) center. The discovery center is an area in the early childhood classroom where children can participate in a variety of informal science activities that stimulate curiosity, exploration, and problem solving.

INCIDENTAL SCIENCE

Incidental science cannot be planned. It sometimes does not take place once a week or even once a month. Just what is incidental science?

A city or town may be struck by a violent windstorm. Limbs of trees are knocked down; whole trees are uprooted. Great sheets of rain fall and streets become flooded. Finally the storm is over.

Is this the time for an incidental science experience? Of course it is! This is the time for children who are interested to learn many things. They can study the roots of trees; they may have the chance to observe growth rings. They are able to examine tree bark. They can observe what happens to water as it drains from a flooded street. Some might want to talk about their feelings as the lightning flashed and the thunder crashed. Some may wish to create a painting about the experience.

Sink and float experiments are always a popular science activity.

A teacher cannot plan such an experience. A good teacher can, however, take advantage of such an opportunity by letting children explore and seek answers to questions.

ART AND SCIENCE

SCIENCE LEARNING AND ART

Children working with art materials make scientific observations, noting, for example, that water makes tempera paint thinner and that crayons become soft if left near the heat. Claire looks at her wet, drippy painting and says, "I wonder if I can blow it dry with my wind." Drew finds that his clay figure left on the windowsill overnight has "gotten all hardened up" because it is no longer wet.

Experimentation with art materials may lead to many other discoveries about cause and effect. Children notice that colors change as they are mixed and that the sponges used for printing absorb liquid. In contrast, other materials such as plastics are found to be nonabsorbent. Children using many materials observe differences between liquids and solids and see that other items such as wax crayons and oil paints resist water. In mixing paint from powder, children learn that some materials dissolve in water. The operations of simple machines

The discovery center is a place to try out ideas and "what if's".

can be understood through using tools such as scissors and hammers. The potential for developing science concepts is in the art materials and in the processes—ready to be discovered and applied.

Animals, science, and art.   Young children's natural love of animals is a good place to begin when planning art activities that encourage science experiences. Children are intrigued with the study of animals. Yet, animals provide more than a science experience for children, as they stimulate children's artistic exploration. Young children, after touching, seeing, hearing, or smelling animals, will be stimulated to use art to represent animals. Children with an emotional attachment to household or school pets will be motivated to create visual images. Teachers create opportunities for learning about animals by providing art media and materials for children to use; engaging children in discussions about animals; and reading stories, showing pictures, and singing songs about animals.

The following sections of this chapter provide ideas which may be used as the basis for planning both formal and informal science activities. These, of course, are meant to be starting points. Teachers will think of many more activities that suit their particular group interests and abilities.

THE DISCOVERY/ SCIENCE CENTER

The discovery center should have things for the children to "do." It is not a center where children just look at objects. Most teachers use a sand and water table in the discovery center. Here various materials—rice,

In science activities, children are free to explore, investigate, and experience the process of finding answers to questions about the world.

beans, cornmeal, sawdust, mud—can be placed in the table for children to explore, measure, and pour. Sand and water activities are usually informal science and open-ended—that is, children can freely explore and manipulate materials with no definite or specified purpose to the activity.

The discovery center can house plants and animals for the children to observe. In addition to caring for them, the children can also record information about them, such as the amount of food given to the gerbil each day, the amount of water used for the plant, or the amount the plant has grown. (See Figure 13–1 for basic materials and supplies for the discovery center.)

In preschool and kindergarten classrooms, and in elementary classrooms organized with learning centers, many science activities can be set up for independent use. Printed activity directions can be prepared to guide reading students. Tape-recorded guides can also be made to reduce the amount of direct supervision needed for small-group learning activities.

Try to locate the discovery center in an area that both invites children's participation yet controls distractions. Varying the location to fit the requirements of the activity builds interest. Science is very popular on the days when it takes place under a blanket-covered table! Careful planning of space, materials, and time for science will allow children to work as safely, independently, and successfully as possible.

Collection of Objects
(Many of which the Children can Bring—Rocks, Shells, Insects, and so on)

Things to classify	Science kits	Flashlight
Magnifying glass	Magnets (horseshoe, bar)	Binoculars, telescope, periscope
Objects that float and sink (an old wash-tub works well to hold the water)	Iron filings	Rope, fibers
	Prisms	Sponges
Different kinds of soil	Tuning forks	Batteries
Seeds to plant and classify	Aquarium	Rubber tubing
Shapes	Terrarium	Animals/animal cages
Compass	Vivarium	Stethoscope
Simple machines	Tactile board/box	Food coloring
Things to take apart and put together (old clocks, toys, motors, etc.)	Plants	Electric bell
	Bug house	Dry/liquid measure containers
Objects to smell, taste, hear, touch, and see	Thermometer (Celsius)	Pendulum frame/bobs
	Kaleidoscope, scanoscope	Scales (kitchen, balance, spring)
Filmstrips about science	Hourglass, clocks, stopwatch	Assorted balancing materials
Collection of books	Color paddles	

FIGURE 13–1 | Discovery center—basic science materials and supplies.

THIS ONE'S FOR YOU   Internet Ideas

As always, the Internet is there at our fingertips with great information on science activities to use with children. Here are some Web sites for sources of science information:

Environmental Resources: Current and environmental education for K–12 includes teaching kits, student masters for classroom instruction, and more than a dozen hot links. Sponsored by the National Cattlemen's Beef Association. www.TeachFree.com.

Earth Science Week: One week in October is generally named Earth Science Week. The American Geologic Institute sponsors the event and serves as a clearinghouse for ideas, activities, special events, and support materials. For more information, visit www.earthsciweek.org or write to American Geologic Institute, 4220 King St., Alexandria, VA 22302.

Space Day: Generally held in May, Space Day is the culminating event of the year-round Embrace Space educational initiative. Space Day encourages people around the globe to advance science, mathematics, and technology education, and to inspire future generations to continue the vision of our space pioneers. To learn more about the event and surrounding activities, visit www.spaceday.com or call (202) 833-8121.

TerraServer: The TerraServer Web site, www.terraserver.com, provides unlimited access to the largest collection of satellite pictures of the Earth. Students and teachers can view areas of interest online, such as a Civil War battlefield, the Grand Canyon, or their own school building.

Friends of Frogs: *A Thousand Friends of Frogs Educational Activity Guide* helps K–12 teachers integrate frog study into classroom curricula. The activities in the guide are aligned with the National Science Education Standards. A grant from the National Fish and Wildlife Foundation, the U.S. Fish and Wildlife Service, and the Best Buy Children's Foundation allows teachers in the United States to receive the guide free of charge. For more information, write to A Thousand Friends of Frogs, Hamline University Graduate School, 1536 Hewitt Ave., St. Paul, MN 55104; call (800) 888-2821; e-mail: frogs@hamline.edu or visit www.enc.org/order/.

ACTIVITIES FOR CHILDREN

Pets, Pets . . . All Kinds of Activities

GOALS: To develop children's interest in animals

To encourage children's creativity

To tie in science to other program areas

MATERIALS: Art supplies as required for each activity

PREPARATION: Have the children share information on pets they have at home. Discuss pets they would like to have, or pets they have had in the past.

PROCEDURE:

1. Encourage children to draw, paint, or model representations of their pets doing something characteristic.
2. Make their drawings, paintings, or cutout animals into booklets, murals, or puppets.
3. Provide scraps of furry fabrics, yarns, and spotted and striped papers in different shapes for children to paste on a background and then add details for real or imaginary pets.

VARIATION:

■ Provide styrofoam trays on which children can draw simple animal forms. Pierce the outline at regular intervals for the younger children to stitch. Older children can pierce through the trays themselves.

■ Transfer children's animal drawings onto felt or burlap. Cut out two duplicate shapes, stitch them together, and fill with beans, seeds, or shredded nylon hose for use as toys to toss.

■ Have the children draw, paint, or model the pet out of clay.

■ Have the children dramatize the pets, movements.

ACTIVITIES FOR CHILDREN

Science and Language Arts

GOALS: To encourage children's interest in science activities

To tie in language arts and science

MATERIALS: Paper, pencils, and markers

PREPARATION: Discuss the way pets feel, how they look, the sounds they make, the way they move, the purpose of various parts of the body, the need for food, their homes, and so on.

PROCEDURE:

1. Have the children write or tell original stories based on the pet.
2. Tape these stories.
3. Have the children act out the story.

VARIATION:

■ Have the children write experience charts about their care and characteristics.

■ Have the children tell animal stories, recite animal poems, and sing animal songs.

■ Show the children pictures of animals. Have the children tell which are tame and which are wild; which fly, hop, swim, and so on; and which live in water, on land, and so on.

■ Have older children keep journals on their daily observations of a classroom pet. They can write stories with the pet as the main character.

ACTIVITIES FOR CHILDREN

Cloud and Sky Watching

GOALS: To encourage children's interest in nature

To develop children's creativity

MATERIALS: None required

PREPARATION: Plan to take a walk outdoors on a mild, partly sunny or cloudy day.

PROCEDURE:

1. Have the children lie on the ground and look up at the sky.
2. Talk about the shapes of the clouds.
3. Talk about how clouds join together.
4. Ask questions like, "Are there many colors in the clouds?" or "How do clouds seem to move?"

VARIATION:

■ Have the children draw or paint a picture about their cloud watching time.

■ Have the children make up a story about the clouds.

ACTIVITIES FOR CHILDREN

The Sounds of Nature

GOALS: To encourage children's interest in science activities

To develop listening skills

MATERIALS: Tape recorder, tape

PREPARATION: Discuss sounds the children hear inside the classroom. Discuss sounds they might hear outside the classroom.

PROCEDURE:

1. Take one or two supervised children outside to an area near the school.
2. Have the children tape as many different sounds as they can hear.
3. Play the tape for the rest of the class.
4. Have the children guess who/what is making the sounds.

ADDITIONAL INFORMATION: Encourage children's interest in sounds by asking questions. Examples may include: Can they hear sounds made by birds? By animals? What do the leaves in the trees sound like? How do trees without leaves sound? What other sounds can be heard? How do noises made by cars differ from noises made by trucks? How does a person feel if there is too much noise?

ACTIVITIES FOR CHILDREN

What Happens to Rain Water?

GOALS: To encourage children's interest in science activities

MATERIALS: None required

PREPARATION: Find an area near the school where children can explore after a rainstorm.

PROCEDURE:

1. After a rainstorm, have the children follow the paths taken by the water.
2. Have the children look to see if all of the water flows into a sewer. Does some of it go into the ground?
3. Observe what happens in paved areas compared to grassy areas.
4. Observe what happens in dirt areas compared to grassy areas.

VARIATION: Older children can learn about erosion and the effects of it in their own parks and playgrounds.

ACTIVITIES FOR CHILDREN

Activities with Seeds

GOALS: To encourage children's interest in science activities

To develop observation skills

MATERIALS: Seeds, potting soil, and tongue depressors

PREPARATION: Have the children plant seeds in pots.

PROCEDURE:

1. Press a stick like a tongue depressor down into the soil by the seed when it sprouts.
2. Put the date and name of the plant on the tongue depressor.
3. When the seed sprouts, have the child mark the height of the sprout each week as it grows.
4. If seeds in some pots don't grow, dig them up to see what happened to them.

VARIATION:

■ Help the children build a model greenhouse in the block center, using plants, large blocks, and packing boxes. They can put their plants in the greenhouse, along with watering cans.

■ Plants can be started from sweet potatoes. Place a sweet potato in a glass so that half the potato is under water. It will produce roots and a vine. (Try to find potatoes that aren't bruised.)

■ Geraniums and philodendrons will produce roots from cuttings placed in water, which can then be potted. Pussy willow twigs will grow roots in water.

■ Top gardens can be made by cutting off about an inch from the top of root vegetables, such as carrots. Place the cut end in water, and new leafy growth will shoot up.

ACTIVITIES FOR CHILDREN   Spray Art

GOALS: To encourage children's interest in science activities

To develop children's creativity

MATERIALS: Spray mist bottles with trigger handles, squeeze bottles of food coloring, large white butcher block paper or a white bed sheet, scissors, tape, a large towel or plastic mat, and water

PREPARATION: Spread the towel or plastic mat on the floor. Cut a large square of butcher block paper. Tape the paper or the sheet to the table top or outside to a wall or fence. Fill the spray bottles with water. Squeeze 10 to 15 drops of food coloring into the spray bottles. Secure the top. Prepare several bottles of water with different colors of the food coloring mixture.

PROCEDURE:

1. Have the child shake the bottle near the paper or sheet.
2. Holding the spray bottle, have the child spray the colored water onto the paper to make a mural.
3. When the children are finished spraying the colors, remove the tape.
4. Let the mural dry before displaying it.

ACTIVITIES FOR CHILDREN   Water Play Ideas

GOALS: To encourage children's interest in science activities

MATERIALS: Water table or large tub, water

PREPARATION: See the Procedure for required preparation.

PROCEDURE: Choose one or more of the following ideas to liven up children's water play activities.

■ Put salt in the water, then try to float and sink objects.

■ Put snow in place of the water.

■ Add foam or rubber alphabet letters and small fishnets. Have the children name the letter they catch, or have them catch the letters that make up their name.

■ Experiment with varying amounts of water and air inside zippered sandwich bags in floating experiments.

■ Make boats out of heavy aluminum foil. See if they float.

■ Make a bridge over a portion of the water using scrap materials.

VARIATION:

■ Provide a large chunk of ice in the water table. Provide safety goggles, rubber mallets, and rock salt.

■ Challenge children to create a boat from found objects, then move it from one end of the water to the other without using their hands.

ACTIVITIES FOR CHILDREN

Pump Bottle and Chalk

GOALS: To encourage children's interest in science activities

To develop children's creativity

MATERIALS: Colored chalk, plastic pump bottles of different sizes

PREPARATION: Fill the plastic pump bottle with water.

PROCEDURE:

1. Have the child color the sidewalk with colored chalk.

2. Have the child press the pump top and let the water splatter over the chalk on the sidewalk, making a design on the chalk.

VARIATION: Use different-sized pump bottles, comparing the different water marks made by each bottle.

ACTIVITIES FOR CHILDREN

Spray Art—Designer T-Shirt

GOALS: To encourage children's interest in science activities

To develop children's creativity

MATERIALS: Spray mist bottle with trigger handle, food coloring, large white butcher block paper, scissors, tape, large towel or plastic mat, and t-shirt

PREPARATION: Spread the towel or plastic mat outdoors, on the floor, or under a table. Place another towel or mat on the table. Tape a white t-shirt to the towel, mat, or to the towel on the table. Fill the plastic squeeze spray bottle with water. Squeeze 10 to 15 drops of food coloring into the bottle and secure the top. Prepare several spray bottles of water with different colors of food coloring. Shake the bottles.

PROCEDURE:

1. Have the child shake the bottle.
2. Standing next to the table with the spray gun bottle in one hand, have the child spray the colored water onto the t-shirt.
3. Have the child use as many colors as desired for the design.
4. When finished, remove the tape and hang the t-shirt to dry.

VARIATION: To be sure of permanent color, use liquid dye instead of food coloring and water.

ADDITIONAL INFORMATION: Add more food coloring if the color is too light.

ACTIVITIES FOR CHILDREN

Rocky Road to Knowledge

GOALS: To encourage children's interest in science activities

To sharpen powers of observation, description, and classification

MATERIALS: Assortment of rocks of all shapes, colors, and sizes

PREPARATION: Collect the rocks. Children may contribute rocks they have found.

PROCEDURE:

1. Have the children sort the rocks by size.
2. Have the children sort the rocks by color.
3. Have the children sort the rocks by texture.
4. Have the children identify them by name.

VARIATION:

■ Take a walk to see the many ways stone is used in buildings.
■ Look for fossils in limestone.
■ Take a field trip to hunt for interesting rocks.
■ Make a 3-dimensional work of art by gluing them together.

ADDITIONAL INFORMATION: Equipment that is useful in studying rocks includes scales of various types, magnifying glasses, and boxes (or egg cartons) for sorting.

ACTIVITIES FOR CHILDREN

Sun Prints

GOAL: To encourage children's interest in science activities

MATERIALS: Large sheets of blueprint paper

PREPARATION: Place sheets in a sunny area.

PROCEDURE:

1. Have the child lie on the paper for a few minutes. When he or she gets up, a body print will be left.
2. Have the child color or decorate the print, if desired.

VARIATION: If the child can't lie still long enough, use objects for the sun prints.

ACTIVITIES FOR CHILDREN   Insect Cages

GOALS: To encourage children's interest in science activities

　　To develop observation skills

MATERIALS: Small plastic or cardboard cartons, netting, tape, and scissors

PREPARATION: Cut an opening in small plastic or cardboard cartons. Cover the opening with fine netting, taping it into place. If appropriate, have the children prepare these boxes.

PROCEDURE: Have the children observe insects inside the insect "cages." Insects are observed more easily if the insect cages are made from clear plastic containers.

VARIATION: A clean, empty, half-gallon milk carton also makes a good insect viewer. Cut rectangular holes on two sides of the milk carton. Slip a nylon stocking over the carton. Fasten the stocking at the top with a rubber band. Insects can be held inside for temporary viewing.

ACTIVITIES FOR CHILDREN   Observing Worms

GOALS: To develop observation skills

　　To encourage children's interest in science activities

MATERIALS: Large glass jar (large peanut butter jar is good), worms, garden soil, black construction paper, and small rocks or sand

PREPARATION: Moisten the sand or soil.

PROCEDURE:

1. Place a layer of small rocks or sand in the bottom of the jar for drainage.
2. Place 2 inches of moist soil and sand in the jar.
3. Pick up the worms and place them in the jar.
4. Cover the worms with more soil.
5. Keep the soil moist.
6. Seal, using a lid with holes punched in it.
7. Wrap black construction paper around the jar.
8. After 24 hours, remove the paper.
9. Allow the children to see the worms tunneling through the soil.

VARIATION:

■ Encourage the children to talk about what interests them about worms.

■ Have older children keep a log of the worms' activity through the week.

■ Have the children write a story, paint a picture, or make a clay model about the worms.

■ Act out how a worm moves.

ACTIVITIES FOR CHILDREN Sky Gazer

GOALS: To encourage children's interest in science activities

To develop skills of observation

MATERIALS: Cardboard tubes from paper towel rolls (one for each child), yarn

PREPARATION: Punch two holes at one end of each tube. Loop an 18-inch piece of yarn through the holes.

PROCEDURE:

1. Have the child hang the telescope around his neck.
2. Have the child go outside on a warm day.
3. Have the child lie down on the grass.
4. Have the child use the telescope to look up into the sky.
5. Have the child describe what he sees.

VARIATION:

■ Have the children look some more. What else do they see? Have them tell each other.

■ Have the children draw a picture about what they saw.

■ Have the children move like clouds they observed.

ACTIVITIES FOR CHILDREN Build a Bird Feeder

GOALS: To develop observation skills

To encourage interest in science activities

MATERIALS: Empty milk carton or plastic soda bottle, twigs, leaves, seeds, non-toxic glue, string, and birdseed

PREPARATION: Cut windows and doors into the empty milk carton or plastic soda bottle.

PROCEDURE:

1. Decorate the carton or bottle in such a way that birds will want to visit.
2. Paste on colored pictures of big juicy worms.
3. Glue on twigs, leaves, and seeds.
4. Tie it to a tree branch.
5. Fill it with birdseed.
6. Watch and see how many birds and what kinds of birds use the feeder.

VARIATION:

■ Pinecones can be used for another type of bird feeder. Spread sugarless peanut butter on pinecones and roll them in wild birdseed. Fasten the pinecones to the branches of a tree using floral wire.

■ Keep a log of how many birds, and what kinds, visit the feeder each day.

ADDITIONAL INFORMATION: Keep decorations to a minimum so as not to frighten the birds.

ACTIVITIES FOR OLDER CHILDREN
Endangered Animals—Language Art Activities
(Grades 4–5)

GOALS: To encourage children's interest in science
To develop writing skills
To develop children's creative thinking

MATERIALS: Pictures of endangered species from magazines

PREPARATION: Discuss endangered species, what they are, and why we are concerned about them.

PROCEDURE:
Choose one or more of the following activities on endangered species.

■ Have the children write a story in which the main character is an endangered animal who is trying to teach his family why the species is endangered.

■ Have the children debate in a small group about the issue of wild animals being captured and put in a zoo. Should they or shouldn't they?

■ Have the children write a short speech (2–4 minutes) about an animal topic they feel strongly about.

■ Have the children write a story in which they become an endangered animal lost in a large city. Have them include how they feel being lost and endangered and what they should do in this situation.

■ Have the children make a clay model of an endangered animal and write a short paragraph telling key facts about the animal.

■ In pairs, have the children design an advertisement that could be published in a newspaper to promote the preservation of an endangered animal.

■ Have the children build a three-dimensional habitat model for an animal of their choice.

ACTIVITIES FOR OLDER CHILDREN
Movement Activity
(Grades 4–5)

GOALS: To encourage children's interest in science activities
To develop children's creativity

MATERIALS: None required

PREPARATION: Have the students think about their favorite animal. Have each choose one animal to "be" for this activity.

PROCEDURE:
1. Pretend that everyone is a different animal.
2. Role-play how each animal might react to meeting the other.
3. Perform a skit with all of the animals—some endangered and some not.
4. Have the animals discuss the problems with being endangered.

VARIATION:
■ Have the students invent a game called the Animal Game.

■ In a group, make up an animal song and record it on a tape recorder.

■ Have the children write a poem or story about an animal and add animal sounds as they read it to other students.

ACTIVITIES FOR OLDER CHILDREN
(Grades 4–5) How Does Water Disappear?

GOALS: To understand evaporation

To encourage children's interest in science activities

MATERIALS: Sponge, blackboard, water, and a heavy piece of cardboard

PREPARATION: Moisten the sponge. Make a wide, damp streak on the blackboard.

PROCEDURE:

1. Have the children observe the blackboard for several minutes.
2. Ask them what happened.
3. Make two streaks about one yard apart.
4. Use the cardboard to fan one of the streaks.
5. Compare the time it took for each streak to disappear.

VARIATION: Put a small amount of water (1/2 inch) in two small jars. Seal the lid of one and leave the other open. Observe for 24 hours. Discuss the differences in water remaining in each jar.

ADDITIONAL INFORMATION: Children should learn from this activity that water is absorbed into the air by a process called evaporation. Increasing the amount of air moving over the water (fanning) increases the rate of evaporation.

ACTIVITIES FOR OLDER CHILDREN
(Grades 4–5) Science: A Different View of Things

GOALS: To develop observation skills

To encourage children's interest in science activities

MATERIALS: Collection of unusual rocks, shells, dried seed pods, other small objects, glue, plastic photo cubes, pencils, and paper

PREPARATION: Glue several objects to the bottom of plastic photo cubes.

PROCEDURE:

1. Challenge children to draw the objects inside the cube from each of the six points they can see when looking straight through one side of the cube.
2. Have the children share their drawings.
3. Talk about the kinds of lines in each drawing.

VARIATION: Create drawings from unusual or imagined vantage points, such as being in a hot air balloon, flying in an airplane, being inside of a mine or a cave, looking at things under water, or looking out the window of a rocket while it is being launched or is nearing a planet.

FOOD FOR THOUGHT

Scientists Tell All

Parents appear to be the biggest single positive factor in stimulating a childhood interest in science, according to a national survey of scientists released by Bayer Corporation and the National Science Foundation (NSF) (1999). "The message to parents is clear: You don't have to be a science expert to help your children love the subject, or all learning for that matter," said Mae C. Jemison, former astronaut and Bayer Corporations science literacy advocate for its Making Science Make Sense initiative. "You just need to encourage and support them as they pursue their interests." The Bayer/NSF survey, the Bayer Facts of Science Education IV: Scientists on Science for the 21st Century, polled more than 1,400 members of the American Association for the Advancement of Science. The survey asked them, among other things, to look back on their own educational and career experiences and forecast trends in science literacy and scientific advances in the new millennium.

More than half of the scientists said they first became interested in science during their elementary school years. Teachers were as influential as parents in sparking an interest in science. And, apart from formal science classes (82 percent), more than 80 percent of the scientists were influenced by science toys and equipment like chemistry sets and telescopes; 78 percent mentioned newspapers, magazines, and other media that covered science; 76 percent said science museum visits; and 69 percent felt that doing science experiments at home was influential.

While all scientists reported informal science activities like playing with science toys and doing experiments at home, these activities were more important for male scientists (85 percent and 71 percent, respectively) than for female scientists (60 percent and 55 percent).

"The fact that chemistry sets and microscopes had an effect on this many men makes perfect sense since they were probably given them as birthday presents," explained Jemison. "What we need to ask ourselves is 'What if more girls had access to and were encouraged to play with the same kinds of toys?' "

Few scientists (25 percent) believe science is given enough emphasis in elementary school, though 74 percent think it should be given the same priority as reading, writing, and arithmetic. In addition, most scientists (85 percent) say that, if asked, they would spend time in the classroom helping students learn and teachers to teach science (Bayer Corporation & NSF, 1999).

The science curriculum at the middle and upper elementary level includes much small group work in problem-solving as well as in discovery.

REFERENCE

Bayer Corporation & National Science Foundation (NSF). (1999). *The Bayer facts of science education IV: Scientists on science for the 21st century*. Pittsburgh, PA: Author.

CHAPTER 14

CREATIVE MATHEMATICS

E verything we know about young children tells us that early math experiences must be hands-on, filled with play and exploration. Young children's meanings and understandings of mathematical ideas take place in an action-based learning environment as they use concrete materials.

All young children need opportunities to explore their world and experience mathematics through play.

In this chapter, the emphasis is on this *active* exploration of mathematical concepts as a natural part of the early childhood program.

 ## DEVELOPMENTAL PATTERN OF LEARNING MATHEMATICAL IDEAS

Long before children formally use numbers, they are aware of them through daily experiences. Through their experiences of living and doing, children are able to tell the differences in the sizes of people, animals, and toys before they have any idea about measurement. They recognize, too, the difference between *one* and *many* and between *few* and *lots* before they acquire real number concepts. They develop a sense of time long before they can tell time by a clock. Their ideas of time grow out of hearing things like: "It's time for lunch." "It's time to go to bed." "We're going for a walk today." "We went to the park yesterday."

This pattern of early use of numbers is similar to the general-to-specific pattern of physical growth (see Part 1). In these early stages of mathematical thinking, the child

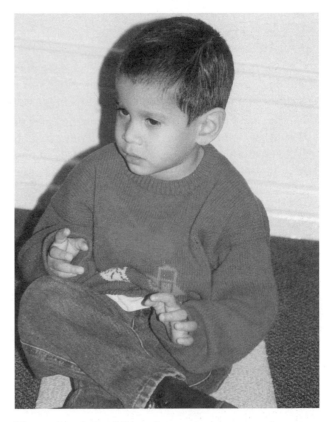

Fingerplays help children learn number concepts.

has a general understanding of numbers which will gradually move toward a more specific understanding as the developmental process continues. Let us now look at how to put mathematics into action in the early childhood program.

THIS ONE'S FOR YOU

Using Children's Books to Teach Math

You will find that children's books can be used to launch many interesting math learning activities. There are many excellent sources of children's books for math. An example of using the book *The Very Hungry Caterpillar* by Eric Carle, which describes the life cycle of a caterpillar through the use of vibrant collage-like designs, will give you an idea of how to include books in math experiences.

Teaching Comparisons. Size comparison is the most obvious prenumber concept that can be drawn from this book. The caterpillar changes from a tiny egg laid on a leaf to a small, hungry caterpillar to a big brown cocoon and finally, to a large, beautiful butterfly. After reading the book, discuss the size relationships. Later, children can compare cutouts of these items and arrange them from largest to smallest.

Teaching Ordering. The prenumber skill of ordering can be related to both the days of the week and the life cycle. Ask children to tell the order of the days of the week or stages of the life cycle told in the book. Ordering the days of the week in this way can promote an interest in the calendar for daily record keeping of days gone by. The life cycle can be used in a gamelike situation in which children order the pictures of the cycle. This can be made self-correcting by placing the numerals 1 through 4 on the back of the pictures.

One-to-One Correspondence. The fact that the caterpillar ate through a variety of foods one by one can be used to emphasize the one-to-one correspondence. A learning center follow-up could require children to match pompom caterpillars to plastic fruits to see if there is an equal match or if there are more caterpillars or fruit.

Rational Counting. Children can also be asked to rationally count the number of pieces of food the caterpillar ate in the story by counting the number of fruits and then the number of other foods eaten. They might also count the number of days of the week and the life cycle changes. A later concrete learning activity would be to have children count out pieces of fruit or other similar foods eaten by the caterpillar for their own particular snack time. Learning center games could involve the counting of food cutouts found in plastic containers.

Cardinal Number. Use the story to emphasize the prenumber skill of recognizing cardinal numbers. As the children look at the book, ask them, "How many things did the caterpillar eat on Saturday?" "How many on Monday?" Later, they can work with a learning center activity that involves counting holes made by the hungry caterpillar in card stock leaves to determine how many bites the caterpillar took. A self-correcting feature can be included by simply writing the answer on the back of the leaves.

MATHEMATICAL CONCEPTS

This section provides a brief description of basic mathematical concepts young children develop through everyday experiences in the early childhood program.

NUMBERS

Before the child is three years old, she often can count to ten in proper order. Such counting (called **rote counting**), however, may have little specific meaning for the child. The words may be only sounds to her, sounds repeated in a particular sequence like a familiar song. This rote counting is similar to a child who can repeat words without really understanding their meaning.

Quite different from and much more difficult than rote counting is understanding the numerals as they apply to a sequence of objects: that each numeral represents the position of an object in the sequence (button 1, button 2, button 3, and so on). Equally or more difficult to understand is the idea that the last number counted in a sequence of objects represents all the objects in the sequence, the total number of objects counted. This is called **rational counting.** For example, in counting six buttons, the child must grasp the idea that six, the last number counted, tells her how many buttons she has—that she has six buttons *in all*.

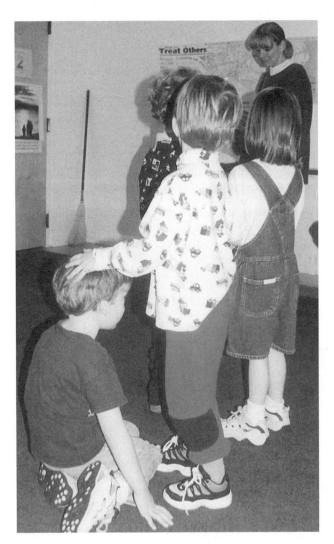

Playtime allows children many chances to extend, explore, and refine their math skills.

Rational counting, a higher-level number understanding, develops slowly for most children. However, carefully structured activities that take one idea and present it to children one step at a time help them grow from a general to a more specific understanding of numbers.

Young children frequently hear counting—as steps are being climbed, objects are being stacked, foods are being distributed, fingerplays are being played, familiar nursery rhymes and songs are being enjoyed, and during many other activities. This repetition helps the child memorize the sequence and sounds of numbers, even before the meanings of these numbers are understood.

True counting ability (rational counting) is not possible until the child understands one-to-one correspondence. In other words, to rote count (to say the number sequence) is one thing, but to count items correctly—one number per item—is more difficult. Very often when a young child is given a series of things to count,

the child counts two numbers for one item or two items while saying only one number. Thus, as rote counting develops, teachers should also encourage the skills of **one-to-one correspondence.**

Having the child touch each object as she counts is one way to encourage one-to-one correspondence. Repeating this exercise in various experiences throughout the day reinforces the concept of one-to-one correspondence.

CLASSIFICATION AND SORTING

Classification and sorting are beginning math activities for young children.

Classification. Putting together things that are alike or that belong together is one of the processes necessary for developing the concept of number. In order to classify, children must be able to observe an object for likenesses and differences.

Before children can classify and sort, they need to understand concepts such as "belongingness," "put together," "alike," and "belong together." These concepts are acquired over time as children have varied hands-on experiences in the early childhood program.

Your role as a teacher is to help children gain these ideas through a variety of experiences with a wide variety of materials selected specifically for classifying and sorting activities.

Materials for children's classifying and sorting may be kept together on a shelf in the manipulative toy or game area of your room. Boxes or sorting trays (plastic dishpans and muffin tins work well) are kept with the materials. Sorting trays can be constructed by either attaching a series of metal jar lids onto a board or piece of cardboard; mounting a number of clear plastic cups onto a board; dividing a board or tray into sections with colored pieces of tape; or by mounting small, clear plastic boxes onto a board. Egg cartons, plastic sewing boxes, tool boxes (such as those used for storing nuts and bolts), and fishing boxes are also useful for sorting trays and stimulate children to use materials mathematically.

COMPARING

The skill of **comparing** seems to come easily and naturally, especially when it is a personal comparison. "My shoes are newer than yours." "I've got the biggest." "My sister is little." "You've got more."

When different size and shape containers are used in sand and water play, children can make comparisons based on volume.

Stories and poems, often the folk tales children are already familiar with, offer other opportunities for informal

FOOD FOR THOUGHT
Web Sites for Math Information and Activities

Try some of the following Internet and software resources to give you some new ideas for math activities.

Counting the Days. A comprehensive resource on calendars by World Book. You'll find an excellent historic background on the calendar with great related web links. Visit www.worldbook.com/fun/calendar/html/calendars.htm.

Timelines. This software allows you to create graphic timelines ranging from one-page representations to a timeline that stretches from one school hallway to the next. There are also dozens of timeline databases on many curricular themes which will help you incorporate timelines in all content areas. For more information on *Timelines* by Tom Snyder Productions, visit their Web site at: www.tomsnyder.com.

Today in History. What better way to examine the changes of time than to explore the events of history? This Library of Congress site gives us a look at the events of history over time. Look at today, or type in your birthday and see what events occurred on that special day in history: lcweb2.loc.gov/ammem/today/.

Once Upon a Time. Incorporate your favorite book characters of time. Who can forget the ticking clock in the belly of the alligator in *Peter Pan*? Or the travel through time in the *Time Machine*? Who is the time character in *Alice in Wonderland*? And don't forget the stroke of midnight in *Cinderella*. How many more can you find? Be sure to check out the time theme from Carol Hurst's Children's Literature Site for many more ideas about time and books: www.carolhurst.com/.

WebMath. This is an exceptional site which uses the immediacy of the Internet to provide students with help for math problems they're working on right now. Using a sophisticated math "engine," the user enters a problem and the engine generates an answer with an explanation of how the problem was solved. Teachers can even create a math quiz online. WebMath can solve more than 80 types of word problems. Want to figure wind chill, convert fractions, or make a graph? These and more are available. Be sure to share this resource with parents, too! Visit www.webmath.com.

Texas Instruments Educational Resources. Calculators anyone? This is a comprehensive collection of math activities for all grades. Click on educators, students, or parents to find resources using math and calculators. An Activity Matrix makes it easy to choose by subject, grade level, or product. This site offers excellent Internet resources for math and science divided by grade level. There is also a free booklet, *Uncovering Math with Your Family,* that can be downloaded and sent home to involve parents in their child's math instruction. Teachers are invited to share ideas for using calculators and math in the classroom and there are discussion groups for sharing. Parents will find books and resources on math. Visit www.ti.com/calc.

comparisons. *The Three Billy Goats Gruff, The Three Bears,* and others offer comparisons on the basis of differing attributes.

Throughout the preschool years, ask children to observe and note differences in the objects of their environment, to name them, and to discuss them with one another.

ORDERING (SERIATION)

Another mathematical idea that is a vital part of mathematic understanding is the idea of **ordering (seriation).**

Ordering the environment into series begins when children are very young and continues throughout adult life. The child begins by perceiving opposite ends of a series:

big	_____	little
heavy	_____	light
cold	_____	hot
long	_____	short

The comparison of the height of two children is beginning ordering, as is the comparison of two sets of things as more or less. Ordering sticks, blocks, or nesting cups in a sequence that leads gradually from the smallest to the biggest helps children see ordered size relations.

For middle elementary level children, sorting and classifying can be done with many more items and categories.

Children enjoy ordering activities and do so spontaneously. Many table toys provide ordering experiences, as do ordinary objects like measuring spoons and cups.

Your role is to provide materials and sufficient time. When children find the existing materials too easy, you can awaken their interest by encouraging them to use the toys differently, by asking them questions, and by providing additional materials.

Ordering activities can include length (sticks), height (bottles), total size (bowls and shoes), weight (stones), color (from light to dark), and other endless possibilities.

SHAPE AND FORM

Young children need many experiences with shapes and making comparisons between shapes before they focus on naming shapes. Usually, it is enough to introduce one new shape at a time. As the new shape is understood, other shapes may be added.

In teaching young children about shape and form, it is important to include more shapes than the common geometric shapes of a circle, triangle, rectangle, and square. Since shapes aid in, or are sources of, identification, limiting instruction to the "basic shapes" excludes from the learning environment important aspects of recognition of shapes in general.

Yet familiar shapes must be taught before uncommon ones. Most of these unfamiliar shapes depend on previous shape identification and recognition. From the basis of understanding simple shapes, the child is able to build more complex structures.

As with the teaching of any ideas, shapes can be found throughout the child's environment. Words defining shapes should be used often. For example, everyday language should include such statements as: "That is a square box," rather than "That is square"; "The clock is round," rather than "This is round"; "Put the book on the square table," rather than "Put it over there." With these phrases, the object and its characteristic shape are made clear to the child. Later on, more characteristics, such as color, size, texture, and number, may be added.

When unfamiliar shapes are introduced, a review of already familiar ones should precede the new introduction. Then the children's thinking can be stimulated with such questions as "How is this new shape the same as. . . ?" or "How is this new shape not the same as (or different from). . . ?" Such comparisons reinforce and review shapes already learned.

MATHEMATICS GRADES 3–5

Mathematics is a subject most students in grades 3–5 like. Students in grades 3–5 see mathematics as practical, are challenged with many new ideas, and believe that what they are learning is important. However, sometime between grades 4 and 8 students' interest in mathematics begins to wane. Although they continue to view mathematics as important, by grade 8 students are less likely to characterize it as interesting or to consider themselves good at math. It is crucial that the mathematics education in the upper elementary and early middle grades be challenging, relevant, and engaging for students.

Because the amount of content in grades 3–5 expands greatly from that of the earlier grades, students need help in building connections and managing the many new concepts and procedures they are encountering. Students in grades 3–5 must also understand and bear responsibility for their learning. In math this means learning how to examine, ask questions, and consider different strategies—all with the goal of making sense of mathematical ideas and fitting them to other, related areas.

In grades 3–5, extending understanding from whole numbers to fractions and decimals is a key dimension of the mathematics curriculum. Students need many and varied experiences in order to understand what fractions and decimals represent, how they are related to each other, and how they are different from whole numbers.

ACTIVITIES FOR CHILDREN

Block Cleanup—Math Time, Too!

GOAL: To encourage children's development of math concepts

MATERIALS: Assortment of blocks

PREPARATION: The teacher can be the cleanup director, or the children can take turns being director.

PROCEDURE:

1. Have the cleanup director direct children to pick up blocks of three different lengths.
2. Have the children pick up blocks that are curved.
3. Have the children pick up blocks according to size.
4. Have the children pick up blocks different from a specific block that the cleanup director names.

5. Have the children put away blocks in groups of twos, threes, fours, and so on.

VARIATION:

- Have the children put away blocks according to size beginning with the biggest or longest and ending with the smallest or shortest.
- Have the children put away all of a particular shape or size block and ask how many of that block the children used.
- Have the children stack all of the blocks that go in the lower left section of the blocks shelf, then stack the lower middle shelf, and so on.
- Select certain people to put away certain shapes, (e.g., rectangles, cylinders, and so on).

ACTIVITIES FOR CHILDREN

Counting . . . The Many Ways

GOALS: To practice counting skills
To encourage children's interest in math activities

MATERIALS: Buttons, bottle caps, or similar objects; paste; paper; and a box

PREPARATION: Place objects in the box. Practice counting the objects with the children. Have the children touch each object counted.

PROCEDURE:

1. Practice counting to *three,* saying the numbers out loud.
2. Take *three* objects out of a box, counting them as they are taken out.

3. Vary the number, taking out *four* objects, then *five,* and so on.

VARIATION:

- Have the child glue the buttons or bottle caps onto a piece of paper to make a picture or collage.
- Play Bean Bag Toss. Have a large target and give each child a turn to try to get a specified number of bean bags into the hole. Have the child choose the specified number of bean bags and count them again as she throws.

ADDITIONAL INFORMATION: In counting activities, have the child touch each object.

ACTIVITIES FOR CHILDREN Snack Time Counting

GOALS: To practice counting skills

To encourage children's interest in math activities

MATERIALS: Snack time food that can be counted, such as raisins, carrot sticks, banana slices, crackers, and so on

PREPARATION: Cut snack foods into pieces that can be counted.

PROCEDURE:

1. Choose a number such as "four."

2. Serve snack items in groups of four, such as four raisins, four carrot sticks, four banana slices, four crackers, and so on.

VARIATION: Choose a geometric shape such as a circle and serve round snack items (round crackers, cucumber slices, round cereal, carrot slices, banana slices, and so on).

ACTIVITIES FOR CHILDREN Count Your Marbles

GOALS: To practice counting skills

To encourage children's interest in math activities

MATERIALS: Ten paper cups, box with lots of marbles in it

PREPARATION: Label paper cups with the numerals 1 through 10.

PROCEDURE:

1. Place the box of marbles and the cups on a table for a minimath center.

2. Have two children work together.

3. Have one child examine the numeral printed on each cup.

4. Have the child drop in the appropriate number of marbles.

5. Have the partner check each cup and count the marbles to see if the correct amount was put in it.

6. Place the marbles back into the box.

VARIATION:

■ Place numerals from 1 to 10 around the room. Show the child a card with objects on it. Ask her to find the numeral that tells how many objects are on the card.

■ Make a number book by pasting the correct number of beans, pieces of macaroni, or colored squares next to the written numerals.

ACTIVITIES FOR CHILDREN

Wearing Numbers

GOALS: To develop number recognition

To encourage children's interest in math activities

MATERIALS: Supply of white paper hats (the kind restaurant workers wear), markers, crayons, glue, and a supply of objects like buttons, seeds, bottle caps, and so on

PREPARATION: Write a number on each hat.

PROCEDURE: Have the children glue different sets of items onto the hat that go with the number on their hat. For example, three buttons on the hat with a "3" on it, four stickers on the hat with a "4" on it, and so on.

VARIATION:

■ Make paper crown hats out of construction paper. Have the children become Number Kings and Queens, using the same activity described in Procedure.

■ Choose a geometric shape such as a triangle. Cut various colors and sizes of triangles out of construction paper. Have the children glue them onto their hats (or crowns).

ADDITIONAL INFORMATION: White paper hats can be purchased through a restaurant supply house. Check with a restaurant manager to find out where to buy them locally. They might even offer to donate them for your children's use!

ACTIVITIES FOR CHILDREN

Number Books

GOALS: To develop number recognition

To develop counting skills

MATERIALS: Four sheets of white paper for each child, colored construction paper, paste, stapler, magazines, and catalogs

PREPARATION: Staple four sheets of white paper together with a colored construction paper cover. Title the cover according to a specific math concept (Number Book, Matching Book, Shape Book, and so on). Number the pages of each book from one to eight.

PROCEDURE:

1. Have the children look through magazines and catalogs to find pictures to glue to the page in the correct number.

2. Have the children glue pictures of one thing on page one, pictures of two things on page two, and so on.

VARIATION:

■ Make a Shape Book. Choose a geometric shape, such as a circle. Have the children glue pictures of circular things throughout their books.

■ Label the pages of the books with different geometric shapes (circles, squares, triangles, and so on). Have the children glue correspondingly shaped pictures onto the appropriate pages.

ACTIVITIES FOR CHILDREN   Fishes in Order

GOALS: To practice ordering skills
To encourage children's interest in math activities

MATERIALS: Construction paper, scissors

PREPARATION: Cut out three fish. Make each fish large enough to totally cover the next smaller fish when placed over it.

PROCEDURE:

1. Tell the children that the fish go in order, with the biggest fish first leading the others.

2. Have the child find the largest fish, then the fish that will follow.

3. Check to see if the largest fish covers the fish that follows.

4. For self-checking, have the child place each fish on top of the next to see if the next fish is smaller.

VARIATION: Order from the smallest fish to the largest fish.

ACTIVITIES FOR CHILDREN   Putting Things in Order

GOALS: To practice ordering skills
To encourage children's interest in math activities

MATERIALS: Nesting materials, such as a set of measuring spoons or measuring cups.

PREPARATION: Place objects on a table in front of the child. Do *not* put them in order.

PROCEDURE:

1. Have the child arrange the objects in the correct order so they will "nest" together. Objects must fit inside the other.

2. Have the child set the objects on the table in order from smallest to largest after she has finished "nesting" them.

VARIATION:

■ Order boxes or cans from smallest to largest by placing them inside one another.

■ Have the children roll balls of various sizes from clay or play dough. They can then order these balls according to size.

■ Make felt or cardboard cutouts in three or more sizes of different heights; for example, trees, houses, and hats. Have the child arrange them in a given order beginning with the shortest or tallest.

■ Use materials such as buttons, gummed stars, lids, beads, feathers, and nails to practice putting things in order of size.

ACTIVITIES FOR CHILDREN

Lots of Ideas to Compare

GOALS: To develop comparison skills

To encourage children's interest in math activities

MATERIALS: See specific activity for materials required

PREPARATION: Discuss how objects can be compared. Use comparison words like "longest," "longer," "shortest," "shorter," "biggest," "bigger," and so on.

PROCEDURE: Choose one or several of the following activities to practice comparing objects.

1. Use string, ribbon, pencils, rulers, or strips of paper. Have the children tell which is longest, longer, shortest, and shorter.

2. Use buttons, dolls, cups, plastic animals, trees, and boats. Have the child identify the biggest one or one bigger than another.

3. Use containers and coffee cans filled with various materials and then sealed buckets or bags of items. Have the child identify which is the heaviest or the lightest, or which is heavier than another.

4. Use toy cars, trucks, and swings. Have the child tell which is the fastest, and slowest, or which is faster than another.

5. Use paper, cardboard, books, pieces of wood, food slices, and cookies. Have the children make or find the item that is thick, thicker, thickest, or thinnest.

VARIATION: Use voices, musical instruments, drums, or other noise makers. Have the children pick out the loud and soft sounds, and the loudest or softest sounds.

ACTIVITIES FOR CHILDREN

Buttons, Buttons, Everywhere!

GOAL: To encourage children's interest in math activities

MATERIALS: Buttons of all shapes and sizes, index cards, and glue

PREPARATION: Ask parents to furnish buttons in all shapes and sizes.

PROCEDURE:

1. Have the children sort buttons by color and by size.

2. Have the children make graphs showing how many buttons of each color have been collected.

VARIATION: Make at least five different designs by gluing buttons to cards. Give children the same size cards and let them use buttons from the classroom supply to duplicate the designs on their cards.

ACTIVITIES FOR CHILDREN   Number Quiz

GOALS: To practice counting skills
To practice comparison skills

MATERIALS: None required

PREPARATION: Discuss the words "more" and "fewer."

PROCEDURE: Have the children make up and exchange riddles about "more" and "fewer." Examples may include: "I'm thinking of a number that is one more than the buttons on my shirt" or "I'm thinking of a number that is one fewer than the windows in our room."

VARIATION: Have the children make up and mentally solve riddles about the same numbers; for example, "I am the same number as the number of points on a triangle."

ACTIVITIES FOR CHILDREN   Sorting Loop

GOALS: To practice sorting skills
To encourage children's interest in math activities

MATERIALS: String or yarn, set of round objects of several colors, and a set of red objects of different shapes and sizes

PREPARATION: Make two big loops with string on a table or on the floor. Put a round object in one loop and a red object in the other.

PROCEDURE:

1. Have the children sort two ways: by round objects, and by red objects.
2. Have the children place red objects in one loop, and round objects in the other loop.
3. Make the loops overlap as shown in Figure 14–1.
4. Tell the children that only objects that are round *and* red can go in the middle loop.
5. Have the children re-sort the objects.

VARIATION: Provide other sets of objects that lend themselves to this type of sorting and let the children determine the sorting rules.

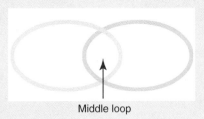

Middle loop

FIGURE 14–1 | Sorting loops.

ACTIVITIES FOR CHILDREN

Sorting Beans

GOALS: To practice sorting skills

To encourage children's interest in math activities

MATERIALS: Bag with about 30 beans of three different kinds, and three small containers, each labeled with a picture of one of the beans (or tape one of the beans onto the container)

PREPARATION: Explain to the children that there is a bag with three different kinds of beans in the math center. Show them the beans and name them together. Show the children the three containers with labels on them.

PROCEDURE:

1. Have the children sort the beans into the three containers.
2. Have each child take the beans out of the bag one at a time.
3. Have each child figure out which container each bean belongs in.
4. Have each child put the bean in the correct container.
5. When the child is finished, have him pour all the beans back into the bag for the next child.

ACTIVITIES FOR OLDER CHILDREN

Junk Mail Math
(Grades 4–5)

GOALS: To practice addition skills

To encourage children's interest in math activities

MATERIALS: Supply of catalogs

PREPARATION: Provide each child with a catalog for this activity.

PROCEDURE:

1. Have the child find two items that total $11.98 (or any other figure you choose).
2. Have the child add up all the items on page 7 (or any page you choose).
3. Ask the child "If you had $25.00 to spend for your friend's birthday, what item would you select?"
4. Have the child figure shipping costs on a given item.

VARIATION: Have the children comparison shop for a specific item through several catalogs. What is the best price for the item, including shipping costs?

ACTIVITIES FOR OLDER CHILDREN Multiplication Art
(Grades 4–5)

GOALS: To practice multiplication skills
To tie in art with math

MATERIALS: Paper, crayons, and markers

PREPARATION: Have each student select five multiplication equations that are especially hard to remember.

PROCEDURE:

1. Have the child draw a picture of the equation and the answer.

2. Have the child draw a picture and put the equation and answer somewhere within the picture. For example, a drawing for 5×6 might consist of a boy who is wearing a shirt with the number 5 on it, standing in front of an apartment door with a 6 on it, talking with a woman who is celebrating her thirtieth birthday with a cake that has 30 written on it.

VARIATION: Have the child choose two multiplication facts that are difficult for them. Build three-dimensional creations that use those equations. For example, the equation $9 \times 6 = 54$ can be shown as a model house with six rooms and nine objects in each room. Have the child share his creation with the class without showing the equation. Have other students study the model and figure out the multiplication fact hidden within.

ADDITIONAL INFORMATION: Memorizing the multiplication facts and understanding the idea of what these facts represent are a necessary foundation for further math learning. This memorization can be particularly difficult for students. This activity and others like it help students with this memory skill.

ACTIVITIES FOR OLDER CHILDREN Multiplication Talk Show
(Grades 4–5)

GOALS: To practice multiplication skills
To encourage children's interest in math activities

MATERIALS: None required

PREPARATION: Discuss how the talk show will work. Tell the children they will participate as the guest audience and/or the featured speakers.

PROCEDURE:

1. Have the show moderated by Mickey Multiplication, with the topic of "The Rough Life of Being a Multiplication Problem."

2. Have the children role-play multiplication problems after giving each number a personality. For example, Freddie Four may discuss how confused he gets when he has to play with Mr. Eight Snowman. The last time they played a game, he caught Mr. Snowman cheating 32 times!

ACTIVITIES FOR OLDER CHILDREN — Multiplication Baseball
(Grades 4–5)

GOALS: To practice multiplication skills

To encourage children's interest in math activities

MATERIALS: None required

PREPARATION: Divide the class into two teams. Designate a first, second, third, and home base in the room. For example, the pencil sharpener can be first base, the blackboard can be second, and so on.

PROCEDURE:

1. Have one group stand at the front of the room (home base) while the other group is seated.

2. Have one student from Team A "at bat," while one student from Team B "pitches" a multiplica-

tion problem. The pitcher must know the answer to their team's problem or it's an automatic home run. After the problem is "pitched," the student at bat gives the answer and moves to first base. This continues until three students answer incorrectly, at which time the teams trade places.

VARIATION: To make the game more challenging, divide the multiplication problems into "singles" (easy), "doubles" (moderate), "triples" (difficult), and home runs (extremely difficult). Have the child at bat choose which type of pitch he or she wants. You can decide how many "innings" time will allow.

ACTIVITIES FOR OLDER CHILDREN — Fun with Fractions
(Grades 4–5)

GOALS: To practice fraction skills

To encourage children's interest in math activities

MATERIALS: See individual activity for required materials

PREPARATION: Review fractions with the children.

PROCEDURE: Try some of these activities to reduce the fear of fractions and to help students understand what a fraction really is.

- Fraction story—Write a story about a fractional family. For example, the "Fourth" family that has four members: 1/4, 2/4, 3/4, and 4/4. Give each member of the family a unique personality relating to its fraction.

- Fraction song—Make up a song to help children learn about fractions. You might want to use a familiar melody. Be sure the lyrics help children understand that fractions are used to break down a "whole."

- Fraction P.E. Game—Redesign a game you already play to include fractions. For example, in softball, every time a player scores, his team could score 2/3 of a point instead of one point.

- Fraction Skit—Write and perform a short skit that teaches students how to reduce fractions. You may want to use props to show that certain fractions are equal even if they look different.

ACTIVITIES FOR OLDER CHILDREN **Art and Math**
(Grades 4–5)

GOALS: To recognize geometric shapes and forms in nature and in the environment

To encourage children's interest in math activities

MATERIALS: Magazines, newspapers, paper, scissors, and paste

PREPARATION: Discuss how artists use their knowledge of measurement and geometric shapes and forms in designing architecture, in planning beautiful vases, and in many other aspects of art.

Discuss radial balance—In radial balance, shapes and lines go out from a center. You see radial designs in many flowers and wheels.

PROCEDURE:

1. Have the children collect and display examples of radial balance and radial designs in human-made and natural forms.

2. Have the children cut examples from pictures in old magazines and newspapers.

3. Have the children bring in actual objects for this activity as well.

VARIATION: Have the children develop a display with their examples of radial balance.

ADDITIONAL INFORMATION: Examples of radial balance include starfish, wheels, snowflakes, many flowers, and the like.

CHAPTER 15

CREATIVE FOOD EXPERIENCES

hildren learn best when they experience the world firsthand—by touch, taste, smell, sight, and hearing. To make the most of any food experience, children must be *directly* involved with real food and given as much responsibility as possible for growing, selecting, preparing, and eating the food.

The use of foods in a classroom can be one of the most creative parts of the program. Foods are a part of each child's experience. Foods and cooking are interesting to children. All of their senses are used in food activities. They see the foods. They smell them, touch them, and taste them. The children can hear many kinds of foods boiling, popping, or frying. Other learning is enhanced by food activities, too. Art, science, and aesthetics are all related to cooking in some way.

Children enjoy food activities at any age.

IMPORTANCE OF FOOD EXPERIENCES TO THE TOTAL PROGRAM

CONCEPT BUILDING

Food activities help children develop new concepts in many areas such as language arts, science, health and safety, and mathematics.

Children learn to describe things. In cooking activities, children experience many shapes, sizes, and colors. They see that some things start out in a round shape and become long and flat during the cooking

process. Many foods change in size when they are heated; some change in texture and color. Foods come in many colors, and the colors sometimes change with mixing, heating, or cooling.

Children learn about tastes. Children find out how heating or mixing changes taste. They learn that some things, such as salt or sugar, can change the taste of foods. They discover that some foods taste good when they are mixed together and that others do not.

Children observe changes. As they did in science activities, children observe that foods change from

205

liquids to solids and from solids to liquids. They also see steam (a gas) rising from liquids that are heated. They smell odors as foods change from solids to liquids to gases. They see how ingredients, when mixed together, form a new substance. In baking, this same substance changes even more.

Children learn to express themselves. Language develops as a result of food experiences. Words like "bitter," "sour," "sweet," and "salty" have real meaning. "Hot," "cold," "warm," and "cool" are part of the food vocabulary. Children may learn the words "delicious" and "tasty." They learn a more complete meaning of terms like liquid and solid, freezing and boiling, smelly and odorless. When the words relate to direct experiences, the child's vocabulary grows.

Children enjoy eating their food creations.

SKILL BUILDING

There are a number of skills that children can learn from working with foods.

Small-muscle coordination. Mixing foods and pouring liquids from one container to another are ways in which children develop coordination. The small muscles in the hands develop as a child holds a large spoon and helps in the mixing process when using a recipe. The measuring, pouring, and mixing of foods all require the use of small muscles as well as hand-eye coordina-

tion. Thus, food activities provide excellent small motor activities for young children.

Simple measuring skills. By using cups and spoons that have marks showing amounts, a child begins to understand measurements. The child is able to observe that a tablespoon is larger than a teaspoon and that a cup holds more than a tablespoon. The child can also begin to realize that by using too much flour, water, or salt, recipes don't turn out quite as well as if the

THIS ONE'S FOR YOU   You May Not Know about Fruit

- Some fruits, especially dried fruits, berries, and solid fruits such as pears are good sources of fiber. Offer children wedges of seedless oranges and apples. They have fiber that's lost when they're made into juice.
- Generally, the more color a fruit (or vegetable) has, the more vitamins and minerals it contains.
- For toddlers, avoid fruits with seeds. Pay special attention as toddlers eat dried or frozen fruits and cut firm fruits to be sure they don't choke on the hard bits of food.
- Bananas and avocados are favorites of young children because the fruits' textures are appealing. Both are rich in potassium and other minerals.
- Products marked "juice" must contain 100 percent juice. "Drinks," "ades," "punches," "cocktails," and other beverages may be little more than fruit-flavored sugar water.
- Giving a child juice made from concentrate is a good way to provide fluoride if your water supply is fluoridated.
- Juice is a food. Give it only once or twice a day so children won't fill up on it and not eat other foods. Encourage plain water for thirst.

correct amounts are used. The child begins to under-stand that the amount of each ingredient used makes a difference in the final product. This realization leads the child to look for ways to figure out amounts. This is when measuring tools are discovered.

Social skills. Food experiences are a natural avenue for social learning. Mixing, measuring, decorating, and eating all provide many opportunities for talking with others, exchanging ideas, sharing likes and dislikes, and learning about each other. You will find that in prepar-ing food, children many times will talk more freely about themselves and their lives in the homey, routine nature of this type of activity.

HEALTH AND SAFETY

As children are involved in food experiences, they learn some basic information on routines and cautions about food and cooking necessary to good health and safety. This information is best learned in the process of work-ing with food and not as a "lecture" type lesson.

Here are some important basic health and safety is-sues to keep in mind.

■ Cleanliness is important in all food preparation. Both children and adults should always wash their hands with soap and water before beginning any food ex-perience.

■ Be sure children keep fingers and utensils out of their mouths while preparing food.

■ Do not allow any tasting of recipes containing raw eggs. Raw eggs are a source of salmonella bacteria and can cause digestive problems.

■ Any cooking adventure involving heat, knives, or operating appliances should be carefully super-vised.

■ Turn utensil handles toward the center of the range at all times.

■ Be sure you know which children have food allergies. Some children may also have ethnic food restrictions that prohibit their eating certain foods as well.

FOOD ACTIVITIES IN THE CURRICULUM AREAS

Cooking does more than build physical, health and safety, and social skills. It is an ideal project for just about all of the curriculum areas. It involves reading, math, sci-ence, creative activities, opportunities for independent learning and following directions, and drawing and writ-ing activities. Let's look briefly at these different areas.

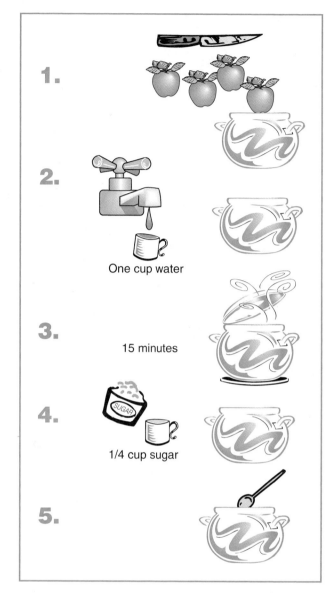

1.

2.
One cup water

3.
15 minutes

4.
1/4 cup sugar

5.

FIGURE 15–1 | Picture recipe for applesauce (recipe at end of chapter).

READING

For pre-kindergarten children, drawings with words and numbers can be used to help children understand the recipe. (See picture recipes in Figures 15–1, 15–2, and 15–3.) This is a good warm-up activity for reading in kindergarten or the primary grades. Older children can read the recipe, which itself is good practice. Many books, for both preschool and elementary age, talk about food and cooking. Display some of these books in your library area for the children to look at. If you find a book that applies to a specific cooking experience, read it to the group before beginning to cook.

In the language arts center, furnish a tape recorder for children's dictation of their real and fantastic recipes.

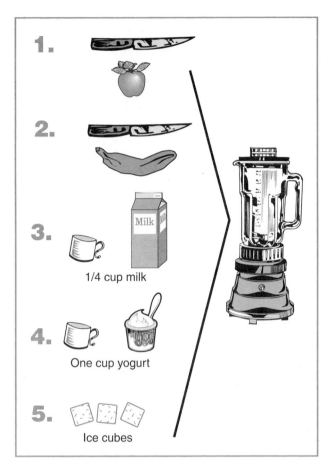

FIGURE 15–2 Picture recipe for banana apple icy (recipe at end of chapter).

FIGURE 15–3 Picture recipe for apple sandwich (recipe at end of chapter).

Provide paper and art materials for later transcription into books.

MATH

For most recipes, measuring instruments—cups, tablespoons, and teaspoons—are required. It's also helpful and interesting to have a food scale for measuring as well. Sequencing (measuring, mixing, and then baking), estimating, counting, adding, fractions, and discrimination of size and shape are all involved in cooking experiences.

Discuss each of these objects and activities as you go along, working with small groups so everyone gets a turn. Children learn better when they *do* than when they merely look and listen.

Older children can handle measuring and mixing ingredients on their own. You can challenge their math skills by asking them to measure the ingredients for one-half of the recipe you're going to use. Or they can figure out how to double or triple the recipe for a larger group.

SCIENCE

Cooking develops sensory skills. It involves physical and chemical changes, the use of simple machines, and predicting the outcome of a cooking experiment. For example, when making cookies, place all the ingredients on the table and give everyone a chance to smell, touch, and taste each one. Then mix the ingredients with spoons or forks. Ask the children about shape and texture as you mix. Ask them to predict the outcome of your cooking experience. Then, after baking, compare your predictions with the results.

Older children can suggest ways to alter the recipe to make it turn out in different ways. They enjoy experimenting with different spices to give their recipes a new and special flavor.

SCIENCE CENTER

Provide open-ended activities for cooking explorations. For instance, try a taste test of all the different ways apples are used in cooking and eating: apple juice, cider,

THIS ONE'S FOR YOU

Individual Cooking Activities in Interest Centers: A Free-Choice Activity

It's John's turn to "cook" during free-choice activity time. First, he washes his hands; second, he puts on a white paper chef's hat, and third, he begins cutting fruit into bite-sized pieces with a plastic knife. He is following a picture recipe and will eventually put the fruit on a skewer to make a fruit kabob for his snack to be eaten later with his classmates. And, he made his snack all by himself! Independent snack preparation can easily be set up in the classroom with some basic equipment and recipes designed for individual portions.

Below are ideas and recipes to help you get started cooking independently in your classroom.

Cut off one of the end flaps of a sturdy cardboard box and cut the box apart at the side seam so it will stand up using the other end flaps as supports. This will be your instruction "board." Cover the entire box with colorful contact papers. The box can be set up on a table to designate your snack and work area.

Sequential picture recipes can be clipped to each section of the box/board. For example, the pictures in sequence would indicate to (1) wash hands, (2) cut fruit into pieces, (3) put fruit on skewer, and (4) place on paper plate with name on plate. Basic equipment for your snack activity center would include measuring cups, small bowls, tongue depressors, small wire whisks, 5-ounce paper cups, plastic serrated knives, electric skillet, blender, and paper chef's hats. AN ELECTRIC APPLIANCE IS OPERATED BY ADULTS ONLY.

After you've designated your snack area and gathered your equipment, you're ready to begin with the recipes that follow. Before each child actually begins the snack preparation, gather the children in a group, tell them briefly about the recipe, and remind them of any specific directions. For example, a direction might be that each child may cut up only one slice of melon. While one or two children are working in the snack area, the teacher always needs to be available for assistance as the children need it.

PEANUT BUTTER PUDDING FOR ONE

You'll need: 2 tablespoons dry milk; 2 tablespoons instant vanilla pudding mix; 1/3 cup water; 1 tablespoon fresh peanut butter (no sugar added)

What to do: 1. Using a tongue depressor for leveling dry ingredients, measure dry milk and pudding mix in 5-ounce paper cup. 2. Add water and stir using a small whisk, 1-1/2 minutes. 3. Add peanut butter and whisk until smooth. 4. Chill.

LETTUCE WRAP-AROUNDS

You'll need: lettuce leaves; any combination of luncheon meats or cheese slices, or spreads such as cream cheese, peanut butter, or egg salad

What to do: 1. Lay lettuce leaf flat on cutting board. 2. Place meat and/or cheese slice on lettuce leaf. 3. Add a spread or other filler and roll up the combination, securing with a toothpick. These may be eaten rolled up or can be cut into bite-sized pieces with a serrated knife.

BANANA SHAKE BAG

You'll need: ¼ cup chopped peanuts; 1 banana

What to do: 1. After peeling banana, cut in one-inch chunks. 2. Place peanuts in a plastic baggie. 3. Put a few banana chunks at a time in the bag and shake. Serve bananas on paper plates.

(Continued)

FOR YOU...(Continued)

E MIX-UP

/4 cup plus 1 tablespoon instant nonfat dry milk; 1/2 cup pineapple juice, chilled; 1/2 cup crac...

What to do: 1. For cracked ice, wrap some ice cubes in a towel and pound with a hammer. 2. Combine all ingredients in a blender and blend on high 30 seconds until thick and foamy.

Watch the food disappear at snack time because the children love these activities. Don't forget the paper chef's hats (available at a party store) or you can make your own hats! The hats make the children feel even more special, like "professional" chefs.

sauce, butter, dried, even apple cider vinegar. Or compare the appearance, taste, and texture of red, green, and yellow apples. You can also explore bananas: Brainstorm a list of how many different ways you can cook or eat them. What can you do with a frozen banana? Make ice cream! (Put chunks of frozen banana in a blender with just a hint of milk, blend until thick, and eat immediately.) How do bananas taste when they're sliced in circles? Try it and see.

CREATIVE ACTIVITIES

Almost all recipes can be extended, modified, changed, or given an unexpected twist. Use your imagination, and, more important, get the *children* to use theirs! Use a soft pretzel recipe (recipe at end of chapter) to make animals or three-dimensional sculptures instead of the traditional pretzel shape. Add food coloring to the coating mixture (in the recipe) and paint your animals or sculptures before baking.

DRAWING AND WRITING

Have the children dictate stories, anecdotes from home, and highlights of their experiences cooking in your classroom. Involve parents and other volunteers in this

activity. Those children who wish to can tell and draw about the day's cooking activity. Older children can keep personal journals of their cooking experiences. They may want to select certain favorite recipes and make up their own cookbooks.

In all areas of the curriculum, there are some things to remember when planning cooking activities:

1. Work out ahead of time a sequence of steps for the activity.

2. Plan a series of activities that are gradually more complex.

3. Encourage the children to talk about what they are doing.

4. Relate the activity to home experiences.

5. Give the names for new foods, processes, and equipment used.

6. When appropriate, involve the children in getting supplies for the activities.

7. Encourage discussion of what has been done. Allow a good amount of time for tasting and touching.

8. Use follow-up activities to reinforce the learning. (See Figure 15–4.)

USING FOOD IN SCIENCE ACTIVITIES

- Plant an outdoor or indoor garden.
- Have a tasting party.
- Arrange unusual foods on a science table.
- Place carrot, beet, or pineapple tops in a shallow bowl of crushed stones or pebbles covered with water.
- Cut off the top third of a sweet potato and put it in water. Allow sprouts to vine at the top. Hold the potato part way out of the water.
- Examine a coconut, then break it open.
- Examine and cut a fresh pineapple.
- Taste baby foods.
- Place seed catalogs on the reading shelf.
- Make a food dictionary.
- Draw pictures of your favorite foods from each food group. Make a meal: Draw a picture of a plate and cup and fill them with your foods to make a nutritious meal. Make sure you label each food.

CREATIVE ART ACTIVITIES WITH FOOD

- fruit-colored play dough
- potato printing
- broken eggshells on paintings
- child-made food books
  Foods I Like
  Fruits I Like
  Foods My Daddy (or Mommy, Sister, etc.) Likes
- a class mural made of pictures of foods
- creating flannel board pictures (have foods cut from flannel for child to arrange on a flannel or story board)
- food pictures cut from newspaper or magazine advertisements to paste on colored paper
- have children paste pictures of foods on a chart with areas for fruits and vegetables, breads, milk, and meats
- make picture charts of favorite recipes

TABLE ACTIVITIES—FOOD EXPERIENCES

- sewing cards with food pictures
- dishpans of beans with funnels, measuring cups
- food scale with beans for weighing
- balance for weighing

FIELD TRIPS—FOOD EXPERIENCES

- grocery store
- vegetable garden
- fruit orchard
- school kitchen
- bakery
- restaurant
- pizza parlor
- ice cream store
- fruit and vegetable stand
- bottling company
- dairy
- canning factory
- hatchery
- cornfield, strawberry or melon patch
- kitchen of one of the children's family

GAMES FOR COOKING EXPERIENCES

- Can You Remember? (display foods on a tray; cover; try to remember where each is)
- How Many? (different foods, etc.)
- Which? (foods that can be eaten raw, foods that are yellow, etc.)
- Grouping (those that are yellow, those that are eaten for breakfast, etc.)
- Touch and Tell (place food in a bag; have child feel and try to identify)
- Smell and Tell (have child close eyes and try to identify food by smelling)
- Guess What? (describe the characteristics of food; children try to identify)

FIGURE 15–4 | Follow-up activities to reinforce learning.

FOOD FOR THOUGHT

"Enriched"—"Fortified"— Good or Bad

Don't worry about giving young children some foods such as white bread and sandwich buns that say *enriched* or *fortified* on the label. Enrichment replaces some of the nutrients lost during processing and fortification adds others. Some people say that white flour and products made with white flour are not nutritious. This is not true. It's just that whole grains are a bit better because they have more of some vitamins, minerals, and fiber. All starches are valuable sources of vitamins, minerals, and calories for young children. Even the youngest child needs at least four servings from the starch group each day. It's best to offer a variety of selections from the list rather than four or more portions of the same starch. This is true of all food groups (Hess et al., 1990).

WHOLE GRAIN STARCH CHOICES

barley	oatmeal	whole-grain Melba toast
brown rice	pumpernickel	wheat germ
bulgar	rye bread	whole-wheat pasta
corn tortilla	Rykrisp	
millet	whole-grain breads	
oat bran	whole-grain cereals	
	whole-grain wafers	

BEST ENRICHED/FORTIFIED STARCH CHOICES

bagel, bialy	cornbread or corn muffins	raisin bread
bread sticks	matzo	rusks
cereals (ready-to eat, not too sweet)	melba toast	spaghetti
	noodles	
cooked cereals (all kinds)	pasta	

OTHER STARCH CHOICES

English muffin	graham crackers	muffins (unenriched)
flour tortilla	french bread (unenriched)	oatmeal cookies
hard rolls	italian bread (unenriched)	pasta salad
biscuits	white bread (enriched)	pretzels
bread stuffing	white rice	rice cakes
fruit/nut bread	Zwieback	

ACTIVITIES FOR CHILDREN

Hot Potato Game

GOAL: To encourage children's interest in games related to food activities

MATERIALS: Potato, tape or CD of music

PREPARATION: Have the children sit in a circle on the floor.

PROCEDURE:

1. Play music as the children pass a real potato around the circle.

2. When the music stops, have the child with the potato leave the circle.

3. Have each child who leaves the circle get a turn to start and stop the music.

VARIATION: Cut up the potato and use it for a printing activity after the game.

ACTIVITIES FOR CHILDREN

Food and Field Trips

GOAL: To encourage children's interest in food activities

MATERIALS: Paper, pencils, tape recorder, and camera (optional)

PREPARATION: Arrange a field trip with a local restaurant, pizzeria, or bakery. Arrange to see at least one recipe being prepared.

PROCEDURE:

1. Before the trip, have the children prepare a list of questions they would like to ask during the visit.

2. Consider taking along a portable tape recorder and camera to record the steps of the recipe the children are learning about.

VARIATION:

■ Have the children make the recipe at school.

■ Have the children write a story about their experiences, using the photos as their inspiration.

■ Have the children draw or paint a picture about their experiences.

ACTIVITIES FOR CHILDREN

Math and Food Experiences

GOALS: To encourage children's interest in food activities

To reinforce learning about shapes

MATERIALS: Crackers in a variety of shapes: gold-fish, oyster, square, and oval; bowl; and paper plates

PREPARATION: Place paper plates for each type of cracker on the table.

PROCEDURE:

1. Have the children work together to sort the crackers onto each plate.

2. Pass the plates around and choose crackers to eat at snack time.

VARIATION: After a food activity, make a bar graph that lists all the recipes you've used in your class. Indicate the names of the children who liked each one. Which recipe did most children prefer? Which recipe was least preferred? Brainstorm with the children how they could change the recipes to make them even better.

ACTIVITIES FOR CHILDREN

Food, Language Arts, and Art Activities

GOALS: To relate food activities to language arts and art activities

To encourage children's interest in food activities

MATERIALS: The book *Pretzel* by Margaret Rey (1997), ingredients for soft pretzel recipe found at the end of this chapter, crayons, markers, paper, and play dough

PREPARATION: Read *Pretzel* by Margaret Rey to the children.

PROCEDURE:

1. Have the children make real pretzels with the recipe for soft pretzels found at the end of this chapter.

2. Have the children create drawings about their pretzel-making experience.

VARIATION:

■ Have the children record their pretzel-making experience.

■ Have the children make their own pretzel books.

■ Have the children make pretend pretzels with play dough or clay, or by twisting brown butcher paper.

ACTIVITIES FOR CHILDREN

Food Riddles

GOALS: To encourage children's interest in food activities

To practice listening and thinking skills

MATERIALS: None required

PREPARATION: Have the children sit in a small group of 4 to 5. Read the entire riddle before the children respond. You may want to write the riddles on index cards to read to the children.

PROCEDURE: Read the following food riddles for the children to guess the answer to:

1. I'm in the dairy group. I'm white. People drink me out of a glass, cup, or carton. You put me on cereal. What am I? (milk).

2. I'm in the vegetable group. I'm long, orange, and crunchy when eaten raw. What am I? (carrot).

3. I'm in the fruit group. I'm round, shiny, and smooth to touch. I'm crunchy to bite into. I grow on a tree. What am I? (apple).

4. I'm in the meat group. I'm flat and round in shape. I often come on a bun. Sometimes people put catsup on me. What am I? (hamburger).

5. I'm in the bread and cereal group. I come in a loaf. You can slice me to make sandwiches. I smell good right after I'm baked. What am I? (bread).

6. I'm a member of the meat and poultry group. I have an oval shape. I come from a chicken. You can fry me, scramble me, or boil me. Inside I am yellow and white. What am I? (egg).

7. I'm a member of the fruit group. I'm tiny, brown, and wrinkled. I used to be a grape. You can eat me in a cereal, in cookies, or just by myself. I'm sweet but not a junk food. What am I? (raisin).

VARIATION:

■ Have the children make up their own food riddles.

■ Have the children concentrate riddles on only one food group.

■ Have the children concentrate riddles on only ethnic foods.

ACTIVITIES FOR CHILDREN

Original Recipes

GOALS: To encourage children's interest in food activities

To practice telling things in a sequence

MATERIALS: Paper, pencil

PREPARATION: Discuss the children's favorite foods. Have the children pick their favorite food.

PROCEDURE:

1. Have the child dictate recipes for his favorite food.

2. Write down *exactly* what the child says. Include mistakes and funny parts, too.

3. Put the recipes together in a booklet for parents.

VARIATION: Draw a picture or make a painting about making the recipe. These can be used as a cover for the recipe booklets.

ACTIVITIES FOR CHILDREN   Great Grapes

GOAL: To encourage children's interest in food activities

MATERIALS: Red, purple, and green grapes

PREPARATION: Place assortment of grapes on the table.

PROCEDURE:

1. Have the children tell about the many grape products they eat or drink (jelly, juice, etc.).

2. Brainstorm new ways to prepare and eat grape snacks.

3. Make one or several of the grape recipes found at the end of this chapter.

VARIATION:

■ Make a grape cookbook, with each recipe signed by the cook.

■ Have the children draw or paint a picture about grapes.

ACTIVITIES FOR OLDER CHILDREN   Potatoes—A Food Unit
(Grades 4–5)

GOAL: To tie in language arts, math, and food activities

MATERIALS: Tomie de Paola's book *Jamie O'Rourke and the Big Potato* (1992), or you could also use McDonald's *The Potato Man* (1996)

PREPARATION: After reading the book to the group, make it available for children to read on their own for at least a week. Discuss the book(s) read about potatoes.

PROCEDURE:

1. Have the children research the history of the potato, as well as Ireland.

2. Have the children write factual reports on these topics.

3. Compile the reports into a class *Potato Book.*

VARIATION:

■ Use a 10-lb. bag of potatoes as a source of math experiences. Have the children estimate the number of potatoes in the bag, then count the potatoes. Discuss their estimates. Compare the actual number of potatoes to these estimates.

■ Make up a summary graph showing the range of numbers between the estimates and the actual number of potatoes.

■ Give each child a potato. Have them count the eyes, estimate the circumference, then measure it. Graph the results.

■ Using a balance scale, have the children weigh each potato.

■ Discuss the nutritional value of potatoes as you make dishes using recipes from children's families.

ACTIVITIES FOR OLDER CHILDREN
Vegetable Soup— Cooking Unit
(Grades 4–5)

GOAL: To tie in language arts, science, and food activity

MATERIALS: *Growing Vegetable Soup* by L. Ehlert (1987) or *Neighborhood Soup* by J. Nelson (1990)

PREPARATION: Read either one or both of the books listed above.

PROCEDURE:

1. Have the children work cooperatively to make the neighborhood soup.
2. Discuss the creation of new soups.
3. Have the children brainstorm ingredients for their original soups.
4. Have the children create labels for their own soup cans.

VARIATION:

■ Have the children work together to present a play based on the *Neighborhood Soup* story, including props and promotional posters.

■ Have the children plant vegetable seeds and observe their growth. Have them keep written records of plant growth under a variety of conditions, including without light and without water.

■ Have the children use seed catalogs and real vegetables to examine the edible parts of various plants.

■ Have the children taste a variety of vegetables—raw and cooked—and compare the nutritional value of each. Then, use the raw vegetables in the art center for making vegetable prints.

ADDITIONAL INFORMATION: Plan to use several weeks to complete this unit on vegetable soup.

ACTIVITIES FOR OLDER CHILDREN
Fruit Science
(Grades 4–5)

GOALS: To encourage children's interest in food activities

To practice observation skills

MATERIALS: Three or four different varieties of apples

PREPARATION: In front of each kind of apple, place a label with the name of it.

PROCEDURE:

1. Have the children read the names of the apples and describe and compare the different varieties.

2. Give the children thin slices of the varieties to name, taste, and compare.

VARIATION:

■ Have the children research facts about apples: uses and food value, growth and environment, and so on.

■ Have the children make a special dessert or salad using the apples. (See recipes at the end of this chapter.) Have the children taste, describe, and enjoy them.

■ Make an apple collage using colored paper depicting the different kinds of apples.

ACTIVITIES FOR OLDER CHILDREN
(Grades 4–5)

Eggs-traordinary!

GOAL: To tie in language arts and food activity

MATERIALS: *Green Eggs and Ham* by Dr. Seuss (1976), paper, pencils, markers, and ingredients to make green eggs and ham

PREPARATION: Read *Green Eggs and Ham.*

PROCEDURE:

1. After reading the story, have the children try to state the moral of the story as clearly as possible. (The moral might be stated: "You never know if you'll like a new food until you try it" or "Try it, you'll like it.")

2. Have the children make green eggs and ham.

VARIATION: Have the children use their imaginations by drawing and coloring a picture of a food. Have them color the picture so that the food looks interesting or fun to them, and then write a paragraph to go with their pictures.

ADDITIONAL INFORMATION: Discuss purchasing environmentally sound egg cartons with the children. Molded pulp cartons are generally made from 100 percent recycled paper. That makes these a better choice than polystyrene egg cartons. Polystyrene is not recyclable, nor is it biodegradable.

ACTIVITIES FOR OLDER CHILDREN
(Grades 4–5)

Food from Animals and Plants

GOAL: To encourage children's interest in where food comes from

MATERIALS: Paper, scissors, paste, magazines or newspapers

PREPARATION: Discuss farms, farm animals, and the plants we eat.

PROCEDURE:

1. Have the children draw or cut out pictures to make a farm scene of plants and animals we eat.

2. Have the children draw another picture of some plants and animals we do not eat.

VARIATION: Have the students think about the grocery store. Are products from plants and animals sold together in one department or are they in separate departments?

ADDITIONAL INFORMATION: Polyvinyl chloride (PVC) is a huge contributor to environmental pollution. Supermarkets package their meat, fish, and poultry in polystyrene trays and then wrap them in PVC wrap. However, the deli counter will cut meat and wrap it in freezer wrap or molded pulp trays, which are better. Have students offer suggestions for alternative ways to buy and package meat.

ACTIVITIES FOR OLDER CHILDREN Food and the Media
(Grades 4–5)

GOALS: To encourage children's interest in food activities

To tie in language arts and food activities

MATERIALS: Newspapers, magazines, paper, scissors, paste, crayons, and markers

PREPARATION: Discuss how food is advertised in the newspapers and in magazines.

PROCEDURE:

1. Have the children cut out food advertisements from newspapers and magazines.

2. Have the children evaluate the food advertised as to its nutritional value.

3. For food poor in nutritional quality, have the children find an advertisement for a better one.

VARIATION:

■ Use this eating advice rhyme to evaluate the food advertised: "Before eating, keep repeating, stop and think, will this help me grow?"

■ Make a poster or bulletin board with the "Eating Advice" rhyme.

ACTIVITIES FOR OLDER CHILDREN Food Groups
(Grades 4–5)

GOAL: To become more aware of foods and food groups

MATERIALS: Paper and pencils

PREPARATION: Review the food groups (bread, fruit, vegetable, meat, and milk). Discuss with the students what they had for breakfast.

PROCEDURE:

1. Have the children list typical foods eaten at breakfast.

2. Have the children write one breakfast menu.

3. Have the children count the number of servings from the bread, fruit, vegetable, meat, and milk groups.

4. Have the children subtract the breakfast servings to determine the food to eat the rest of the day.

VARIATION: After lunch, have the children determine how many servings from each food group have been eaten, and how many servings need to be eaten at supper in order to meet their food requirements.

RECIPES FOR FOOD EXPERIENCES

Frozen Grapes.   Place washed grapes on a cookie sheet with spaces between each one. Cut them in half to avoid choking. Freeze. When frozen, place in a plastic bag. Eat frozen.

Grapes to Raisins.   Wash and dry a large bunch of green grapes. Place in a basket in a warm sunny spot for four to seven days. You will then have raisins!

Grape Fruit Cocktail.   Slice grapes in half with plastic knives. Add sliced grapes to a can of fruit cocktail. Add fresh fruit chunks as desired.

Grape Surprises.
A. Ingredients:
   1/2 cup peanut butter
   1/2 cup nonfat dry milk powder
   2 tablespoons honey
   grapes
B. Procedure:
   1. Mix peanut butter, milk powder, and honey until a soft, non-sticky "dough" is formed.
   2. Knead dough, then press out pieces into 2-inch circles.
   3. Place a grape in the center. Wrap dough around grape and seal well.
   4. *Variation:* Place grapes inside cream cheese balls, then roll in chopped nuts.

Grapes and Yogurt.
A. Ingredients:
   small bunch of grapes
   1 cup yogurt or sour cream
B. Procedure: Slice grapes with plastic knife and add to yogurt (or sour cream).

Cheesy French Fries.
A. Ingredients:
   1 package (9 ounces) frozen french fried potatoes
   1/2 teaspoon salt
   dash pepper
   1/2 cup grated sharp cheese
B. Procedure:
   1. Preheat oven to 450°F.
   2. Arrange potatoes on cookie sheet.
   3. Sprinkle with salt and pepper.
   4. Bake uncovered 15 minutes.
   5. Sprinkle cheese over potatoes.
   6. Bake 2–3 minutes longer or until cheese is melted.

Soft Pretzels.
A. Ingredients:
   1-1/2 cups warm water
   3 cups flour
   1 pkg. yeast
   1 tablespoon sugar
   1 teaspoon salt
   1 tablespoon vegetable oil
B. Procedure:
   1. Mix together all the ingredients.
   2. Add small amounts of flour until mixture does not stick to your hand.
   3. Roll out 12 small balls of dough to make snakes or worms.
   4. Loop ends together to make a pretzel knot.
   5. Coat with a mixture of one egg yolk and two tablespoons of water.
   6. Sprinkle a few pieces of salt on each pretzel.
   7. Place on a slightly greased cookie sheet.
   8. Bake at 425° for 10 to 12 minutes.

Applesauce.   Picture recipe in Figure 15–1.
A. Ingredients:
   4 to 6 medium apples
   1/4 cup sugar
   1/2 stick cinnamon (or 1–2 whole cloves, if desired)
B. Procedure: (if food mill is not used)
   1. Peel and core the apples.
   2. Cut apples into quarters, and place in pot.
   3. Add a small amount of water (about 1 inch).
   4. Cover the pot and cook slowly (simmer), until apples are tender. The cooked apples can then be mashed with a fork, beaten with a beater, or put through a strainer.
   5. Add sugar to taste (about 1/2 cup to 4 apples), and continue cooking until sugar dissolves.
   6. Add 1/2 stick of cinnamon (or 1 to 2 cloves) if desired.
      Note: If a food mill is used, it is not necessary to peel and core the apples. After the apples are cooked as above, they are put through the food mill. Children enjoy turning the handle and watching the sauce come dripping out of the holes.
   7. *Variation:* For fun, add a few cinnamon candies. What happens to the color of the applesauce? Is the flavor changed? Be sure to add them while the applesauce is still hot.

Banana Apple Icy.   Picture recipe in Figure 15–2.
A. Ingredients:
   1 apple
   1 banana
   1/4 cup milk

1 cup plain yogurt
3 ice cubes
B. Procedure:
1. Peel and core 1 yellow apple.
2. Cut it into small cubes.
3. Peel and slice 1 banana.
4. Put these in a blender with the milk and yogurt.
5. Add 3 ice cubes.
6. Blend until smooth.
7. Makes enough for 2 small glasses.

Apple Sandwich. Picture recipe in Figure 15–3.
A. Ingredients:
1 apple
peanut butter
B. Procedure:
1. Peel and core an apple.
2. Cut it crosswise into slices.
3. Spread peanut butter on one apple slice and top with another apple slice.

Fruit Soup.
A. Ingredients:
honeydew and/or cantaloupe melon
1 banana
1 plum
kiwifruit
grapes and other fruits
1 cup of orange juice
1 scoop of frozen yogurt
B. Procedure:
1. Scoop balls from melons with a melon baller. (Kids love doing this.) Use a honeydew melon or cantaloupe or some of each.
2. Cut up banana with a butter knife.
3. Add the orange juice for the base of the soup and put in a blender.
4. Add banana pieces and whirl on high for 30 seconds.
5. Pour soup into 3 or 4 bowls—or into 8–10 small cups.
6. Add cut-up fruit to each and then top it off with a scoop of frozen yogurt.

Beautiful Bagels.
Use bagels as your "easel." Take 1/2 of a bagel, let the child spread it with cream cheese. Have available a variety of sliced vegetables such as carrots, cucumbers, bean sprouts, cherry tomatoes, green or red bell peppers, or black olives. Children can decorate their snack to their own "taste" both artistically and health-wise.

Stuffed Baked Apples.
A. Ingredients:
4 tart apples
1/4 cup crunchy breakfast cereal
1/4 cup chopped walnuts
1/4 teaspoon cinnamon
1 cup raisins
2 tablespoons honey
B. Procedure:
1. Core apples.
2. Combine ingredients and spoon equal amounts into each apple cavity.
3. Place apples in shallow baking dish and add 1/4 cup of water.
4. Bake uncovered for 40 minutes at 300°F.

Banana Breakfast Split.
A. Ingredients:
1 banana, sliced lengthwise
1/2 cup cottage cheese
1 tablespoon wheat germ
1 tablespoon raisins
1 tablespoon chopped nuts
B. Procedure:
1. Place banana slices in a bowl.
2. Put scoops of cottage cheese on top.
3. Sprinkle with wheat germ, raisins, and nuts. Makes one serving.

Pear Bunnies.
A. Ingredients:
ripe pear, cut in half lengthwise
1 lettuce leaf
1 teaspoon cottage cheese
1 red cherry
raisins
almond slivers
B. Procedure:
Place pear half on lettuce half, rounded side up. Decorate, using cottage cheese for "cottontail," cherry for nose, raisins for eyes, and almond slivers for ears.

Fruit Leather. This recipe reinforces the concept that fruits like apricots, peaches, raspberries, apples, etc., can be changed and used in new ways.
A. Ingredients:
1 quart or 2 pounds of fresh fruit
sugar
cinnamon
plastic wrapping paper
B. Procedure:
1. Help children break open, peel, and seed or pit fruit.

2. Puree prepared fruit in blender until smooth.

3. Add 2 tablespoons sugar and 1/2 teaspoon cinnamon to each 2 cups of puree.

4. Pour mixture onto sheet of plastic wrap that has been placed on a large cookie sheet. Spread mixture thinly and evenly.

5. Cover mixture with a screen or a piece of cheesecloth and place in the sun until completely dry—about one or two days. It can then be eaten or rolled and stored.

Peanutty Pudding.

A. Ingredients:
1 package regular pudding
2 cups milk
peanut butter

B. Procedure:
1. Prepare pudding as directed on package. (You may choose to use the sugar-free type.)
2. Pour cooked pudding into individual bowls.
3. While still warm, stir in 1 tablespoon peanut butter to each bowl.

Fruit Kabobs.

A. Ingredients:
1 cup vanilla or lemon yogurt (low fat, low-sugar variety)
2 cups fresh or canned fruit (chunk-style)
pretzel sticks

B. Procedure:
1. Thread fruit chunks onto pretzel sticks. Talk about how colors and sizes look next to each other.
2. Dip each end piece into the yogurt before eating, or spoon yogurt over the entire kabob.

Strawberry Yogurt Shake.

A. Ingredients:
1/2 cup frozen unsweetened strawberries, thawed
2 tablespoons frozen orange juice concentrate, thawed
1/2 cup banana (optional)
1 cup vanilla or lemon yogurt

B. Procedure:
1. Puree strawberries in blender.
2. Add remaining ingredients to blender and mix until frothy.
3. For holidays or special occasions, stick straws through colorful paper shapes and serve with shakes. Makes two servings, 3/4 cup each.

Peanut Butter Banana Smoothie.

A. Ingredients:
1 cup vanilla yogurt
1 to 2 tablespoons peanut butter
1 banana

B. Procedure:
1. Combine all ingredients in blender.
2. Whip for 30 to 60 seconds or until smooth.
3. Serve in custard cup or small bowl to eat with a spoon, or pour into cups to drink.

Broccoli Trees and Snow.

A. Ingredients:
3/4 cup small curd cottage cheese
1/2 cup plain yogurt
1/4 cup fresh minced parsley
1 bunch broccoli

B. Procedure:
1. Mix cottage cheese and yogurt in blender until smooth.
2. Add parsley and refrigerate until cool.
3. Cut broccoli into "dippers." (Cucumbers, zucchini, celery, carrots, radishes, and green peppers make good "dippers," too.)
4. Dip vegetables into yogurt mix and enjoy.

Fruit Sun.

A. Ingredients:
grapefruit, sections
muskmelon, balls
cherries
raisins

B. Procedure:
1. Arrange grapefruit sections in a ring around muskmelon balls.
2. Cherries and raisins may be used to make a face.
3. Amounts depend on the number to be served; 1/2-cup servings are appropriate.

Pigs in a Blanket.

A. Ingredients:
frankfurters
bread slices
American cheese
butter
mustard

B. Procedure:
1. Spread butter on bread.
2. Place bread slices on ungreased baking sheet and top each with a slice of cheese.
3. Place frankfurters diagonally on cheese.
4. Fold bread over to form triangle. Brush with butter.
5. Set broiler at 550°F.
6. Broil about 2 minutes.

Meatballs.

A. Ingredients:
1 pound hamburger
1 cup bread crumbs

1 or 2 eggs
3/4 teaspoon salt
1/8 teaspoon pepper
1/4 cup milk

B. Procedure:
1. Mix ingredients well.
2. Shape into small balls.
3. Brown until cooked through in electric skillet.

Carrot and Raisin Salad.

A. Ingredients:
3 cups shredded carrots (teacher to prepare)
3/4 cup raisins
juice of one lemon
3 tablespoons sugar
dash of salt

B. Procedure:
1. Mix ingredients thoroughly.
2. Serve immediately.

Banana Bake.

A. Ingredients:
1 banana, peeled
butter, melted

B. Procedure:
1. Place peeled banana in shallow baking dish and brush with melted butter.
2. Bake in moderate oven (375°F) from 10 to 15 minutes (until tender).
3. Serve hot as a vegetable.
4. Yield: 1 serving.

French Toast.

A. Ingredients:
8 slices bread
4 eggs
1/4 tablespoon salt
2 cups milk

B. Procedure:
1. Beat eggs slightly. Add salt and milk.
2. Dip slices of bread in egg mixture and fry in electric skillet.
3. Serve hot with jelly, honey, or syrup.

Carob-Nut Snack.

A. Ingredients:
1 cup dry-roasted unsalted peanuts
1 cup unsweetened carob chips
1 cup unsweetened dried banana chips
1 cup unsweetened cereal

B. Procedure:
Children can take turns shaking ingredients in a plastic container with lid to mix. Serve in small cups, or carry in plastic bags on field trips. Can be stored in container for several weeks.

No-Bake Brownies.

A. Ingredients:
1 cup fresh peanut butter (no sugar added)
1 cup nonfat dry milk
1/4 cup soy protein powder (plain, no dextrose or other sugar substitutes)
1 teaspoon vanilla
2 tablespoons carob powder (or cocoa if you don't mind the caffeine)
1/2 cup fructose
3/4 cup water
1/2 cup raisins (optional)
coconut or chopped nuts (optional)

B. Procedure:
1. Mix peanut butter, dry milk, carob (or cocoa), fructose, and vanilla with mixer or pastry blender.
2. Add water, a little at a time, mixing after each addition. At first it may seem too wet, but the water will be absorbed.
3. Add raisins. Add more water if needed.
4. Press mixture into 8″ × 8″ pan sprayed with nonstick coating.
5. Sprinkle coconut or chopped nuts on top.
6. Cut into squares. Refrigerate unused portion.

Chow Mein Crunchies.

A. Ingredients:
1 package chocolate chips (or 1 package butterscotch chips)
1 can chow mein noodles
1 cup salted peanuts

B. Procedure:
1. Melt chocolate chips in a double boiler or in a saucepan over very low heat.
2. Add chow mein noodles and salted peanuts.
3. Stir until the noodles are coated with chocolate mixture.
4. Drop by spoonfuls on waxed paper.
5. Place in refrigerator until cool.

Jam Brown-n-Serve.

A. Ingredients:
6 brown-n-serve rolls
1 teaspoon melted margarine
6 teaspoons apricot preserves

B. Procedure:
1. Brush butter over top of rolls.
2. Make lengthwise cuts in top of roll.
3. Insert 1 teaspoon of preserves.
4. Bake in greased shallow pan at 200°F for 10 to 12 minutes.

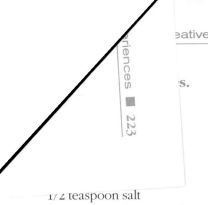

1/2 teaspoon salt
1 teaspoon baking powder
B. Materials: fork, cookie sheet
C. Procedure:
1. Mix butter and sugar.
2. Add cottage cheese and vanilla.
3. Add flour, salt, and baking powder.
4. Stir. Smooth into balls.
5. Put on greased cookie sheet. Flatten with fork. Bake at 375°F for 10 to 15 minutes.

Scrambled Eggs.
A. Ingredients:
eggs, one per child
milk, salt, pepper as desired
B. Materials: fry pan or electric skillet
C. Procedure:
1. Permit each child to break an egg into a bowl.
2. Beat the egg with a fork.
3. Add milk, salt, and pepper as desired.
4. Cook in fry pan or electric skillet.

Peanut Butter Balls.
A. Ingredients:
1/2 cup fresh peanut butter
1 tablespoon jelly
1/2 cup dry milk powder
1 cup bran or corn flakes
1/3 cup bran or corn flakes (crushed)
B. Procedure:
1. Mix the peanut butter and jelly in bowl.
2. Stir in milk powder and 1 cup bran or corn flakes. Mix well.
3. With your hands, roll the mix into small balls. Roll the balls in the crushed flakes.

Peanut Butter Apple Rolls.
A. Ingredients:
1 8-ounce can refrigerated crescent rolls
2 tablespoons fresh peanut butter
1 apple, peeled and finely chopped
B. Procedure:
1. Separate dough into 8 triangles.
2. Spread a thick layer of peanut butter on each triangle.
3. Top with 1 tablespoon of apple.
4. Start at the shortest side of each triangle and roll to other side. Place on cookie sheet.
5. Bake at 350°F for 10–15 minutes.

Peanut Grahams.
A. Ingredients:
graham crackers
fresh peanut butter
one or more of the following toppings—nuts, sunflower seeds, raisins, chocolate chips, sliced bananas, sliced apples
B. Procedure:
1. Break each graham cracker in half.
2. Spread some peanut butter on one half.
3. Place your favorite topping on the peanut butter.
4. Spread some peanut butter on the other graham cracker half.
5. Press the two halves together to make a sandwich.

Peanut Logs.
A. Ingredients:
1 cup creamy peanut butter
1 cup honey
1 cup instant nonfat dry milk
1 cup raisins
1 cup graham cracker crumbs
B. Procedure:
1. Blend peanut butter, honey, and dry milk.
2. Add raisins and mix well.
3. Stir in graham cracker crumbs.
4. Roll teaspoonfuls of mixture on waxed paper to shape into logs.
5. Refrigerate 1 hour. Makes about 50.

Nutty Swiss Cheese Spread.
A. Ingredients:
2 cups Swiss cheese, shredded
1/2 cup fresh peanut butter
1/2 cup sour cream
1/4 cup raisins
B. Procedure:
1. Mix all ingredients well.
2. Use spread on bread or crackers.

Graham Cracker Bananas.
A. Ingredients:
4 bananas
1/4 cup evaporated milk
1/2 cup graham cracker crumbs
1/4 cup butter or margarine, melted
B. Procedure:
1. Peel bananas and cut in half lengthwise.
2. Roll bananas in milk, then roll in graham cracker crumbs.
3. Place in greased baking dish. Pour melted butter over top.
4. Bake at 450°F for 10 minutes.

Broiled Bananas.

1 banana (unpeeled)
1 tablespoon plain lowfat yogurt

Make a small slit in the banana skin. Place unskinned banana slit-side up on a piece of aluminum foil. Broil for 5 to 10 minutes, until softened. Open skin to expose banana. Serve with a dollop of yogurt. Most children like bananas, so this recipe should be a hit. In this recipe, the banana is eaten with a spoon and the skin becomes the dish.

Frozen Banana Coins.

An excellent use for a very ripe banana. Peel bananas. Freeze bananas on a tray. Place frozen banana in a freezer bag or freezer container. Return to freezer until ready to use. To serve, remove banana from freezer and slice into 1/4″ pieces. Serve immediately, or pieces will become soggy. Yield: ½ banana per serving.

Frozen Banana Pop.

Cut banana in half horizontally. Carefully push one popsicle stick into each banana half. Freeze. Serve directly from freezer.

Popcorn Mix.   For children over three years of age.
A. Ingredients:
    2 cups plain popped popcorn
    1/4 cup quartered dried apricots
    1/4 cup raisins
    1/4 cup peanuts
    Mix all ingredients together. Store in a tightly covered container. Yield: 2¾ cups.

Rice Pudding.
A. Ingredients:
    4 tablespoons uncooked rice
    4 cups milk
    1 tablespoon butter
    3 tablespoons sugar (optional)
    1/2 teaspoon vanilla extract
    nutmeg
B. Procedure:
    1. Combine all ingredients except nutmeg in buttered casserole.
    2. Sprinkle nutmeg on top.
    3. Bake at 300°F for 1½ hours.

Baked Popcorn Treat.
A. Ingredients:
    1/2 cup butter
    1/2 cup brown sugar
    3 quarts popped corn
    1 cup peanuts
B. Procedure:
    1. Mix butter and sugar until fluffy.
    2. Combine corn and peanuts. Stir into butter-sugar mixture.
    3. Place in baking dish and bake at 350°F for 8 minutes. Pour into bowl and serve.

Crunchy Fruit Munch.
A. Ingredients:
    3 quarts popped popcorn
    2 cups natural cereal with raisins
    3/4 cup dried apricots, chopped
    1/4 teaspoon salt
    1/3 cup butter or margarine
    1/4 cup honey
B. Procedure:
    1. Preheat oven to 300°F. Combine first four ingredients in large baking pan; set aside.
    2. In small saucepan, combine butter or margarine and honey. Cook over low heat until butter or margarine is melted.
    3. Pour over popcorn mixture, tossing lightly until well coated.
    4. Place in oven. Bake 30 minutes, stirring occasionally. Makes 3 quarts.
    5. Store in tightly covered container up to 2 weeks.

Popcorn with Peanut Butter.
A. Ingredients:
    2 quarts popped popcorn
    1 tablespoon fresh peanut butter (creamy or chunky)
    2 tablespoons butter or margarine
B. Procedure:
    1. In small saucepan, melt butter or margarine and peanut butter until smooth.
    2. Pour over popped corn and mix well.

Popcorn Cheese Snacks.
A. Ingredients
    2 quarts popped popcorn
    1/2 cup butter or margarine
    1/2 cup grated American or Parmesan cheese—or both
    1/2 teaspoon salt
B. Procedure:
    1. Spread freshly popped popcorn in a flat pan; keep hot and crisp in oven.
    2. Melt butter and grated cheese and add salt.
    3. Pour mixture over popcorn. Stir until every kernel is cheese flavored.

Turtle Pancakes.

A. Ingredients:
   pancake or biscuit mix
   1/3 cup nonfat dry milk
   2 cups milk
B. Procedure:
   1. Follow package directions. (For extra nutrition, add 1/3 cup nonfat milk to the standard recipe calling for 2 cups milk.)
   2. The batter should be in a bowl rather than in a pitcher; the child puts the batter on the griddle by spoonfuls, sometimes deliberately dribbling for effect.
   3. A turtle is made by adding four tiny pancakes (the legs) around the perimeter of one round pancake about 3 inches in diameter.

ONE-STEP COOKBOOK

These are one-process recipes. They require some preparation but the actual recipe uses one method that demonstrates what happens when food is prepared in that manner.

Carrot Curls. For this activity, you will need carrots, a vegetable peeler, and ice water. Show the children how to use a vegetable peeler safely. When peeling carrots, the peeler should be pushed down and away from the body, rather than toward the body or face.

Help children peel off the outside skin of the carrot, then make additional carrot peels. Place peels in ice water in the refrigerator until they curl. Use the carrot curls for a snack.

Apples—with Cheese. Halve and core apples. Fill hollowed center with smooth cheese spread. Chill for 2 to 3 hours before serving.

Yogurt and Cereal Parfait. In a tall glass, layer lemon, vanilla, or fruit-flavored yogurt with a favorite breakfast cereal.

Banana Breakfast Bites. Peel bananas and cut into bite-sized pieces. Dip each piece in yogurt, then drop into a plastic bag filled with wheat germ. Shake to coat. Serve as finger food.

Fruit Cubes. Make frozen cubes with fruit juice, placing a small piece of fruit in each cube before it freezes. Add a popsicle stick to each cube to make individual fruit treats on a stick.

Banana on Ice. This is a tasty, low-calorie treat—only about 85 calories per banana. Simply peel a banana and wrap it in plastic wrap. Place it in the freezer for several hours or until hard. (Don't leave it in the freezer too long.) Eat frozen. It tastes exactly like banana ice cream.

Smiling Sandwich. Spread peanut butter on a rice or corn cake. Use two raisins for eyes and a banana or apple slice for a smiling mouth.

Ants on a Log. Fill celery sticks with peanut butter, cream cheese, or pimento cheese. Use raisins or nuts as the "ants."

Apple Bake. Place a cored apple in a dish with a small amount of water. Cover with foil (for oven) or cover loosely with plastic wrap (for microwave) and bake at 350°F for 20 minutes (oven) or on HIGH for 5 minutes (microwave). Add a sprinkle of cinnamon if desired.

Juice Freeze. Fill a 6-ounce paper cup with sugar-free fruit juice, cover with plastic wrap, and push a plastic spoon through the center of the wrap. Freeze. Tear away cup to eat.

Dried Banana Chunks. Slice bananas into 3/4-inch thick slices. If desired, roll in chopped nuts. Place on baking sheet in 150°F oven with oven door open about 2 inches. Dry until shriveled, or about 12 hours.

Cheese Melt. Cut Monterey Jack cheese into small cubes. Place far apart on baking sheet and place in 375°F oven for a few minutes until cheese melts and spreads wafer thin. Cool and remove.

Milk Mix. Pour cold milk into an almost empty jelly or jam jar. Shake vigorously. Drink.

Peanut Butter. Place 1 cup shelled roasted peanuts and 1 tablespoon oil in blender and blend to peanut butter.

Popcorn. Pour a handful of popcorn kernels into heavy pan with 1 tablespoon oil. Cover and heat until popcorn is popped.

REFERENCES

de Paola, T. (1992). *Jamie O'Rourke and the big potato.* New York: Scholastic.

Ehlert, L. (1987). *Growing vegetable soup.* New York: Harcourt Brace.

Hess, M. A., Hunt, A. E., & Stone, B. M. (1990). *A healthy start: A worry-free guide to feeding young children.* New York: Holt.

McDonald, M. (1996). *The potato man.* Chicago: Children's Press.

Rey, M. (1997). *Pretzel.* Boston: Houghton Mifflin.

Seuss, D. (1976). *Green eggs and ham.* New York: Random House.

CHAPTER 16

CREATIVE SOCIAL STUDIES

Learning to be part of a social group is not something that is natural or inborn in human beings. The fact is that learning about oneself, about others, and about how to act with others is a long process.

Social studies are an important part of a child's education. They help the child understand the complex world in which she lives and enable her to be productive and happy within society's framework.

SOCIAL CHARACTERISTICS AT DIFFERENT AGES

While it is impossible to predict with any certainty the developmental pattern of any individual, there are general characteristics common to age groups. The following is a summary of age-level social characteristics.

PRESCHOOL AND KINDERGARTEN

Socially at this age level, friendships are usually limited to one or two "best" friends, but these may change frequently. Play groups are not too well organized and tend to change often. Although quarrels are frequent, they tend to be of short duration. There is great pleasure in dramatic play and beginning awareness of sex roles.

Emotional development is at a volatile stage—emotions are expressed freely and outbursts of anger are common. A vivid imagination frequently leads to grossly exaggerated fears. Competition for adult affection breeds jealousy. Mentally, students are developing rapidly in the acquisition of language. They enjoy talk-

ing to each other and in front of groups. Imagination and fantasy are at their peak.

PRIMARY GRADES (6–9 YEARS)

Although friendship patterns are still likely to be characterized by "best friends," greater selectivity is now evident in the choice of friends. Games are more organized, but there is great emphasis on "rules." Quarrels are still frequent as are physical aggression, competition, and boasting. Although the difference in interests of boys and girls becomes more pronounced at this age, there is great variation in behavior from one classroom to another because of influences exerted by teachers.

Emotionally, children become very sensitive during this period. Criticism, ridicule, and failure can be devastating. Despite their own sensitivity, they are quick to hurt others. Generally, students are eager to please the teacher and want to do well in school, for which reasons they require frequent praise.

Eagerness to learn is common to this age group. Learning occurs primarily through concrete manipulation of materials. Eagerness to talk is still evident and there is much experimentation with language—including obscene language. Concepts of reciprocity, fairness, and right and wrong develop during this period.

ELEMENTARY GRADES (9–12 YEARS)

Peer groups begin to replace adults as sources of behavior standards and the recognition of achievement. Interests become more sharply different between the sexes—frequently resulting in "battles" between them

Being able to get along with others is a key social learning skill.

Dramatic play allows children to try on social roles in a safe environment.

for recognition and achievement, as well as the exchange of insults. Team games become more popular, along with class spirit. Crushes and hero worship are common.

This is the period when the conflict between adults and the group code begins to emerge. Instead of a rigid following of rules, youngsters at this age begin to understand the need for exceptions. Frequently they set very high standards for themselves—sometimes unreal standards—hence feelings of frustration are common. While the desire for independence grows, the need for adult support is still strong—therefore unpredictable behavior often results. Curiosity still remains strong at this age.

With these social developmental characteristics in mind, let us now look at how the early childhood program can include both developmental levels and the social studies themes/standards.

 ## LEARNING ABOUT ONE'S WORLD

A child's universe begins with himself, extends to his family, and then moves out to the larger community. The development of a child's self-concept, his awareness of self, is the important beginning point in social studies for young children.

To know oneself in a social sense involves learning such things as one's name, one's ethnic background, family grouping, and occupations in one's family. In the early childhood years learning about oneself is at a ba-

sic level; that is, young children are learning about how their lives fit into the larger social group.

Children learn about where they live—in a house, an apartment, or a condominium—and how it is like and unlike the residences of their peers. They learn the similarities and differences among families in form, style of living, and values.

Those who work with young children from preschool through the early and later elementary years can help them discover and appreciate their own uniqueness by beginning with a positive acceptance of each child.

In the early childhood years, young children need opportunities to *live* important experiences, to learn in an *active* way. The activities in this chapter are designed to help children learn about themselves and others.

 ## PEOPLE IN THE COMMUNITY

As a child meets people in the community, he learns about the many roles people play in his life. He becomes involved in relationships in which adults play varied roles and people depend upon each other. He passes a firehouse in the neighborhood and sees where the firefighters are stationed. He goes to the garage with his mother and sees the mechanic fix their car. He goes to the post office with his brother and mails a letter to Grandmother. Children learn, through everyday experiences such as these, that others help them and they help others.

A good place to begin a discussion about understanding others in the child's world then is to learn about people in the child's most immediate environment. This includes the people who serve the school

THIS ONE'S FOR YOU   **Virtual Field Trips**

The Internet is a powerful tool for learning about the world. Older students will enjoy the following virtual field trips and other social studies-related Web field trips.

Visit the White House. On this White House Web page, kids can send an e-mail message to the President, take an online tour of the First Lady's garden, read current press releases, and access information about other government agencies: www.whitehouse.gov.

Visit Other Countries. To find out about www servers in other countries and information about those countries, visit the Virtual Tourist Web page: www.xmission.com/~kinesava/webmap/.
    You can also visit this site for information using interactive maps.

Have a Mayan Adventure. At the Science Museum of Minnesota, explore the ancient and modern Maya Culture: www.sci.mus.mn.us/sln/ma.
    There you will find online exhibits, science activities, and other resources in the exhibit halls. Also check out their sister site, the Thinking Fountain, at: www.sci.mus.mn.us/sln for more creative activities.

Look into the Daily Almanac. Find out many fun and interesting facts on the Daily Almanac Web site: www.nova.edu/Inter-Links/fun/alamanc.html.
    You can find out what is the current U.S. national debt and how much of it each citizen is responsible for. Other facts you'll find are current U.S. population, as well as fun stuff like your "humorscope" at the Daily Almanac page.

Have a Ball at KidsCom! Don't miss this site at www.kidscom.com! KidsCom is a communication playground just for kids ages 8–12, but adults will have fun here, too. The page is available in French, German, English, or Spanish with lots of tips and ideas for teachers and parents. Children can find keypals, enter contests, play geography games, and ask Tobie Wan Kenobi, an Internet guru, technical Internet questions.

and community. There are many people in the child's immediate environment. It is important to emphasize the importance of all of these individuals. Each member helps to make the whole community where we live and go to school what it is; all jobs are important. Activities at the end of this chapter are designed to help develop the idea of the importance of community workers.

TRIPS INTO THE COMMUNITY

Every school is located in a community. An excursion into the community helps young children gain new information and extends children's experiences.

Any planned excursion should be either an outgrowth of children's experiences or meet a specific need.

Within the same group of children, needs will differ. For instance, a teacher taking four children to the zoo found that for three of them the short bus trip back and

forth was the exciting part of the trip because they had never been on a bus before. For the other child, the bus ride was an everyday event, and the giraffe was the highlight of the trip.

PLANNING FOR TRIPS

A teacher needs to plan for a trip. The purpose of a trip is to provide children with firsthand experiences. A child should not only be able to see, hear, and smell, but he should be able to touch and taste as well. A teacher also needs to know the children and their special interests and concerns.

Familiarize yourself with the community in which the school is situated before planning excursions. Become familiar with street signs and working people who come and go from the school, shops, business establishments, buildings, and service. Talk with people in the community. As you plan, try to anticipate the children's reactions, remembering that you are planning for *young*

FOOD FOR THOUGHT

Field Trip Videos

Field trips are important to children's learning. "Field trip" videos may be the next best thing. Although they are not interactive (as a CD-ROM tour might be), videos can be stopped at certain points for discussion, plus they generally offer supplemental in-class exercises. The videos listed below are characterized by remarkable variety in design, approaches, and applications.

Although field trip videos are not substitutes for the real thing, they may provide preparation for an actual excursion, or they can serve as reinforcement, or an enjoyable opportunity for a second visit. When reality and video meet, a veritable explosion of learning opportunities can occur, and learning can become vital, relevant, and limitless. Field trip videos can even assist the teacher in demonstrating field trip safety, manners, protocol, and preparation (e.g., remembering to bring hats, sunscreen, lunch, water, binoculars, a magnifying glass . . .).

Field trip videos strongly recommended include: *Kids Express, Moody Video Collections,* and *Schoolworks.*

Kids Express. Field trips also can mean making friends and bonding with others through a common experience. Miss Shirley Bowers, an author with many years' experience as an early childhood educator, communicates great warmth in *Kids Express.* Her field trip context is carefully designed to stimulate young minds, and to build independence and self-reliance. *Kids Express* field trips are built on the philosophy that children need exposure to varied and integrated experiences in a safe environment. You will meet a great staff of friends and helpers in these videos. *Happy Campers* offers assistance for the young child exploring nature, and *Little Rodeo Wranglers* spends a day at the ranch with good music and good friends.

Each video integrates music, literature, art, cooking, history, science, and math. Ultimately, Miss Shirley tries to prepare children to be part of society by modeling how to better interact with one another. More Miss Shirley videos include: *Science Ooze and Awes, Finishing School for Young Ladies & Gentlemen, Americana,* and *Kids Can Cook.* The series is geared for children ages 3–8. For more information to purchase these videos, contact Kids Express at 1-888-492-5437, or by e-mail at misshirley@kidsexpress.com.

Moody Video Collections. Moody Science Videos were some of the first visual learning excursions into the ocean, space, caves, and even the honeybee hive. They include such scenes as time-lapse photography of plants actively germinating and growing miraculously, becoming full grown in a matter of seconds. Such sequences have since become classics. Moody has updated its many science video library contributions for home and school with appealing titles in the Science Adventure Series, such as *Treasure Hunt, Flying on Wings of Beauty, The Clown-Faced Carpenter, The Long Journey,* and *The Wonder of You.* They feature topics such as caves, spiders, butterflies, seeds, woodpeckers, space, water, animal migration, blood circulation, the human body, and more. Children ages 3–10 will enjoy these videos, which are suited for both home and school.

Contact Moody Video at 1-800-842-1223 or visit the Web site at www.moodyvideo.org.

Schoolworks. Seldom do we get the chance while on a field trip to interview the zookeeper or the museum curator. This is where the *Video Field Trip Series* is particularly valuable. The videos conveniently supplement field trips in a more up-close-and-personal fashion, for all to enjoy. Another advantage is the chance to visit sites that may be too distant to visit in person. *The Video Field Trip Series* cleverly explores careers as well. Series titles now available include *To the Zoo, To the BFI Recyclery,* and *To a Glassmaking Studio.* McDonald's and Longs Drugstores have cooperated in supporting and encouraging the development of the *Video Field Trip Series.* In addition, Schoolworks donates a percentage of their profits to public schools. K–8 students will find insights about the real world from these adventurous and fun videos.

Schoolworks videos are available by calling 1-800-396-8754.

THIS ONE'S FOR YOU

Folktales: Learning about Other Cultures

Children's literature offers young children another way to identify and empathize with others. Over the centuries, all people have told stories. Introducing young children to the folktales of other cultures may help them feel better connected to people far away in time and space—a far cry from a tourist curriculum.

You may find that reading different versions of the same folktale helps children see that people the world over share the same feelings, hopes, dreams, and concerns. An example is *The Three Billy Goats Gruff* (Blair, 1964) and the Mexican tale *Borrequita and the Coyote* (Aardema, 1991), which have similar themes.

You may find that fables can also help teach young children about values. *Carmine the Crow* (Holder, 1993) conveys more about why people should be kind to the elderly than any number of more obvious tales about nice little children visiting nursing homes:

Carmine the crow lives alone with his tinfoil collection and his little habits: a cup of tea to drink and old ballads "to cheer himself up." After rescuing a gorgeous swan, he is given a small box of stardust with which he can fulfill his dreams. As he hurries through the meadow, however, he discovers a mouse, a frog, and a rabbit all in need of wishes answered. He gives away his stardust and heads home to his old-man chair and his little bed of nettles. Although the story has a happy ending, it will haunt the reader with its sensitive depiction of being old and set in one's ways.

An authentic Navajo legend, *Ma'ii and Cousin Horned Toad* (Begay, 1993), teaches the importance of generosity. The story details how the lazy coyote Ma'ii tries to outwit his industrious toad cousin. The coyote finds out that small and generous is not necessarily stupid. A true sense of the Southwest is intertwined by the Navajo poems woven throughout the story.

The Fortune-Teller (Alexander, 1993) tells the story of a lucky young carpenter who desperately wants more out of life than nails and elbow grease in his village in Cameroon, Africa. Through a series of happy accidents, he ends up rich and blessed. But what makes the folktale so memorable is the expressive African faces, the rich hues of the villagers' garb, and the pictures that convey a true sense of tribe and extended family.

children. This means that you will need to keep in mind these basic guidelines in planning all excursions.

- Keep it simple.
- Discuss, read about, and organize play around the places to be visited in advance.
- Encourage close observations while on the outing.
- Give small amounts of information if children are interested.
- Provide time, materials, and enthusiasm for follow-up plans and projects.

PERSONAL CELEBRATIONS

Celebrations are part of a child's life. A child becomes more sensitive about his own feelings and of the feelings of others when he rejoices with them in celebration. Through celebrations, a child in his own way can be part of a group and acknowledge a special day or event.

In the life of any child, there are events that deserve celebrations. When a teacher observes that a child is moved by a situation, the experience is worth emphasizing with a small but **personal celebration.** For example, a child ties his shoes by himself for the first time. For many children, this is a very special event. The teacher may take time to say, "Great! You did it!" or "Show me how you did it!" or "How does it feel to do it all by yourself?" You might want to share a new accomplishment of your own at a time like this. "I just learned how to drive a car and I feel so good when I can go out in the car and drive all by myself!" Share good feelings with children, and a child begins to learn

that feelings are important and worth celebrating. When a child ties his shoes, the teacher's knowing glance the next day reaffirms his positive feelings about himself.

Birthday celebrations for young children need to be simple events. Large parties are overstimulating and confusing for young children. Young children are happy with small recognitions; a child counts the candles on the cake and then blows them out—a very exciting event for the child.

ACTIVITIES FOR CHILDREN

Community Workers

GOALS: To develop awareness of helpers in the community

To encourage children's interest in social studies activities

MATERIALS: None required

PREPARATION: Find out when the garbage is collected at the school.

PROCEDURE:

1. Have the children present when the garbage truck comes.
2. Have the children talk to the workers about their job and the service they perform.
3. Have the children ask about the truck and its operation and care.

4. Have the children ask how citizens can help get the garbage ready for the collector. Don't overlook that these helpers are also people with personal lives.

VARIATION: Have the children follow the same procedure for postal workers, grocery store clerks, mechanics, painters, laundry workers, bus drivers, cooks in the cafeteria, and custodians.

ADDITIONAL INFORMATION: If the people you talk with can be persuaded to visit the classroom informally, the experience will be all the more effective.

ACTIVITIES FOR CHILDREN — Be A Worker

GOALS: To develop an awareness of community workers

To encourage children's interest in social studies activities

MATERIALS: Hats, dress up clothing, and objects workers would use

PREPARATION: Talk about community helpers and workers in the community. Discuss what they wear, how they look, and what they do.

PROCEDURE:

1. Put hats and clothing that community workers wear in the housekeeping center.
2. Have the children dress up. Costumes can be simple, with only a hat or mask, or an object to carry suggesting the worker.
3. Have some children bring in an article of clothing to serve as a costume.

VARIATION:

■ Playing the role of community workers may take the form of a parade, a guessing game, a pantomime, or a play.

■ Have the children draw or paint a picture of their favorite worker.

ADDITIONAL INFORMATION: Such experiences help broaden the child's understanding of life in the local community.

ACTIVITIES FOR CHILDREN — How Do I Look?

GOALS: To develop a child's self-awareness

To encourage children's interest in social studies activities

MATERIALS: Unbreakable mirror, paper, crayons, markers, paint, and brushes

PREPARATION: Talk about how we are more alike than different. Talk about how we all have the same body parts: eyes, nose, mouth, hair, hands, and so on.

PROCEDURE:

1. Discuss the color, size, and shape of eyes, hair, nose, mouth, ears, and so on.
2. Have the children draw or paint pictures of their faces.
3. Have the children cut out pictures, mount them on a low board, and label the faces.

VARIATION:

■ Use magnifying makeup mirrors to produce interesting reactions from the children when they see their enlarged images.

■ Supply children with pictures of people with missing body parts. Have the children describe what part is missing.

ADDITIONAL INFORMATION: A full-length mirror in a safe, but clearly visible, place at child level is one way for children to see themselves and each other. Many children don't have the chance to see their reflections because mirrors in their homes are too high.

ACTIVITIES FOR CHILDREN

Policeman, Where Is My Child?

GOALS: To develop a child's self-awareness

To encourage children's interest in social studies activities

MATERIALS: None required

PREPARATION: Talk about how everyone has different colors of eyes and hair, different skin color, different sizes, how everyone is wearing different clothes, and so on.

PROCEDURE:

1. Have one child be the policeman, and another the mother.
2. Have the mother describe the physical appearance of her missing child (dress, hair, eyes).
3. Involve all the children as they look at themselves to see if they're being described.
4. Have the policeman try to guess which child in the room belongs to the mother.

ACTIVITIES FOR CHILDREN

Flannelboard Game

GOALS: To develop a child's self-awareness

To encourage children's interest in social studies

MATERIALS: Flannelboard cutouts of a boy and girl, and body parts for each (arms, legs, eyes, etc.)

PREPARATION: Deliberately place body parts in the wrong area, such as an arm in the leg's place.

PROCEDURE:

1. Have the children discover what is in the wrong area.
2. Have the children place parts in the right location.

VARIATION: Have the children take turns deliberately putting parts in the wrong place for other children to fix.

ACTIVITIES FOR CHILDREN — Whose Voice Is It?

GOALS: To develop awareness of other's voices

To encourage children's interest in social studies activities

MATERIALS: Tape recorder, tape

PREPARATION: Tape each child's voice.

PROCEDURE:

1. Play the tape.
2. Discuss how each person has a different voice tone.
3. Have the children guess who each speaker is.

VARIATION:

■ Record children telling their favorite stories (examples: *The Three Bears, Three Billy Goats Gruff, Little Red Riding Hood*). Use different voices for different characters.

■ Play the game "Who Am I?" Have one child in the center of the circle be "it." "It" tries to guess who the speaker is. The speaker disguises her voice after the children have mastered the game with their natural voices.

ACTIVITIES FOR CHILDREN — Trips into the Community

GOAL: To develop awareness of community and community workers

MATERIALS: None required

PREPARATION: For all of the suggested trips, check out the place to be visited *before* visiting. Tell them the number of children and adults in the group, your time of arrival, and what you will be looking at.

PROCEDURE:

Go on one or more of the following trips in the nearby community.

■ **Supermarket.** Do not try to do too much in one visit. Make several trips, each with a different focus. Watch the goods being delivered. Watch the boxes being unpacked and merchandise being stamped. Look at all the different kinds of machines in the store.

■ **Produce Department.** What are some things displayed on special cardboard or wrapped in individual papers? Why are some things displayed on crushed ice or refrigerated? See if you and the children can name the fruits and vegetables.

■ **Dairy Department.** What kinds of things are sold here? Why are they kept cold? Where do the products come from?

■ **Meat Department.** Watch the butcher cut and package meat. Why is the meat kept cold? Is it cold in the back, too? See how many varieties of meat you can name.

■ **Bakery Department.** Compare the ovens with the ovens at home, or the size of the flour sacks with the sacks at home. Notice the quantities of baked goods and the process of baking. What kinds of clothes do the bakers wear? Why?

ACTIVITIES FOR CHILDREN

Our Crossing Guard

GOALS: To develop awareness of community workers

To encourage children's interest in social studies activities

MATERIALS: None required

PREPARATION: Find out where the crossing guard is on duty at your school. Arrange a time when you can visit the crossing guard.

PROCEDURE:

1. Have the children watch what the guard does.
2. Have the children identify how she tells the vehicles and pedestrians to go. To stop.
3. Have the children talk with the officer.
4. Have the children get a good look at her uniform.

VARIATION:

- Have the children draw pictures or paint pictures of the crossing guard.
- Have the children dictate stories of the experience to go along with the drawings.
- Have the children act out being a crossing guard with a group of children.

ACTIVITIES FOR CHILDREN

All about Me

GOALS: To develop children's self-awareness

To encourage children's interest in social studies activities

MATERIALS: Magazines, paper, and paste

PREPARATION: Have children think about how they look. Have them look in a mirror to see how they look.

PROCEDURE:

1. From magazines, have the children cut pictures that they like or that remind them of themselves.
2. Have the children paste these pictures on a sheet of paper for an "All About Me" collage.

VARIATION:

- Have the children guess who the "All About Me" collage is about.
- Make up "Guess Who?" riddles describing individual children from their collages. Suggest clues that reflect the child's positive characteristics.

ACTIVITIES FOR CHILDREN

How Do I Look?

GOALS: To develop a child's self-awareness

To develop a child's awareness of others

MATERIALS: Photos of the children, alone or in groups

PREPARATION: Talk about differences between boys and girls.

PROCEDURE: Ask children the following questions:

1. Do girls look different from boys? How?
2. Do girls dress different from boys?
3. Are there differences in hair? What else?
4. Do men look different from ladies? How?
5. Do they sound different?

VARIATION:

■ Take photos of the children, alone or in groups, and mount them on a bulletin board or in a scrapbook. Print the names of the children beneath the photos.

■ Use the photos as a starting point for a discussion about how we all have the same body parts, even though we all look different.

ADDITIONAL INFORMATION: If a child brings out the difference in sex organs, accept it very matter-of-factly. In this and other such activities, the teacher can bring out that we are more alike than different. Natural points in such a discussion are color, size, and shape of eyes, hair, nose, mouth, and so on.

ACTIVITIES FOR CHILDREN

Self-Study: How the Children See You

GOALS: To develop a child's awareness of others

To understand how the children see you

MATERIALS: Paper, crayons, and markers

PREPARATION: Select one or two children who are at least four years old. Seat them individually at a table with paper, crayons, and markers.

PROCEDURE:

1. Have the children draw a picture of you.
2. Encourage them to take their time.
3. Have them include as many details as they want.
4. When they are finished, give them another sheet of paper.
5. Have the children draw a self-portrait.
6. When both pictures are completed, cut them out and paste them side by side.

ADDITIONAL INFORMATION:

■ Look at each child's drawing of you. What features appear to be most important to the children? Did they overlook any important characteristics, such as a beard, long hair, or glasses?

■ Compare the drawing of you with the self-portrait. How are they similar? How are they different? Is there more detail in your picture or in the self-portrait? Is one bigger than the other?

■ Is there a difference in emotional expression?

■ Do these drawings reveal anything about how these children view themselves and you?

ACTIVITIES FOR OLDER CHILDREN Names and Identity
(Grades 4–5)

GOALS: To develop awareness of others' opinions and ideas

To develop a child's self-awareness

MATERIALS: Paper and pencils, crayons, or markers

PREPARATION: Have a discussion in which the children share what others may think about them. Help them consider if and why it is important what others think.

PROCEDURE:

1. Have the children brainstorm how they may change what others think.

2. Have each child write his or her name vertically on a piece of paper.

3. Beside each letter, have the child write a word or phrase that describes or tells about herself or himself. For example: M—Michigan is my home state; A—always running around; R—really hard working; Y—yellow is my favorite color.

VARIATION:

■ *Have the students write in words or phrases that describe other students' names.*

■ Have the children draw or paint self-portraits using the words or phrases from this activity.

■ *Have the children draw or paint pictures of other students using the words or phrases from this activity.*

ACTIVITIES FOR OLDER CHILDREN History Makers
(Grades 4–5)

GOALS: To develop understanding of important members of our society

To encourage children's interest in social studies activities

MATERIALS: Classroom calendar, paper, and pencils

PREPARATION: On the classroom calendar, mark and label the birthdays of Betsy Ross (January 1) and Martin Luther King, Jr. (January 15).

PROCEDURE:

1. Have half of the class research Betsy Ross.

2. Have the other half research Dr. King.

3. Have the Ross group present a research fact.

4. Have the King group present a finding in the same (or a similar) category (e.g., birthplace).

5. Continue the activity until no further similarities can be found.

VARIATION: Have the children choose two historical figures they want to research.

ACTIVITIES FOR OLDER CHILDREN Freedom
(Grades 4–5)

GOALS: To appreciate important events in our history

To develop children's interest in social studies

MATERIALS: Paper and pencils

PREPARATION: Call attention to the anniversary of the Emancipation Proclamation (January 1st). Discuss what it meant to the country.

PROCEDURE:

1. Guide the children in considering and finding meanings of *emancipation* and *proclamation*.

2. Help them research the historical actions and decisions associated with the Emancipation Proclamation.

3. Look for and emphasize reasons the proclamation was needed.

VARIATION: Have the children write "Just Suppose" stories about what would have happened in our country if there was never an Emancipation Proclamation.

ACTIVITIES FOR OLDER CHILDREN Telephone Book
(Grades 4–5) Research

GOALS: To appreciate differences in the local community

To encourage children's interest in social studies activities

MATERIALS: Telephone book, Yellow Pages

PREPARATION: Discuss the different ethnic groups in the local community.

PROCEDURE:

1. Have the children study the Yellow Pages. What names are predominant? What might these names tell you about early settlers in the area?

2. Divide the class into groups to consider sources of peoples last names—occupation, animal names, colors, where they live, and so on.

3. Get information on local industries from the Yellow Pages.

4. Watch for unusual advertising wording.

VARIATION:

■ Have the children make a graph showing the various ethnic groups represented in the community.

■ Have the children research the history of the names of streets in the community and their ethnic background.

■ Have the children make a group mural showing the various ethnic groups in their community.

ACTIVITIES FOR OLDER CHILDREN **Regional Crafts**
(Grades 4–5)

GOALS: To learn to appreciate local arts and crafts

To develop children's interest in social studies

MATERIALS: Reference materials showing crafts created in your area in the last 100 years (Local art museums and libraries are a good source for these materials)

PREPARATION: Discuss how these objects are both functional and beautiful.

PROCEDURE:

1. Break the class up into small groups of 3–4.
2. Have the small groups each choose one craft that they find especially appealing.
3. Have each group choose a different craft.
4. Have each group list questions about the craft such as the following:

• How was this (basket) made?
• How long have people been making these (wooden boxes) by hand?
• Do people still make these (silver buttons) today?
• What tools were needed to create the (lace on this apron)?

5. Have the children do research to find the answers to their questions.

VARIATION:

■ Have the children interview craftspeople in addition to using nonfiction books, encyclopedias, and multimedia sources.
■ Have the children report their findings about the craft to the class.
■ Have the children make similar crafts in art activities.

ACTIVITIES FOR OLDER CHILDREN **Tie-Dyeing: An**
(Grades 4–5) **Historical Fiber Art**

GOAL: To learn about tie-dyeing as an ancient fiber art

MATERIALS: Art smocks, 10-inch squares of muslin (at least one per child), acrylic or tempera paint, containers for water-paint mixture, string, safety scissors, and rubber gloves

PREPARATION: Prepare several tubs of dye by mixing tempera paints or acrylic paints with water. Give each child a fabric square and string. Have children put on the rubber gloves.

PROCEDURE:

1. Place the cloth on a flat surface.
2. Have the children use their fingertips to gather a clump of material.

3. Have the children tie the clump by tightly wrapping string around it.
4. Have the children repeat the procedure until several clumps have been created.
5. Have the children submerge the cloth in dye for about 20 minutes.
6. Have the children remove the cloth and untie or cut away the string.
7. Dry the cloth on a flat surface.

ADDITIONAL INFORMATION: Tie-dyeing is a fiber art form originated in China between A.D. 617 and 906. Tie-dyed fabrics created at that time were mainly worn by the nobility and priests.

REFERENCES

Aardema, V. (1991). *Borrequita and the coyote.* New York: Alfred A. Knopf.

Alexander, L. (1993). *The fortune-teller.* New York: Dutton.

Begay, S. (1993). *Ma'ii and Cousin Horned Toad.* New York: Scholastic.

Blair, S. (1964). *The three billy goats gruff.* Boston: Houghton-Mifflin.

Holder, H. (1993). *Carmine the crow.* New York: Farrar, Straus & Giroux.

APPENDIX A

Gross and Fine Motor Skills*

BY TWO YEARS

GROSS MOTOR

- walks forward (average age 12 months)
- walks backward (average age 15 months)
- walks upstairs with help (average age 17 months)
- moves self from sitting to standing (average age 18 months)
- seats self in small chair (average age 18 months)
- uses rocking horse or rocking chair with aid (average age 18 months)

FINE MOTOR

- builds tower of two blocks (average age 15 months)
- builds tower of three or four blocks (average age 19 months)
- places pellet in bottle (average age 15 months)
- places blocks in cup (average age 15 months)
- places four rings on peg or large pegs in pegboard (average age 18 months)
- imitates vertical line stroke (average age 20 months)
- turns pages of book, two or three at a time (average age 21 months)

BY TWO AND ONE-HALF YEARS

GROSS MOTOR

- kicks ball forward (average age 20 months)
- jumps in place (average age 23 months)

*90 percent of children at a specific age level will have acquired skill. Adapted from Gesell, A., Ilg, F. L., Ames, L. B., & Rodell, J. L. (1974). *Infant and child in the culture of today: The guidance of development in home and nursery school.* New York: Harper and Row.

- runs (stiffly) (average age 2 years)
- hurls small ball overhand, one hand, without direction (average age 22 months)
- pedals tricycle (average age 2 years)

FINE MOTOR

- builds tower of six cube blocks (average age 23 months)
- imitates circular motion with crayon, after demonstration (average age 2 years)
- turns pages of book, one at a time (average age 2 years)

BY THREE YEARS

GROSS MOTOR

- walks up and down stairs without adult help, but not alternating feet (average age 22 months)
- walks four steps on tiptoe (average age 2¼ years)
- jumps from bottom step (average age 2 years)
- walks backward 10 feet (average age 28 months)
- broad jumps 24–34 inches (average age 2½ years)
- balances on one foot one second (average age 2½ years)

FINE MOTOR

- imitates vertical line from demonstration (average age 22 months)
- imitates vertical or horizontal line (average age 2½ years)
- imitates V stroke from demonstration (average age 2½ years)
- strings four beads in two minutes (average age 2½ years)
- folds paper (average age 2½ years)
- builds tower of seven or eight cubes (average age 2¼ years)

BY THREE AND ONE-HALF YEARS

GROSS MOTOR

- walks on tiptoe 10 feet (average age 3 years)
- balances on one foot for five seconds (average age 3¼ years)

FINE MOTOR

- imitates bridge of three blocks from demonstration (average age 3 years)
- copies circle from picture model (average age 3 years)
- imitates cross from demonstration (average age 3 years)
- closes fist, wiggles thumb (average age 35 months)
- picks longer of two lines (average age 3 years)

 ## BY FOUR YEARS

GROSS MOTOR

- hops, preferred foot (average age 3½ years)
- walks up stairs, one foot on each step, holding rail (average age 3½ years)
- walks downstairs, one step per tread (average age 3½ years)
- throws ball with direction (average age 3½ years)
- balances on toes (average age 3½ years)
- jumps over rope 8″ high (average age 3½ years)
- swings on swing independently (average age 3½ years)
- jumps from height of 12 inches (average age 3½ years)
- holds standing balance, one foot advanced; eyes closed, 15 seconds (one of two tries by 4 years)

FINE MOTOR

- buttons up clothing (average age 3 years)
- cuts with scissors (average age 3¾ years)
- touches point of nose with eyes closed (by age 4, two of three tries)
- puts 20 coins in a box, separately (by age 4, one of two tries)

 ## BY FOUR AND ONE-HALF YEARS

GROSS MOTOR

- balances standing on one foot for five seconds (average age 3¼ years)

- does forward somersault with aid (average age 3½ years)
- catches ball in arms, two of three tries (average age 4)
- catches bounced ball (average age 4 years)
- heel to toe walk (average age 3¾ years)
- jumps from height of 2½ feet (average age 4 years)

FINE MOTOR

- copies cross from picture model (average age 3¾ years)
- draws a man, three parts (average age 4 years)
- copies square from demonstration (average age 4 years)

 ## BY FIVE YEARS

GROSS MOTOR

- balances on one foot for 10 seconds (average age 4½ years)
- hops on nonpreferred foot (average age 4½ years)
- bounces ball two times successively with one hand (average age 4½ years)
- catches large bounced ball, two of three tries (average age 4 years)
- somersaults forward without aid (average age 4¾ years)
- balances on tiptoes for 10 seconds, one of three tries (by age 5 years)
- jumps over cord at knee height, feet together, one of three tries (average age 4½ years)
- walks heel to toe (average age 4¾ years)
- walks heel to toe, backward (average age 4¾ years)
- walks 2″ × 4″ balance beam, 3″ off floor, without falling (average age 4½ years)

FINE MOTOR

- draws man, three parts (average age 4 years)
- builds pyramid of six blocks after demonstration (average age 4½ years)
- clenches and bares teeth (by age 5 years)
- draws diamond after demonstration (average age 4½ years)
- copies square from picture model (average age 4¾ years)
- ties any knot that holds with lace (average age 5 years)

APPENDIX B

Language Development Objectives and Activities for Infants and Toddlers

LEVEL	OBJECTIVE	ACTIVITY
Birth to 1 month	1. To develop intimacy and awareness of communication based on personal contact. 2. To introduce the concept of oral communication. 3. To introduce verbal communication. 4. To stimulate interest in the process of talking.	1. Whisper into the child's ear. 2. Coo at the child. 3. Talk to the child. 4. Let the child explore your mouth with his or her hands as you talk.
1 to 3 months	1. To develop oral communication. 2. To develop auditory acuity. 3. To develop the concept that different people sound different. 4. To develop the concept of oral and musical communication of feelings.	1. Imitate the sounds the child makes. 2. Talk to the child in different tones. 3. Encourage others to talk and coo to the child. 4. Sing songs of different moods, rhythms, and tempos.
3 to 6 months	1. To develop the concept of positive use of verbal communication. 2. To stimulate excitement about words. 3. To develop the concept that words and music can be linked. 4. To develop the ability to name things and events.	1. Reward the child with words. 2. Talk expressively to the child. 3. Sing or chant to the child. 4. Describe daily rituals to the child as you carry them out.
6 to 9 months	1. To develop use of words and reinforce intimacy. 2. To develop the concept that things have names. 3. To develop the concept that there is joy in the written word. 4. To develop the concept that language is used to describe.	1. Talk constantly to the child and explain processes such as feeding, bathing, and changing clothes. 2. Name toys for the child as the child plays, foods and utensils as the child eats, and so on. 3. Read aloud to the child, enthusiastically. 4. Describe sounds to the child as they are heard.
9 to 12 months	1. To develop the concept that body parts have names. 2. To reinforce the concept that things have names.	1. Name parts of the body and encourage the child to point to them. 2. Describe and name things seen on a walk or an automobile trip.

(Continued)

LEVEL	OBJECTIVE	ACTIVITY
	3. To stimulate rhythm and interest in words. 4. To stimulate experimentation with sounds and words.	3. Repeat simple songs, rhymes, and fingerplays. 4. Respond to sounds the child makes, and encourage the child to imitate sounds.
12 to 18 months	1. To develop the ability to label things and follow directions. 2. To expand vocabulary and lay the foundation for later production of sentences. 3. To reinforce the concept of names and the ability to recognize names and sounds. 4. To encourage verbal communication. 5. To reinforce the concept of labels and increase vocabulary.	1. Link up various objects and, naming one, ask the child to get it. 2. Act out verbs ("sit," "jump," "run," "smile," etc.). 3. Use animal picture books and posters of animals. 4. Let the child talk on a real telephone. 5. Describe things at home or outside on a walk or an automobile trip.
18 to 24 months	1. To stimulate imitation and verbalization. 2. To improve the ability to name objects. 3. To encourage repetition, sequencing, and rhythm. 4. To develop auditory acuity, passive vocabulary, and the concept of language constancy. 5. To stimulate verbalization, selectivity, and—eventually—descriptive language. 6. To stimulate conversation.	1. Tape-record the child and others familiar to the child, and play the tapes back for the child. 2. On a walk around the home or neighborhood with the child, point out and name familiar objects. 3. Play counting games, sing songs, and tell and retell familiar stories. 4. With the child, listen to the same recording of a story or song over and over. 5. Cut out of magazines and mount on stiff cardboard: pictures of foods, clothing, appliances, and so on. Have the child identify them as you show them. Use memorable descriptions: "orange, buttery carrots," "the shiny blue car." 6. With the child, prepare and eat a make-believe meal.
24 to 36 months	1. To practice descriptive language and build vocabulary. 2. To encourage verbalization, repetition, comprehension, and speaking in sentences. 3. To develop the concept of written symbols. 4. To encourage specific and descriptive language. 5. To increase understanding of the relation between spoken and written language, and to stimulate the use of both.	1. Keep a box of scraps of materials and small objects. Have the child select objects, using words to describe them ("fuzzy," "big," "red," etc.). 2. Ask the child: "Show me the floor," ". . . the door," and so on. When the child points, say "Here's the floor," and so on, and encourage the child to imitate you. 3. Label the child's possessions. Use the child's name repeatedly: "Mike's bed," "Mike's toy chest." 4. Ask "Which one?" when the child gives a single-word description, and expand on the child's language (e.g., Child: "Cookie." You: "Yes, this is a ginger cookie."). 5. Call to the child's attention familiar brand names or identifying symbols on products, buildings, and so on.

APPENDIX C

Basic Program Equipment and Materials for an Early Childhood Center

 ## INDOOR EQUIPMENT

The early childhood room should be arranged into well-planned areas of interest, such as the housekeeping and doll corner, block building, and so on. This encourages children to play in small groups throughout the playroom, engaging in activities of their special interest, rather than attempting to play in one large group.

The early childhood center must provide selections of indoor play equipment from all the following areas of interest. Selection should be of sufficient quantities so that children can participate in a wide range of activities. Many pieces of equipment can be homemade. Consider the age and developmental levels of the children when making selections.

PLAYROOM FURNISHINGS

- tables—seat four to six children (18" high for three-year-olds, 20"–22" high for four- and five-year-olds)
- chairs—10" high for three-year-olds, 12"–14" high for four- and five-year-olds
- open shelves—26" high, 12" deep, 12" between shelves
- lockers—12" wide, 12" deep, 32"–36" high

HOUSEKEEPING OR DOLL CORNER

Item	Number Recommended for 10 Children
Dolls	3
Doll Clothes	Variety
Doll bed—should be large enough for a child to get into, bedding	1

Item	Number Recommended for 10 Children
Doll high chair	1
Small table, four chairs	1 set
Tea party dishes	6-piece set with tray
Stove—child size, approximately 24" high, 23" long, 12" wide	1
Sink—child size, approximately 24" high, 23" long, 12" wide	1
Refrigerator—child size, approximately 28" high, 23" long, 12" wide	1
Pots and pans, empty food cartons, measuring cups, spoons, and so on	Variety
Mop, broom, dustpan	1
Ironing board and iron	1
Clothespins and clothesline	1
Toy telephones	2
Dress-up box—men's and women's hats, neckties, dresses, pocketbooks, shoes, old scarves, jewelry, and so on	Variety
Mirror	1

ART SUPPLIES

Item	Number Recommended for 10 Children
Newsprint paper 18" × 24"	1 ream
Colored paper—variety	3 packages
Large crayons	10 boxes
Tempera paint—red, yellow, blue, black, white	1 can each
Long-handled paintbrushes— making a stroke from ½" to 1" wide	10–12
Easels	1

247

Item	Number Recommended for 10 Children
Finger paint paper—glazed paper such as shelf, freezer, or butcher's paper	1 roll
Paste	1 quart
Blunt scissors	10
Collage—collection of bits of colored paper, cut-up gift wrappings, ribbons, cotton, string, scraps of fabric, and so on for pasting	Variety
Magazines for cutting and pasting	Variety
Clay—play dough, homemade dough clay	50 pounds
Cookie cutters, rolling pins	Variety
Smocks or aprons to protect children's clothes	10

FINGER PAINT RECIPES*

1. *Starch and Soap Finger Paint*

1 cup starch	1 tablespoon glycerine
1½ cups boiling water	(optional, makes it
½ cup soap flakes (not soap powder)	smoother)

   Method: Mix starch with enough water to make smooth paste. Add boiling water and cook until glossy. Stir in soap flakes while mixture is warm. When cool, add glycerine and coloring (powder paint, poster paint, or vegetable coloring).

2. *Flour and Salt Finger Paint, Cooked*

2 cups flour	3 cups cold water
2 teaspoons salt	2 cups hot water

   Method: Add salt to flour, then pour in cold water gradually and beat mixture with egg beater until it is smooth. Add hot water and boil until it becomes glossy. Beat until smooth, then mix in coloring.

3. *Flour and Salt Finger Paint, Uncooked*

1 cup flour	1 cup water
1½ teaspoons salt	

   Method: Combine flour and salt, add water. This has a grainy quality unlike the other finger paints, providing a different sensory experience.

4. *Argo Starch Finger Paint*

½ cup boiling water	6 tablespoons cold
2 tablespoons Argo starch	water

   Method: Dissolve starch in cold water in cup. Add this mixture to boiling water, stirring constantly. Heat until it becomes glossy. Add color.

5. *Wheat Flour Finger Paint*

3 parts water	1 part wheat flour

   Method: Stir flour into water, add food coloring. (Wheat flour can be bought at low cost in wallpaper stores or department stores.)

6. *Tempera Finger Paint*

dry tempera paint	½ cup liquid starch or ½ cup liquid dishwashing detergent

   Method: Mix the tempera paint with the starch or detergent, adding starch gradually until desired thickness is reached. Paint extender can also be added to dry tempera paint.

7. *Easy Finger Painting*

   clear liquid detergent
   dry tempera paint

   Method: Mark off sections on a table with masking tape the size of the paper to be used (newsprint works fine). Squirt liquid detergent on this section and add about 1 teaspoon of dry paint. After the picture has been made, lay the paper on the finger paint and rub. Lift off carefully.

8. *Cold Cream Finger Paint*

   Dry tempera paint can be mixed with most brands of cold cream. This is good for a first experience with a child reluctant to use colored paint with his fingers.

PASTE RECIPES

1. *Bookmaker Paste*

1 teaspoon flour	1 heaping teaspoon oil of cloves
2 teaspoons salt	
¼ teaspoon powdered alum	1 pint cold water

   Method: Mix dry ingredients with water slowly, stirring out lumps. Slow fire; cook over double boiler until it thickens.

2. *Hobby Craft Paste*

¾ cup water	½ cup Argo starch
2 tablespoons light Karo syrup	¾ cup water
1 teaspoon white vinegar	¼ teaspoon oil of wintergreen

   Method: Combine first ¾ cup water, corn syrup, and vinegar in a medium-sized saucepan; bring to a full boil. Stir cornstarch into second ¾ cup water until smooth. Remove boiling mixture from heat. Slowly pour in cornstarch-water mixture, stirring constantly until smooth. If lumps form, smooth them out with back of spoon against side of saucepan. Stir in oil of wintergreen. May be used immediately but will set to paste consistency in 24 hours. Store in covered jar. Keeps two months. Makes about 2½ cups.

---

*Interesting smells can be obtained by adding different food flavorings (mint, cloves) or talcum powder to finger paint if desired.

3. *Flour Paste*

Mix together:
¼ cup flour
cold water—enough to make creamy mixture

Method: Boil over slow heat for 5 minutes, stirring constantly. Cool. Add cold water to thin if necessary. Add a few drops of oil of peppermint or oil of wintergreen.

4. *Co-op Paste*

1 cup sugar   1 cup flour
1 tablespoon powdered   1 quart water
   alum   oil of cloves

Method: Mix and cook in double boiler until thick. Remove from heat and add 30 drops of oil of cloves. This mixture fills a juice container (8–10 oz.) about ¾ full. Needs no refrigeration.

RECIPES FOR DOUGH AND OTHER PLASTIC MATERIALS

1. *Cooked Dough*

½ cup flour   2 cups boiling water
½ cup cornstarch (blend   ½ cup salt
   with cold water)

Method: Add salt to boiling water. Combine flour with cornstarch and water. Pour hot mixture into cold. Put over hot water and cook until glossy. Cool overnight. Knead in flour until right consistency, adding color with flour.

2. *Cooked Dough*

4 tablespoons cornstarch ½ cup boiling water
½ cup salt

Method: Mix cornstarch and salt. Add color if desired. Pour on boiling water, stir until soft and smooth. Place over fire until it forms a soft ball. In using, if it sticks to fingers, dust hands with cornstarch.

3. *Sawdust and Wheat Flour*

4 parts sawdust   1 part wheat flour

Method: Make paste of wheat flour and water. Add sawdust. Presents interesting sensory appeal.

4. *Uncooked Play Dough*

3 cups flour   1 cup water
¼ cup salt   1 tablespoon oil
coloring

Method: Mix flour with salt; add water with coloring and oil gradually. Add more water if too stiff, add more flour if too sticky. Let the children help with the mixing and measuring. Keep dough stored in plastic bags or a covered container.

5. *Salt Dough*

1 cup salt   ¾ cup cold water
½ cup cornstarch

Method: Combine all ingredients in a double boiler placed over medium heat. Stir the mixture constantly; in about two to three minutes it should become so thick that it follows the spoon in mixing it. When the consistency is similar to bread dough, place on wax paper or aluminum foil to cool. When dough is cool enough to handle, knead for several minutes. It is then ready to use. To store for up to several days, wrap in wax paper or place in plastic bags.

6. *Ornamental Clay* (Suitable for Dried Objects)

1 cup cornstarch   1¼ cups water
2 cups baking soda

Method: Cook ingredients together until thickened, either in double boiler or over direct heat—*stir constantly*. When it is cool enough, turn it out and let children knead dough and make it into whatever they wish. If used for ornaments, make hole for hanging ornament while dough is still moist.

7. *Baker's Dough* (Suitable for Dried Objects)

4 cups flour   1 to 1½ cups water
1 cup salt

Method: Mix ingredients to make a dough easy to handle. Knead, and shape as desired. Bake at 350° for 50 to 60 minutes. Material will brown slightly, but baking at lower temperatures is not as successful.

BLOCK BUILDING AREA

Item	Number Recommended for 10 Children
Unit blocks—purchased or homemade (directions are available)	276 pieces, 11 shapes
Large, lightweight blocks	Variety
Small wooden or rubber animals and people	Variety
Small trucks, airplanes, cars, and boats	12
Medium airplanes	3
Medium boats	2
Medium-sized trucks— 12" to 24"	3

MUSIC CORNER

■ record player, tape player, CD player
■ suitable records, tapes, and CDs
■ rhythm instruments
■ dress-up scarves for dancing

MANIPULATIVE TOYS

Item	Number Recommended for 10 Children
Wooden inlay puzzles— approximately 5 to 20 pieces	6
Color cone	1

Item	Number Recommended for 10 Children
Nested blocks	1
Pegboards—variety of shapes and sizes	1
Large spools and beads for stringing	2 sets
Toys that have parts that fit into one another	2
Lotto games	2
Dominoes	1

BOOKS AND STORIES (20–30 BOOKS)

A carefully selected book collection for the various age levels should include the following categories.

■ transportation, birds and animals, family life
■ community helpers, science, nonsense rhymes
■ Mother Goose rhymes, poems, and stories
■ homemade picture books
■ collection of pictures classified by subject
■ library books to enrich the collection

NATURE STUDY AND SCIENCE

■ aquarium or fish bowls
■ plastic materials
■ magnifying glass, prism, magnet, thermometers
■ growing indoor plants, garden plot
■ additional material such as stones, leaves, acorns, birds' nests, caterpillars, worms, tadpoles, and so on

WOODWORKING CENTER

Basic woodworking operations are

■ sanding
■ gluing
■ hammering
■ holding (with a vise or clamp)
■ fastening (with screws)
■ drilling
■ sawing

Materials for a woodworking center include:

■ sturdy workbench (or table)
■ woodworking tools: broad-headed nails ¾″ to 1½″ long, a C-clamp or vise (to hold wood), flat-headed hammer weighing about 12 ounces for beginning woodworking experiences, later a claw hammer may be added, 14″ saw with ten teeth to the inch
■ soft white pine lumber scraps (it is difficult to drive nails into hardwood; plywood is not suitable either). Packing boxes of soft pine can be disassembled and used for hammering work.

SAND PLAY

In an outdoor area, sand should be confined so it does not get scattered over the rest of the playground. The area should be large enough so several children can move about in it without crowding each other. A 10″ to 12″ ledge around a sandbox can serve as a boundary and at the same time provide children with a working surface or a seat. If sand is about 6″ to 8″ below the top of the ledge, it is less likely to spill onto the playground. Sand should be about 18″ deep so children can dig or make tunnels. Four or five inches of gravel on the bottom of the sandbox provides drainage.

Basic equipment: Ordinary plastic or metal kitchen utensils—cups, spoons, pails, shovels, sifters, funnels, scoops, and bowls.

WATER PLAY

Water play can be either an indoor or an outdoor activity, depending upon the climate. Clear plastic water basins can be used for water play. When they are on a stand with wheels, they can be moved easily to any area of a room. When these plastic containers are used, children have the advantage of being able to see through the sides and the bottom. If a table stands on a carpeted floor, a plastic runner can be used to protect the carpet, and spillage will not be a serious housekeeping problem.

Materials: Clear tubing, sponges, strainers, funnels, corks, pitchers, and measuring cups. For added interest, rotary beaters, spoons, small bowls, plastic basters, and straws.

 OUTDOOR EQUIPMENT

The outdoor play equipment should be grouped according to use. For example, plan for both active and quiet play; allow for free areas for use of wheel toys. The following is a list of suggested basic outdoor play equipment for the early childhood program.

■ climbing structure(s)
■ large and small packing boxes
■ slide
■ swings with canvas seats
■ wagons and wheelbarrows
■ pedal toys—tricycles, cars, and so on
■ sandbox with spoons, shovels, pails, and so on
■ balls
■ a variety of salvage material, such as rubber tires, tire tubes, lengths of garden hose, ropes, and cardboard boxes, to enrich the play

Many activities, such as housekeeping play and art activities, at times can be transferred to the outdoor area.

Use the following checklist to evaluate your playground setup.

___ There are clear pathways and enough space between areas so that traffic flows well and equipment does not obstruct the movement of children.

___ Space and equipment are organized so that children are readily visible and easily supervised by adults.

___ Different types of activity areas are separated. (Tricycle paths are separate from swings, sand box is separate from the climbing area.)

___ Open space is available for active play.

___ There is some space for quiet play.

___ Dramatic play can be set up outdoors, as space is available.

___ Art activities can be set up outdoors.

___ A portion of the play area is covered for use in wet weather.

___ A storage area is available for play equipment.

___ A drinking fountain is available.

___ The area has readily accessible restrooms.

APPENDIX D

Room and Yard Organization, Exhibitions, and Displays

 ROOM AND YARD ORGANIZATION*

LARGE CARDBOARD CARTONS

Puppet theaters, post offices, and stores are easily constructed by slicing or sawing out a rectangular portion in the top half of the front section of a large carton. When folded to the inside, the flap can be cut back to the desired width for a stage or shelf. The flap is supported by a dowel or a length of heavy cord strung from one side of the box to the other. Leftover latex wall paint is ideal for painting these large structures. This type of paint conceals advertising, does not smear when dry, and can be washed off a brush or child's hands with water. Use old postage stamps, greeting cards, and envelopes if this is to be a post office. Paper tickets, signs, money (bottle tops, etc.) can be used if the structure is to be a theater.

CABLE SPOOLS

Empty cable spools are fun additions to the outside play area. Two or three spools may be secured one on top of another with a plumber's pipe inserted through the center of each; a second pipe can be sunk in concrete close enough to the structure to be used as a firefighter's pole. A rope ladder attached to the top spool adds to the climbing challenge.

CARDBOARD BOXES

To create a table easel from a large cardboard box, measure one side the equivalent length of the bottom and mark. Cut diagonally across from this mark to the bottom corner on both sides. This produces a sturdy

*These suggestions are taken from Jean W. Quill's *A World of Materials,* Washington, DC: National Association for the Education of Young Children, 1969.

cardboard triangle that serves as a table easel once two slits have been made for clothespin clips at the top. The children themselves will be able to remove or replace newsprint for paintings.

The same triangular arrangement covered with a piece of flannel makes a nontipping flannelboard for children's and teacher's use. A show box containing flannelboard figures may be stored beneath the triangle for the child's convenience. It can be used for retelling stories or reworking number experiences in small groups or as a solitary, self-selected activity.

WOODEN CRATES

Wooden crates are durable and good for school use. At a minimal cost, these crates may be transformed into a stove, sink, sofa, work bench, or locker arrangement. To form a solid front, it is necessary only to tap the wooden slats loose, add a few additional slats, and replace side by side. To create a stove, individual pie tins can be turned upside down to simulate gas burners. These are especially effective when painted black to look like "grating." Painted bottle tops add stove controls. A spool set on top of a scrap of wood and painted silver makes a faucet; the entire "sink" may cost little more than the price of the required pan. Many leftover aluminum foil pans are suitable for this purpose. The ends of cantaloupe crates make sturdy frames for children's drawings or trays for the doll corner or science table.

WOODEN AND PLASTIC SOFT-DRINK AND MILK CRATES

These crates, sometimes available at a small charge, are excellent substitutes for commercial hollow blocks. Paint them bright colors with latex paint. A set of casters on one crate can produce a durable wagon for hauling friends or blocks. Set the casters far enough in to allow stacking at those times when the crates are not in use. They also make excellent "cubby holes" for storage.

BOATS

At the beginning or end of the boating season, some rowboats may be destroyed or abandoned as no longer seaworthy. These boats are often donated by marina managers to a school or playground, if transportation is provided by the school. When stored safely, these boats can be made into useful playground equipment.

RECYCLED TIRES

Used tires, hung either horizontally or vertically, make excellent swings. Inflated tubes can be rolled from place to place, bounced on, and used for various movement games.

ICE CREAM CONTAINERS

A circular, spatter-paint screen may be created from the three-gallon containers discarded by ice cream stores or restaurants. Cut the bottom from one of these containers, leaving only a narrow edge to which the edges of a circular piece of screen may be glued. A matching narrow circle, cut from another piece of cardboard, placed over the first and glued down, will secure the screen. A paint-dipped toothbrush is scraped across the screen; any object placed beneath will leave a design on the paper on which it is resting. The carton should be cut down to leave approximately one quarter of its original length; this gives a satisfactory height for spatter painting.

Ice cream containers can also be converted to wastebaskets, space helmets, and diver's masks. To make the latter, simply remove an area from an upside-down carton large enough for the child's face to appear. Allow the child to paint in a choice of colors. Ice cream containers can also be used as storage space, when bolted together.

SAWDUST

Sawdust is available from the lumber mill for use in making sawdust clay. Simply mix a small amount of wallpaper paste in water and add sawdust until a pliable consistency has been reached. This clay hardens over a period of time.

EXHIBITIONS AND DISPLAYS

It is stimulating and educational for children to see their work displayed. Whether the purpose of the exhibit is to introduce new ideas and information, to stimulate interest in a single lesson, to show the children's work, or to provide an overview of their work, the subject of the exhibition should be directly related to the children's interest. Exhibits should be changed often to be of educational and decorative value.

LABELS

- Make large, bold letters that can be easily read.
- Keep titles brief. Descriptive material should be in smaller letters.
- Label children's work with their names as a means of creating pride through recognition of their work.
- Vary the material in making letters. In addition to paper letters, labels can be made of paint, ink, crayon, chalk, cloth, fancy papers, string, rope, yarn, and other three-dimensional materials.

COLOR

- Choose a basic color scheme related to the visual material displayed. Seasonal colors can be used, such as warm colors for fall (yellow, orange, red), cool colors for winter (blue, blue-green, gray), and light and cool colors for spring (colors with yellow in the mixture, such as yellow-orange).
- Use colors for mounting that are more subdued than the materials mounted. This may be accomplished by using lighter, darker, or grayer colors.
- Select a bright color for accent, as in bands or other pleasing arrangements on the larger areas of gray, lighter, or darker colors.
- Create a contrast to emphasize or attract attention. Intense color makes a visual impact, such as orange against black.
- Use both light and dark color values.
- Create color patterns that lead the eye from area to area.

BALANCE

Balance can be achieved formally or informally. To create formal balance, the largest piece of work may be placed in the center with similar shapes on either side. Informal balance is more interesting, subtle, and compelling. Material may be grouped in blocks of different sizes, colors, or shapes, and still be balanced. Margins of the bulletin board should be wider at the bottom.

UNITY

Unity in design is the quality that holds the arrangement together in harmony.

- Ideas can be unified with background paper, lettering, strips of construction paper, yarn, or ribbon.

- Repetition of similar sizes, shapes, colors, or lines can help to create harmony.
- Shapes can be arranged to lead the eye from one part of the board to another.
- One large unusual background shape helps unify the design.
- Avoid cluttering the display; items placed at all angles destroy the unity.

VARIETY

Variety in arrangement prevents monotony. Use interesting combinations of color, form, line, and texture.

EMPHASIS

Emphasis is the main idea or center of interest. This can be achieved by using larger letters, a brighter color, a larger picture, an unusual shape, texture, or a three-dimensional object. Other material should be grouped into subordinate areas.

LINE

Line is used to draw the eye to a specific area; suggest direction, action, and movement; and to hold the display together. Use thick or thin lines; solid, dotted, or dashed lines. Diagonal lines are used to show action; zigzag lines suggest excitement; and slow-moving curves are restful. Lines may be painted, cut from paper, or formed with string, yarn, ribbon, or tape.

TEXTURE

Texture may be created with a variety of materials.

- paper and cardboard—textured wallpaper, sandpaper, metallic foil, egg containers, corrugated cardboard
- fabrics—netting, flannel, burlap, fur, felt, carpet remnants, assorted felt scraps
- miscellaneous—chicken wire, metal screen, sheet cork

THREE-DIMENSIONAL EFFECTS

- Pull letters or objects out to the head of the pin.
- Staple a shallow box to the board as a shelf to hold lightweight three-dimensional items.
- Mount a picture on a box lid and fasten it to the board.
- Use shallow boxes as buildings, animals, and people.
- Pleat a strip of paper in an accordion fold with pictures attached.

- Use paper sculpture—strips of paper can be twisted, curled, folded, rolled, fringed, perforated, or torn. Puppets, animals, birds, flowers, people, abstract forms, and masks can also be made.
- Use three-dimensional materials in displays—styrofoam, egg cartons, paper plates, paper cups, soda straws, cupcake cups, paper lace, toweling tubes, and other discarded materials.
- Use objects from nature—branches, shells, bark, driftwood, feathers.

BACKGROUND MATERIALS

- display paper, tissue paper, burlap, corrugated cardboard, construction paper
- egg carton separators, blotters, textured wallpaper, shelf paper

DISPLAY BOARDS FOR TWO-DIMENSIONAL WORK

- standard cork boards or sheet of plywood to which cork tiles have been glued
- builder's wallboard with wood strip nailed to the top with hooks for hanging
- thick cardboard that will hold pins
- a pasteboard box open for standing on a table or the floor, depending on size
- a folding screen made from an old crate or packing box
- wide strips of binding tape attached along a blank wall; pin pictures to tape
- wire stretched across an empty space with pictures attached to it

 MORE ON BULLETIN BOARDS

The most immediate evidence of an art program is the display of children's artwork. A teacher's creative approach to display is an extension of the art program in the physical environment. Bulletin boards are the most frequent form of display. Consider the following fairy tale.

> Once upon a time there was a carpenter who was building a classroom. When he was on the very top of his ladder, a hammer fell and crashed into the wall, making a very large hole. The carpenter did not know what to do since he had no materials left to repair the wall. Suddenly he had an idea! He found a 4′ × 8′ slab of cork and hung it over the hole. Then he tacked wood strips around the edges and said, "I am well pleased." He named his creation "Bulletin Board."

The dictionary defines a bulletin board as "a board on which bulletins and other notices are posted." Teachers often have other definitions for this term: (1) a surface that must be covered before the first day of school and before parents' night; (2) a board that is always three inches wider than the paper just cut for it; and (3) a rectangle that has a width never sufficient for the number of letters needed to be pinned across it.

Whatever your definition, a bulletin board is much more than a board on which notices are posted. It is a visual extension of a learning experience, a visual form of motivation, and a reflection of a curriculum area. Because bulletin boards are a visual phenomenon, teachers should be concerned about their content and appearance.

Thirty spelling papers or fifteen identical paper pumpkins hanging up like someone's laundry do not constitute a good bulletin board. Mimeographed pictures, commercial cardboard turkeys, and corrugated cardboard trim are *not* visually appealing and certainly are not reflections of the children whose interest you are trying to catch.

A display designed for the eye is also designed for the mind. Children are very much attuned to symbols. Television commercials, billboards, posters, and cereal boxes attest to the impact of images. Bulletin boards should attract constructive attention. Stereotypical smiley faces and dog-eared paper letters with a thousand pin holes will not do it. Ideas and paper fade. Stereotyped versions of an upcoming holiday do absolutely nothing for children's art development.

For an early childhood teacher, one of the best solutions is to display the children's artwork. Art is a visual extension of the child and her own unique ideas and expression. It is the result of the child's own experience and serves as a motivation for others and the child herself. Any subject can be the theme for an effective bulletin board, but one rule of thumb is that all boards should be student oriented and entice student participation. Boards that ask questions, have games to play, or have objects to be handled can be fun *and* valuable learning experiences.

Eye-catching photographs (of the children, if possible) and short stories, poems, and cartoons are exercises for both the eye and mind. Whatever the mode, the key is visual impact. In order for a bulletin board to be a learning experience, it first must get the child's attention. Bright colors, bold design, legible, catchy, succinct phraseology, and relevant themes are vital to bulletin boards by, for, and about the children.

Try some of these suggestions for improving your bulletin boards.

- Take advantage of interest in the World Series, Olympics, or other big sports events for a variety of projects. Find bulletin board space for newspaper clippings, pictures of heroes and heroines, and posting of scores and relative standings. Have the children write reports or draw pictures of games in which they are interested. Make up graphs with scores for each team. Vary these activities according to the level of the children's interest and abilities.

- If you have a bulletin board too big to cope with, cut it down to size by covering it with wallpaper samples, outlining each sample with black construction paper in a kind of giant patchwork quilt effect. Each child can use one of these squares as a personal bulletin board. Or you could use each of the squares to depict a different aspect of one main theme: symbols of Christmas, kinds of animals, favorite people, and so on.

- Be sure all your bulletin boards and other kinds of displays are at the children's eye level.

- When your classroom closet is awash with caps and mittens, why not bring their splashy colors and designs into the open with a self-portrait mural for a bulletin board? On a strip of butcher paper, draw a circle for each child. Have the students add features to turn these circles into self-portraits. Two lines looping down from each face become instant arms. Finally, have each child draw her own hat and mittens on the heads and hands. Encourage the young artists to copy the actual styles, colors, and designs of their own apparel as exactly as possible. This mural not only makes a colorful bulletin board, but also helps you easily identify the owners of any stray clothing.

DISPLAY AREAS FOR THREE-DIMENSIONAL WORK

- Use tops of cupboard or built-in shelves.
- Build shelves with boards supported by cigar boxes or brick, used permanently or temporarily.
- Attach a shelf of wood or particleboard underneath a bulletin board.
- Cigar boxes nailed together make display shelves.
- Dioramas are especially useful where exhibit space is limited.
- A card table can be used for temporary exhibits, then folded up when not in use.
- If obtainable, a small showcase is valuable for displaying museum-type objects.
- Cardboard boxes fastened to bulletin boards make a display place for lightweight objects.
- Use driftwood as an interesting display for weaving and jewelry.
- Puppet display rods can be made with a board and some dowel sticks.
- Mobiles are attractive display devices. Coat hangers can also be used.
- Cover cardboard or cigar boxes and use them as bases for displaying art objects.
- Use a pegboard with brackets.

APPENDIX E

Recycled Materials

Creative teachers find that art possibilities abound everywhere, including a new look at old, discarded materials. For example, in the following teaching suggestions, one kind of discarded item—gallon milk containers—provides a wealth of storage, display, and equipment possibilities.

TEACHING SUGGESTIONS: EMPTY CONTAINERS FULL OF PROMISE

When that plastic gallon milk container is out of milk, it is full of potential for classroom implements you can make yourself. Scoops, funnels, sorting trays, display or storage containers, and carrying baskets are just waiting to be cut out.

Outline the area you wish to cut with a felt-tip marker and use a sharp knife or a small pencil-type soldering iron to do the cutting. (If you use the iron, be sure to work in a ventilated area and avoid the fumes.)

The containers are so readily available you can afford to experiment with a few to find just the shapes you are after. Here are directions for some basic cuts to get you started.

- Scoop—Cut away the handle and part of the side below it. The container's handle instantly becomes the scoop's handle, while the section below becomes the scoop itself.
- Sorting trays—Cut off the bottom or the entire side opposite the handle to make trays of varying depths. These are perfect for sorting small objects, such as pebbles or shells, or for examining small amounts of sand or soil.
- Funnel—Cut the handle a few centimeters from the top. Then cut around the base of the handle to make the funnel's body from the curved section of the jug. The top of the handle becomes the spout. For a larger funnel, just cut the bottom from the container and use the top as the spout.
- Carrying basket—Cut away the upper portion of the side opposite the handle. The children then carry the jug by the handle and use it to transport all kinds of items.
- Display or storage container—Cut the bottom off the jug just below the handle. You'll end up with a square container about 3″ deep, perfect for displaying or storing the specimens that students collect on their outings.

EQUIPMENT FOR MOVEMENT ACTIVITIES FROM RECYCLED MATERIALS

A valuable addition to the movement program in the early childhood classroom is equipment made from recycled materials. For example, empty plastic gallon milk jugs can be used as safe game goals, pins for indoor/outdoor bowling games, or cut out for scoops (see Figures E–1 and E–2) to toss yarn or other light balls in classroom movement activities.

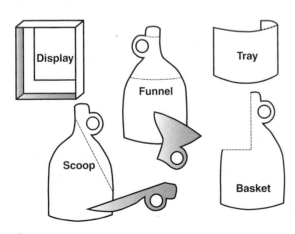

256

Plastic
Bleach
Bottle

Tape
Around
Edge

STYLE 1

Plastic
Bleach
Bottle

Tape
Around
Edge

STYLE 2

FIGURE | Equipment using recycled materials:
E–1 | scoops.

Old pantyhose can be used to make light child-sized rackets for great hand–eye coordination practice in racket games. These rackets are especially good for young children as they are light enough to handle and yet sturdy enough to hit a yarn, Nerf, or plastic ball.

Using recycled materials has an obvious cost benefit in addition to demonstrating the importance of conservation to young children. Young children can possibly use these same materials at home for their own play experiences.

Even better, you can enlist parent participation and involvement in the program by asking parents to donate recycled materials to make movement equipment. Perhaps parents and children together could even get involved at home in making some of the equipment for the class's use, such as yarn balls or pantyhose rackets.

 ## OTHER IDEAS FOR RECYCLING MATERIALS

Just as recycled materials were used for making movement equipment in Chapter 16, these same "discards" can be valuable art materials. Both conservation and creativity can be practiced in ways like these:

■ Be a scavenger. (But remember that the word is "scavenger," not beggar or receiver of junk goods.)

FIGURE | Plastic scoop and yarn ball.
E–2 |

■ Begin your scavenger hunt by making a list of the equipment and supplies that you feel you might find in your community at little or no cost.

■ Search for your treasures in attics, basements, garages, thrift or Goodwill Industry stores, and at garage sales.

■ Ask parents to contribute to the needs of creative children, or send a "want ad" home being specific about what you need. Your ad may read something like the ad in the box below.

PLEASE SAVE...

— yarn and ribbon scraps
— large empty spools
— shirt cardboards
— leftover wallpaper
— men's shirts—we will turn them into smocks
— juice cans with smooth edges
— plastic squeeze bottles
— bits of fabric, trim
— buttons, old jewelry

THEY WILL BE USED BY YOUR CREATIVE CHILD(REN) IN THE EARLY CHILDHOOD PROGRAM.

■ Check with wallpaper and carpet dealers. Wallpaper dealers will sometimes give you their old sample books, and carpet dealers will often sell their sample swatches for a very small sum. These carpet swatches are useful as sit-upons, as rugs for houses the children build, as colorful mats under items on display, and as working mats for use under table toys.

■ Trim the bristles from 1″-wide house painting brushes to about 1″ in length and use these in place of more expensive easel brushes.

■ Gather paper from a variety of sources:

Be a bag grabber. Collect plain paper bags. Cut them open and use them for painting, crayoning, and so on.

Save old newspapers for easel painting. Bright tempera (watercolor) paint on a newsprint background makes a very attractive and interesting work of art.

Check with your community or local newspaper office. They may donate or sell newsprint or old newspapers to you at a minimal cost.

Other materials listed in Figure E–3 can be valuable in the art center.

SANDBOX TOYS FROM THE KITCHEN

From the cupboard—use plastic storage containers such as scoops, molds, or buckets. Foam cups are good scoops or molds. A plastic flowerpot with drainage holes can be a sifter.

Cut an egg carton into individual egg cups for molds.

Make an egg-carton sifter by cutting the lid off an egg carton and cutting the egg cup section in half the short way. In the bottom of each cup, poke a hole. The holes may be the same size or of varying sizes.

MUSICAL INSTRUMENTS FROM RECYCLED MATERIALS

Recycling egg cartons for tambourines. Young children can make a simple tambourine from egg cartons and bottle caps. Simply put a few bottle caps in each egg carton, tape the carton closed, and you have an instrument that players can shake or hit. Children will love playing it both in rhythm and creative movement activities.

Recycling nuts and bolts for rattles. For an unusual set of musical instruments, assemble an assortment of large nuts, bolts, and washers. Young children will get excellent practice in fine finger

The following materials can be valuable instructional tools in the art program as well as in other curriculum areas.

1. Empty plastic containers—detergent bottles, bleach bottles, old refrigerator containers. These can be used for constructing scoops, storing art materials, and so on.

2. Buttons—all colors and sizes. These are excellent for collages, assemblages, as well as sorting, counting, matching, and so on.

3. Egg shells. These can be washed, dried, and colored with food coloring for art projects.

4. Coffee or shortening can lids and cans themselves. These can be covered with adhesive paper and used for the storage of art supplies, games, and manipulative materials.

5. Magazines with colorful pictures. These are excellent for making collages, murals, and posters.

6. Scraps of fabric—felt, silk, cotton, oil cloth, and so on. These can be used to make "fabric boards" with the name of each fabric written under a small swatch attached to the board, as well as for collages, puppets, and so on.

7. Yarn scraps. These can be used for separating buttons into sets; also for art activities.

8. Styrofoam scraps.

9. Scraps of lace, rick rack, or decorative trim.

10. Bottles with sprinkler tops. Excellent for water play and for mixing water as children finger paint.

11. Wallpaper books of discontinued patterns.

12. Paper doilies.

13. Discarded wrapping paper.

14. Paint color cards from paint/hardware stores.

15. Old paintbrushes.

16. Old jewelry and beads.

17. Old muffin tins. These are effective for sorting small objects and mixing paint.

18. Tongue depressors or ice cream sticks. Counters for math, good for art construction projects, stick puppets, and so on.

19. Wooden clothespins. For making "people," for construction projects, for hanging up paintings to dry.

FIGURE E–3 | Beautiful junk list.

movements when they create musical rattles out of these. All you have to do is place several washers on each bolt and loosely turn the nut onto the bolt. Place these inside empty adhesive bandage boxes, tape shut, and use as interesting sound instruments (rattles).

Making music with bottles. Gather a collection of bottles with both small and large mouths, soft drink bottles, ketchup bottles, quart canning jars, mayonnaise jars, and so on.

Show the children how different sounds can be made with different-sized bottles by blowing across the various openings. Have them listen for high and low sounds. Stand the bottles on a table and gently tap them with a spoon. The children can explore different sounds the bottles make by blowing across them and by tapping them with a spoon.

Rhythm instruments from recycled materials. The following are suggestions for simple rhythm instruments the children can make to use in their musical experiences. Creating rhythm instruments from found objects gives young children another opportunity for self-expression. They receive satisfaction and pleasure from beating rhythmic sounds and keeping time to music with instruments they have created.

Materials:

paper plates	plastic egg-shaped
empty spools	containers
pebbles	small plastic bottles
nails	sticks
toweling rolls	old Christmas bells
embroidery hoops	bottle caps
small boxes or cartons	peas or corn
dried beans	wire

Bottle cap shaker
Remove plastic from inside bottle caps. Punch a hole in the center of the bottle cap. String bottle caps on a string and attach to a package handle. Paint if desired.

Spool shaker
Paint designs on a large spool. Force four pipe cleaners through the center of the spool. Attach a Christmas bell to the end of each cleaner by bending.

Plate shaker
Decorate two paper plates with crayons or paint. Put pebbles, dried corn, peas, or beans between them and staple or sew the plates together with bright yarn or string. Bend wire to form a handle, and fit the ends inside.

Box shaker
Place small pebbles, beans, or seeds in a small box or empty clean milk carton to make a shaker. It can be used with or without a handle. Decorate as desired.

Flute
Use a paper towel or tissue paper roll. With a pencil, punch three or four holes (about one inch apart) in the cardboard tube. Cover one end of the roll with a piece of waxed paper, as described later in the instructions for the Hummer. Hum a tune in the open end, moving your fingers over the holes.

Sandpaper blocks
Paint two small wooden blocks. Place a strip of sandpaper on the surface, allowing an overlap on each end for fastening with thumbtacks. Sandpaper may replace carpet on old eraser blocks. Rub together to make a sound.

Clappers
Nail bottle caps to a painted eraser block.

Cymbals
Decorate two lids from tin cans. Fasten a small spool or block of wood on for a handle.

Tambourine
Tie bottle caps by thin wire, pipe cleaners, or string to a decorated paper or tinfoil plate.

Hummer
Decorate a tube from a waxed paper or paper toweling roll. Fasten a piece of waxed paper over one end of the tube. Humming through the waxed paper is fun. Be sure to change the paper after each use.

Circle shakers
Stretch two layers of plastic cloth with uncooked rice or tapioca between them over one half of an embroidery hoop. Fasten with the other half of the hoop to make a circle shaker. (When making any shaker-type toys, be sure that the small objects used are sealed securely inside. Small objects like beans, peas, and rice can pose a serious choking risk to young children.)

Egg shakers
Fill plastic egg-shaped containers (either panty hose containers or plastic Easter eggs) with dried beans. Tape the halves together and use them as maracas.

Bottle shakers
Collect empty small plastic bottles. Fill with rice, beans, or nuts until half full. Seal bottles that don't have child-proof lids with tape. These are excellent shakers for tiny hands.

Drums
Glue lids to salt boxes, cereal boxes, or ice cream boxes and decorate with paint to use as drums. Older children

may make drums from restaurant-size tin cans with canvas or heavy paper stretched and laced to cover the ends.

Kazoo

Use a piece of waxed paper over a clean comb. Play by pressing your lips against the paper and humming.

Gong

Use an old license plate (the older the better). Strike with a mallet to play. Describe the sounds.

Jingle instrument

Use a set of metal measuring spoons. Play by slapping them into your hand.

Wrist or ankle bells

Lace two or three bells through a shoestring. Tie to wrist or ankle. Move to shake your bells.

Rubber band box.   Another addition to rhythm instruments is a rubber band box. Gather together one cigar box (or similar-sized and weight box), five rubber bands of several lengths and thicknesses, and 10 brass fasteners.

Punch five holes, 1½″ apart in each end of the box. Attach a rubber band to a brass fastener, push through one of the holes, and open the fastener on the inside of the box to hold it down. Stretch the rubber band tight to the other end of the box and attach it in the same way. Attach the rest of the rubber bands. To use: The rubber band box can be held, placed on a table, or placed on the floor. Encourage the children to pluck the rubber bands with their fingers or strum the bands with their thumbs. They can experiment with sounds and beats: high-low, fast-slow, and loud-soft.

Sound box.   Another rhythm instrument is the sandpaper sound box. Gather together four pieces of sandpaper (of various grades from fine to coarse), glue, scissors, and a dowel ½ × 6″ long). Glue the top and bottom of the box closed. Allow enough time for it to dry completely. Cut the sandpaper to fit all sides of the box. Glue the sandpaper strips to the box. To use: Rub the dowel on the sandpaper. While the children are using the sound boxes, you can introduce such musical concepts as loud-soft and fast-slow. The dowels can also be used alone in a rhythm band or in a parade. Extend this activity by having the children make their own sound boxes if they are interested.

APPENDIX F

Criteria for Selecting Play Equipment for Young Children

1. *A young child's playthings should be as free of detail as possible.*
   A child needs freedom to express himself by creating his own childlike world; too much detail hampers him. Blocks are the best example of "unstructured" toys. Blocks, construction sets, and other unstructured toys and equipment such as clay, sand, and paints allow the imagination free rein and are basic playthings.

2. *A good plaything should stimulate children to do things for themselves.*
   Equipment that makes the child a spectator, such as a mechanical duck, may entertain for the moment but has little or no play value. The equipment provided for play should encourage children to explore and create or offer the opportunity for dramatic play.

3. *Young children need large, easily manipulated playthings.*
   Toys too small can be a source of frustration because the child's muscular coordination is not yet developed enough to handle the smaller forms and shapes. A child's muscles develop through her play. A child needs equipment for climbing and balancing.

4. *The material from which a plaything is made has an important role in the play of the young child.*
   Warmth and pleasurable touch are significant to him. The most satisfactory materials have been established as wood and cloth.

5. *The durability of the plaything is of utmost importance.*
   Play materials must be sturdy. Children hate to see their toys break. Axles and wheels must be strong to support a child's weight. Some materials break so readily that they prove to be very expensive.

6. *The toy must "work."*
   It's frustrating when a door or drawer won't shut, wheels get stuck, or figures won't stand up. Be sure parts move correctly and that maintenance will be easy.

7. *The construction of a plaything should be simple enough for a child to comprehend.*
   This strengthens his understanding and experience of the world around him. The mechanics, too, should be visible and easily grasped. Small children will take them apart to see how they tick.

8. *A plaything should encourage cooperative play.*
   As we seek to teach children to work and play together, we should supply the environment that stimulates such play.

9. *The total usefulness of the plaything must be considered in comparing price.*
   Will it last several children through several stages of their playing lives?

What are some good toys and play materials for young children?

All ages are approximate. Most suggestions for younger children are also appropriate for older children.

	SENSORY MATERIALS	ACTIVE PLAY EQUIPMENT	CONSTRUCTION MATERIALS	MANIPULATIVE TOYS	DOLLS AND DRAMATIC PLAY	BOOKS AND RECORDINGS	ART MATERIALS
2-year-olds and young 3-year-olds	Water toys: food coloring, pumps, funnels Sand toys: containers, utensils Harmonica, kazoo, guitar, recorder Tools for working with clay	Bicycle Outdoor games: bocce, tetherball, shuffleboard, jump rope, Frisbee	More unit blocks, shapes, and accessories Props for roads, towns Hollow blocks Brace and bits, screwdrivers, screws, metric measure, accessories	More complex puzzles Dominoes More difficult board and card games Yarn, big needles, mesh fabric, weaving materials Magnets, balances Attribute blocks	Cash register, play money, accessories, or props for other dramatic play settings: gas station, construction, office Typewriter	Books on cultures Stories with chapters children can read Favorite stories Children's recipe books	Watercolors, smaller paper, stapler, hole puncher Chalkboard Oil crayons, paint crayons, charcoal Simple camera, film
Older 3- and 4-year-olds	Water toys: measuring cups, egg beaters Sand toys: muffin tins, vehicles Xylophone, maracas, tambourine Potter's clay	Larger 3-wheeled riding vehicle Roller skates Climbing structure Rope or tire swing Plastic bats and balls Various sizes rubber balls Balance board Planks, boxes, old tires Bowling pins, ring toss, bean bags and target	More unit blocks, shapes, and accessories Table blocks Realistic model vehicles Construction set with smaller pieces Woodworking bench, saw, sandpaper, nails	Puzzles, pegboard, small beads to string Parquetry blocks Small objects to sort Marbles Magnifying glass Simple card or board games Flannel board with pictures, letters Sturdy letters and numbers	Dolls and accessories Doll carriage Child-sized stove or sink More dress-up clothes Play food, cardboard cartons Airport, doll house, or other settings with accessories Finger or stick puppets	Simple science books More detailed picture and story books Sturdy record or tape player Recordings of wider variety of music Book and recording sets	Easel, narrower brushes Thick crayons, chalk Paste, tape with dispenser Collage materials
5- and 6-year-olds	Water and sand toys: cups, shovels Modeling dough Sound-matching games Bells, wood block, triangle, drum Texture matching games, feel box	Low climber Canvas swing Low slide Wagon, cart, or wheelbarrow Large rubber balls Low 3-wheeled, steerable vehicle with pedals	Unit blocks and accessories: animals, people, simple wood cars and trucks Interlocking construction set with large pieces Wood train and track set Hammer (13 oz. steel shanked), soft wood, roofing nails, nailing block	Wooden puzzles with 4–20 large pieces Pegboards Big beads or spools to string Sewing cards Stacking toys Picture lotto, picture dominoes	Washable dolls with a few clothes Doll bed Child-sized table and chairs Dishes, pots, and pans Dress-up clothes: hats, shoes, shirts Hand puppets Shopping cart	Clear picture books, stories, and poems about things children know CDs or tapes of classical music, folk music, or children's songs	Wide-tip watercolor markers Large sheets of paper, easel Finger or tempera paint, ½" brushes Blunt-nose scissors White glue
7- to 10-year-olds	Modeling materials, papier-mâché, wire for sculpture, potter's clay	Jump ropes, roller skates, skateboards, equipment for team sports and ball tossing and catching	Woodworking bench; full range of tools and equipment	Computer games, puzzles, crochet and knitting supplies	Materials for skits and short dramatic activities	CDs, tapes of classical, folk, jazz, and popular music Wide range of fiction and nonfiction books	Full range of materials for easel painting, printing, sculpting, collage, rubbings Computer programs for graphic design experiences

APPENDIX G

Puppet Patterns

 HAND PUPPET PATTERN

Hand puppets can be an essential part of your curriculum and are fun for children to use. Hand puppets can be made with or without mouths, but puppets with mouths are usually preferable. The following pattern can be adapted to make people- or animal-shaped puppets (see Figure G–1). Encourage the children to use their imaginations to add faces, ears, hair, and clothes. Features can be glued, sewed, or written on the puppet.

Materials:

Felt, upholstery fabric, Velcro fabric
Glue, needle and thread, scissors
Other decorative materials (yarn, feathers, plastic eyes, etc.)

Directions:

Cut out two pattern shapes using the type of fabric you choose. Sew or glue them together leaving the bottom open. If you use Velcro fabric, glue or sew the wrong sides together. This fabric will not fray. Velcro hook can be attached to decorative items to change a puppet's personality.

This type of puppet is fun and easy for children to use. Show them how to insert their hand the first time they use one. Keep the puppets in a puppet house in the story corner as well as in the home center for the children to use.

MITTENS AND GLOVE PATTERNS

For each mitten or glove: ½ yard (.5m) Velcro fabric, fabric glue or thread and sewing machine, scissors.

Directions:

Following the patterns (see Figures G–2 and G–3), cut material to the size you need. Place wrong sides together and stitch or glue.

Paste cut-out character's pictures to a sturdy piece of paper (cardboard, poster board). Glue a piece of Velcro hook on the back of each character. Children wear the mitten and attach story characters to them during storytelling.

Child Size

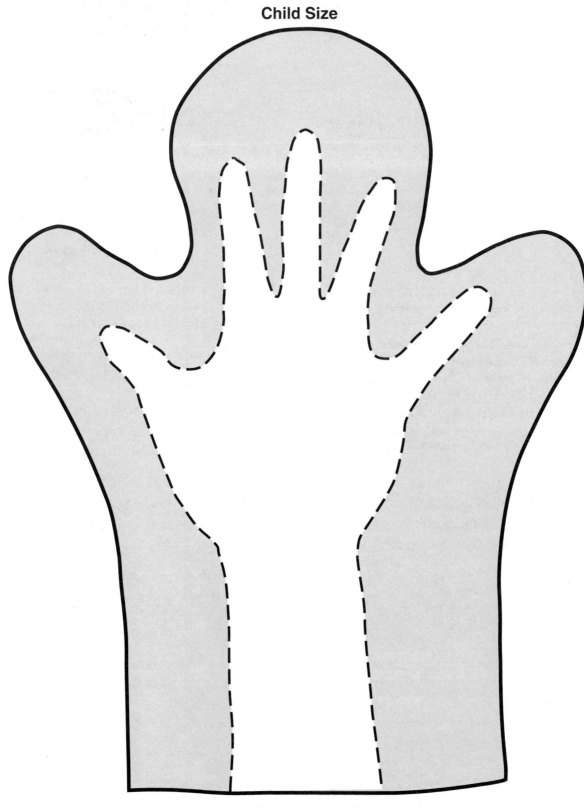

Shorten or lengthen

FIGURE | Hand puppet pattern.
G–1

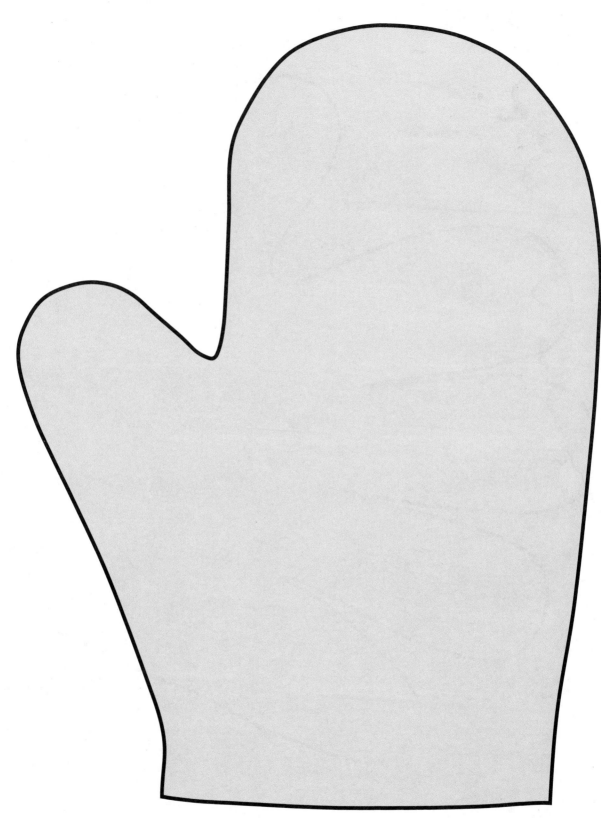

FIGURE | Mitten pattern.
G–2 |

Lengthen here.

FIGURE | Glove pattern.
G–3 |

APPENDIX H

Motor Skills and Characteristics of Children, Ages Two through Ten Years, with Suggested Activities to Encourage Physical Development

SKILLS AND CHARACTERISTICS	SUGGESTED ACTIVITIES
	The Two-Year-Old
Very active, short attention span	Provide pushing and pulling toys. Encourage play with pounding bench, punching bags, and soft clay. Provide opportunities both indoors and outdoors for active free play that involves climbing, running, sliding, and tumbling.
Interest in physical manipulation, ability to stack several items, pull apart, fill, and empty containers	Provide stacking cups or blocks for stacking and unstacking. Provide pop-apart toys, such as beads, for taking apart. (Large enough *not* to swallow.) Provide opportunities for filling and emptying containers with sand, water, rice, beans, rocks, and so on.
Increased development of fine motor skills	Provide crayons, chalk, paint, and paper for scribbling and painting. Be sure all materials are lead-free and nontoxic. Allow the child to "paint" the sidewalk, building, wheel toys, and so on with clear water and a brush large enough to handle. Provide opportunities to play with play dough, finger paint, paper for tearing, and so on.
Increased development in language skills	Encourage the child to talk with you. Use pronouns such as "I," "me," "you," "they," and "we." Encourage the child to use these words. Talk with the child about pictures. Ask her to point to objects or name them. Always give the correct name for objects. Give directions to follow: "Close the door," "Pick up the doll." Be sure to make this a fun game. Teach the child the names of unusual objects such as fire extinguisher, thermometer, screwdriver, trivet.
Likes to imitate	Encourage finger plays. Recite nursery rhymes. Encourage the child to repeat them. Play "I am a mirror." Stand or sit facing the child and have him copy everything you do.
Shows interest in dramatic play	Provide dolls, dress-up clothes, carriage, doll bed, and toy telephones for pretend conversations.
	The Three-Year-Old
Increased development of large motor skills	Provide opportunities for vigorous free play indoors and outdoors. Provide opportunities for climbing, jumping, and riding wheel toys. Play "Follow-the-Leader," requiring vigorous body movements.
Greater control over small muscles	Provide opportunities for free play with blocks in various sizes and shapes. Provide a variety of manipulative toys and activities such as pegboard and peg sets, tinker toys, or puzzles with 3–8 pieces. Encourage children to dress and undress themselves, serve food, set the table, and water the plants.
Greater motor coordination	Provide art activities. Encourage free expression with paint, crayons, chalk, colored pens, collage materials, clay, and play dough. Be sure all materials are lead-free and nontoxic.
Increased development of language skills and vocabulary	Provide opportunities each day for reading stories to children in a group or individually. Encourage children to tell stories. Tape record their stories. Encourage children to talk about anything of interest.

Motor skills and characteristics of children, ages two through ten years, with suggested activities to encourage physical development.

SKILLS AND CHARACTERISTICS	SUGGESTED ACTIVITIES
Beginning to understand number concepts. Usually can grasp concepts of 1, 2, and 3. Can count several numbers in a series but may leave some out.	Count objects of interest (e.g., cookies, cups, napkins, or dolls). When possible, move them as you count. Allow children to count them. Display numbers in the room. Use calendars, charts, scales, and rulers.
Enjoys music and is beginning to be able to carry a tune, express rhythm	Provide music activities each day. Sing songs, create rhythms. Move body to music. Encourage children to make up songs. Tape record them and play them back for the children to dance to or to sing along with.
Curious about why and how things happen	Provide new experiences that arouse questions. Answer the questions simply and honestly. Use reference books with the child to find answers. Conduct simple science activities: What will the magnet pick up? Freeze water, make ice cream, plant seeds, make a terrarium, or fly a kite on a windy day.

The Four-Year-Old

SKILLS AND CHARACTERISTICS	SUGGESTED ACTIVITIES
Good balance and body coordination; increased development of small and large motor skills	Provide opportunities each day for vigorous free play. Provide opportunities for the child to walk on a curved line, a straight line, or a balance beam. Encourage walking with a bean bag on the head. Games: "See how fast you can hop," "See how far you can hop on one foot," "See how high you can jump." Provide opportunities to throw balls (medium-sized, soft), bean bags, or yarn balls.
Small motor skills are developing most rapidly now. Drawings and art express world about them.	Provide an opportunity for a variety of artwork. Encourage children to tell a story or talk about their finished projects. Encourage children to mix primary colors to produce secondary colors. Name the colors with them.
Increasing hand–eye coordination	Encourage children to unzip, unsnap, and unbutton clothes. Dressing self is too difficult at this point. Encourage children to tear and cut. Encourage children to lace their shoes.
Ability to group items according to similar characteristics	Play lotto games. Group buttons as to color or size. Provide a mixture of seeds. Sort as to kind. At cleanup time, sort blocks according to shape. Play rhyming word games.
Increased understanding of concepts related to numbers, size and weight, colors, textures, distance and position, and time	In conversation, use words related to these concepts. Play "Follow Direction" games. Say, "Put the pencil beside the big block," or "Crawl under the table." Provide swatches of fabric and other materials that vary in texture. Talk about differences. Blindfold the children or have them cover their eyes and ask them to match duplicate textures.
Awareness of the world around them	Build a simple bird feeder and provide feed for birds. Record the kinds of birds observed. Arrange field trips to various community locations of interest (park, fire station, police station).

(Continued)

Motor skills and characteristics of children, ages two through ten years, with suggested activities to encourage physical development.

SKILLS AND CHARACTERISTICS	SUGGESTED ACTIVITIES
Has a vivid imagination; enjoys dramatic play	Provide variety of dress-up clothes. Encourage dramatic play through props such as cash register and empty food containers, tea set, and child-sized furniture.

The Five- and Six-Year-Old

Good sense of balance and body coordination	Encourage body movement with records, stories, rhythms. Encourage skipping to music or rhymes. Teach them simple folk dances.
A tremendous drive for physical activity	Provide free play that encourages running, jumping, balancing, and climbing. Play tug-of-war. Encourage tumbling on a mat.
Development and coordination of small muscles in hands and fingers	Encourage opportunities to paint, draw, cut, paste, or mold clay. Provide small peg games and other manipulative toys. Teach sewing with large needle and thread into egg cartons or punched cards. Provide simple carpentry experiences.
Increased hand–eye coordination	Allow children to copy designs of shapes, letters, and numbers. Show a child how his name is made with letters. Encourage catching small balls.
Ability to distinguish right from left	Play games that emphasize right from left. Games can require responses to directions such as "Put your right hand on your nose" or "Put your left foot on the green circle."
Can discriminate between weights, colors, sizes, textures, and shapes	Play sorting games. Sort rocks as to weight; blocks as to weight or shape; marbles or seeds as to colors. Match fabric swatches.
Increased understanding of number concepts	Count anything of interest—cookies, napkins, cups, leaves, acorns, trees, children, teachers, boys, chairs, and so on. Identify numbers visible on a calendar, clock, measuring containers, or other devices.
Enjoys jokes, nonsense rhymes, and riddles	Read humorous stories, riddles, or nonsense rhymes.
Enjoys creative, dramatic activities	Move body to dramatize opening of a flower, falling snow, leaves, rain, wiggly worms, snakes, or blowing wind. Dramatize stories as they are read. Good stories to use are: *Caps for Sale, Three Billy Goats Gruff,* and *The Three Bears.*

The Six- to Ten-Year-Old

Good sense of balance and body coordination	Encourage movements that challenge the child such as horizontal and vertical jumps. Introduce more complex motor skills such as relay runs, obstacle courses, and so on.
More directed in their drive for physical activity	Encourage free play that allows running, jumping, balancing, throwing, and catching. Introduce basic sports such as baseball, basketball, and soccer.
Good development and coordination of small muscles in hands and fingers	Provide many challenging and diverse art activities that allow for fine motor exercise. Encourage three-dimensional projects such as woodworking, papier mâché, costume-making, and so on.

Motor skills and characteristics of children, ages two through ten years, with suggested activities to encourage physical development.

SKILLS AND CHARACTERISTICS	SUGGESTED ACTIVITIES
Improved hand–eye coordination	Continue to encourage tossing, throwing, and catching skills. Use activities that incorporate several skills such as dodge ball.
Learns to apply and refine perceptual skills developed earlier	Challenge children in art activities to see and express shape, form, color, and line in a variety of media. Provide activities that allow them to learn to identify and analyze relationships such as how light affects perception of colors, textures, and form.
Growing facility with use of numbers; can think more flexibly	Introduce the use of calculators for math problems. Challenge them with basic probability and estimation activities/problems. Allow them to work in small groups for problem-solving.
Has an increasingly sophisticated sense of humor	Provide jokebooks, humorous books, and nonsense riddle and rhyme books. Encourage them to write their own humorous pieces.
Enjoys dramatic activities, but self-consciousness is becoming an issue	Encourage children to express themselves in short performances such as sketches, vignettes, "freeze-frame" scenes, and pantomime. Provide opportunities for them to see dramatic activities of other students (i.e., middle school play, dance rehearsal, and so on). Provide books, music, and artwork of great artists for children to experience. (Gallaghue & Ozmun, 1997)

Motor skills and characteristics of children, ages two through ten years, with suggested activities to encourage physical development.

INDEX